A World of
Fiction 2

THIRD EDITION

TIMELESS SHORT STORIES

Sybil Marcus
University of California, Berkeley

Daniel Berman

A World of Fiction 2

Pearson Education, 10 Bank Street, White Plains, NY 10606

Staff Credits: The people who made up the *A World of Fiction 2* team—representing editorial, production, design, and manufacturing—are Tracey Cataldo, Rosa Chapinal, Aerin Csigay, Nancy Flaggman, Amy McCormick, Joan Poole, and Jane Townsend.

Development: Page Designs International
Project management and text composition: S4Carlisle Publishing Services
Cover photo: "Mountain Sentinel" by Ronald Berman
Text font: Palatino LT Std Roman

Library of Congress Cataloging-in-Publication Data
A World of Fiction 2 : Timeless Short Stories/[compiled by] Sybil Marcus, University of California, Berkeley ; Daniel Berman.—Third Edition.
    pages cm
 ISBN 978-0-13-304617-5
 1. English language—Textbooks for foreign speakers.   2. Short stories.   I. Marcus, Sybil.   II. Title.
 PE1128.W7599 2014
 428.6'4—dc23
                            2013039671

For text credits, please turn to the back of the book.

Printed in the United States of America

ISBN 10: 0-13-304617-6
ISBN 13: 978-0-13-304617-5

1 2 3 4 5 6 7 8 9 10—V011—19 18 17 16 15 14

Dedication

To Helen, who believed in us
and
To Ron, whose loving support never wavers

Brief Contents

Husbands, Wives, and Lovers   1

  1 Can-Can   Arturo Vivante   3

  2 The Cranes   Peter Meinke   13

  3 The Kugelmass Episode   Woody Allen   27

  4 An Intruder   Nadine Gordimer   47

Parent and Child   65

  5 Powder   Tobias Wolff   67

  6 Mother   Grace Paley   81

  7 Eveline   James Joyce   91

  8 My Oedipus Complex   Frank O'Connor   105

Loneliness and Alienation   127

  9 Disappearing   Monica Wood   129

  10 A Pair of Silk Stockings   Kate Chopin   143

  11 Everyday Use   Alice Walker   157

  12 The Red Convertible   Louise Erdrich   177

Social Change and Injustice   195

  13 EPICAC   Kurt Vonnegut   197

  14 Like a Winding Sheet   Ann Petry   215

  15 A Drink in the Passage   Alan Paton   233

  16 The Catbird Seat   James Thurber   251

Contents

Preface   xi

How to Use This Book   xiii

Acknowledgments   xvii

Husbands, Wives, and Lovers   1

1 Can-Can   Arturo Vivante   3

A husband arranges a secret meeting with a woman and is surprised by the outcome.

Analyzing Style	Irony
	Symbol
Grammar in Context	Forms Ending in *–ing*
Vocabulary Building	Fixed Expressions with *and*
	Unfamiliar Words

2 The Cranes   Peter Meinke   13

A husband and wife embark on a mysterious outing.

Analyzing Style	Inference
	Setting
	Simile
	Black Humor
Grammar in Context	Wishes
Vocabulary Building	Prepositions
	Oxymoron

3 The Kugelmass Episode   Woody Allen   27

When a New York professor has his deepest wish granted, his life takes an unexpected turn.

Analyzing Style	Dialogue
	Flat Characters
	Anachronism
	Allusion
Grammar in Context	The Passive Voice
Vocabulary Building	Verbs That Introduce Dialogue
	Idioms

4 An Intruder   Nadine Gordimer   47

A home is invaded under mysterious circumstances, changing the lives of its occupants.

Analyzing Style	Simile and Metaphor
Grammar in Context	Adjective Clauses
	Restrictive and Nonrestrictive Adjective Clauses
Vocabulary Building	Adjectives

Parent and Child   65

5   Powder   Tobias Wolff   67

A boy and his father bond in an unusual way.

Analyzing Style	Repetition
	Alliteration
Grammar in Context	Participial Phrases
	Dangling Modifiers
	Sentence Fragments
Vocabulary Building	Alliterative Expressions
	Prepositions

6   Mother   Grace Paley   81

Years after her death, a mother is remembered by her child.

Analyzing Style	Flashback
	Tone
Grammar in Context	Past Tenses
Vocabulary Building	Words in Context

7   Eveline   James Joyce   91

A young woman is faced with a life-changing decision.

Analyzing Style	Imagery
	Flashback
Grammar in Context	Parallel Structure: Coordinating Conjunctions
	Parallel Structure: Correlative Conjunctions
Vocabulary Building	Descriptive Verbs
	Idiomatic Expressions

8   My Oedipus Complex   Frank O'Connor   105

A small boy's world is turned upside down when his father returns home from the First World War.

Analyzing Style	Humor
Grammar in Context	Linking Verbs
	Phrasal Verbs
Vocabulary Building	Denotation and Connotation

Loneliness and Alienation   127

9 Disappearing   Monica Wood   129

An obsession with swimming radically changes the life of an extremely overweight woman.

Analyzing Style	Ellipsis
	Imagery
Grammar in Context	Agreement of Pronoun and Antecedent
	Indefinite Pronouns
Vocabulary Building	Dealing with Unfamiliar Words

10 A Pair of Silk Stockings   Kate Chopin   143

A struggling mother gives in to temptation.

Analyzing Style	Inference
Grammar in Context	Reflexive Pronouns
Vocabulary Building	Collocations with Noncount Nouns
	Adjectives

11 Everyday Use   Alice Walker   157

Family tensions come to a head in a dispute over the ownership of some quilts.

Analyzing Style	Round Characters
	First-Person Narration
Grammar in Context	Prepositional Phrases
	The Expression *Used To*
Vocabulary Building	Phrasal Verbs

12 The Red Convertible   Louise Erdrich   177

A distinctive car plays a key role in the lives of two brothers.

Analyzing Style	Point of View
	Voice
	Foreshadowing
Grammar in Context	Compound Sentences
Vocabulary Building	Phrasal Verbs with Multiple Meanings

Social Change and Injustice   195

13 EPICAC   Kurt Vonnegut   197

A young mathematician uses unorthodox methods to win a woman's heart.

Analyzing Style	Personification
	Colloquialisms
Grammar in Context	Adverbs
	Irregular Adverbs
Vocabulary Building	Confusing Word Pairs
	Idioms Containing Body Parts

14 Like a Winding Sheet   Ann Petry   215

The accumulated stress of living in a racist society takes a terrible toll on a factory worker.

Analyzing Style	Dialect
	Imagery
Grammar in Context	Adverbial Clauses
	Punctuation of Adverbial Clauses
Vocabulary Building	Synonyms

15 A Drink in the Passage   Alan Paton   233

A chance encounter in a divided country leaves two men feeling shaken.

Analyzing Style	Frame Story
	Irony
	Inference
Grammar in Context	Conditionals
Vocabulary Building	Prepositions

16 The Catbird Seat   James Thurber   251

A man whose job is threatened takes drastic and ingenious measures to protect himself.

Analyzing Style	Understatement
Grammar in Context	Noun Clauses
Vocabulary Building	Idioms Containing Colors
	Legal Vocabulary

Text Credits   269

Preface

A World of Fiction is entering its third edition. After nearly twenty years, the feedback from the many users of the book continues to be invaluable. Teachers and students alike have frequently expressed appreciation for a textbook whose core vision is to take nonnative speakers' critical abilities seriously. For this updated edition, I have been joined by Daniel Berman, who has brought a discerning eye to once again deciding which beloved stories to sacrifice in favor of new material, as well as to choosing their replacements and creating the exercises that follow.

The guiding principle behind our selection is the same as before: to offer complex stories with a strong voice, which reveal themselves in layers through careful reading and serious thought. The sixteen stories in this book represent a variety of themes, styles, and perspectives that give rise to intensive literary analysis and diverse cross-cultural discussion. They are unabridged. Each was originally written in English, and many are recognized masterpieces of the genre.

I have used short fiction now for four decades in the classroom. As an English as a second language/English as a foreign language (ESL/EFL) tool, the story has proven itself magnificently. Its form offers nonnative students a complete work of literature with the essential elements of character, setting, plot, motive, and theme, but with a brevity that is nonthreatening. Short stories present the opportunity to reflect on a number of different subjects during a limited course of study, as well as to grapple with a variety of styles that all represent English used in an authentic way. In the process, students enhance their reading, speaking, writing, grammar, and vocabulary skills in a sophisticated and engaging way.

This book arises from the conviction that literature in ESL/EFL education is not just a means to an end, but rather that close scrutiny of a fine literary text is a richly satisfying and rewarding endeavor in itself. We encourage students to think of themselves as archaeologists whose aim is to dig out the buried meanings in the text. In the process, advanced students of English will sharpen their critical thinking and heighten their intercultural sensitivity as they come to understand that there are universal truths and sentiments that bind us all. The stories in this collection offer so many avenues of attack, so many opportunities for curiosity and excitement, that they will naturally inspire even the shyest students to think, discuss, compare, and debate.

This anthology is loosely divided into four thematic sections: Husbands, Wives, and Lovers; Parent and Child; Loneliness and Alienation; and Social Change and Injustice. Many of the stories easily straddle more than one category, but we have attempted to place each one according to its dominant theme. Each section starts with an accessible piece, easier by virtue of its length or content, and works up to stories of greater thematic and/or stylistic complexity.

An underlying premise of our approach is that students read each story twice at home, making full use of any word glosses as they familiarize themselves with the plot and themes. At this level of advanced language achievement, we encourage students to respond freshly and individually to each story. Therefore, there are no prereading questions that alert the students to the story's content, although the capsule summary under the title does provide a clue. Teachers who prefer a more directed method may point students in advance to the *Thinking About the Story* section, which contains one or more questions designed to promote thought and discussion.

After a first reading, students should be equipped with the vocabulary to understand and discuss the plot, while after a second reading they are poised to explore the story's themes. They can then move on to consider the distinctive style of the piece. After this, students are led to express their judgments on the characters' decisions, as well as to ponder the larger issues through their individual cultural prisms.

The transition to studying a story's grammar and vocabulary is a smooth one, as students generally find it much easier to absorb and implement grammatical and lexical items that they have encountered in context. Finally, students should be ready to write short essays in which they integrate what they have learned.

NEW TO THIS EDITION

This new edition of *A World of Fiction* features five new stories: "Eveline" by James Joyce, a classic story of torn loyalties; "The Cranes" by Peter Meinke, a subtle and mysterious story that raises contemporary questions; "The Red Convertible" by Louise Erdrich, a Native American coming-of-age story with sociopolitical undercurrents; "A Pair of Silk Stockings" by Kate Chopin, a moving story of struggle and temptation; and "A Drink in the Passage" by Alan Paton, a poignant and humanist examination of racial segregation in South Africa.

The many revisions in this third edition include updated author biographies; an increased focus on critical thinking; the creation of a new vocabulary-building section in each chapter; new style, grammar, and vocabulary elements; as well as new writing assignments. In addition, extra explanatory text introduces the style, grammar, and vocabulary sections. We believe that the new format and the new two-color design will make it easier for both teachers and students to work their way through each chapter.

How to Use This Book

Each chapter in this anthology is based on a complete short story and is divided into five sections, which call upon the diverse language and critical thinking skills of the student.

Part 1: First Reading

A Thinking About the Story

Students are encouraged to express their visceral responses to the story. The aim is to stimulate an immediate and personal reaction in which students relate to a character or situation.

B Understanding the Plot

The questions in this section lead students through the story in chronological order, eliciting their understanding of its characters, events, motive, and setting. Students who experience difficulties with a story during their first reading may wish to refer to these questions to guide them as they read. This section may be completed orally or in writing, depending on the needs of the class.

Part 2: Critical Thinking

The critical thinking questions in this part of the chapter can be answered orally or in writing. We recommend that students first write their answers to the theme and style questions, and then share these answers with a partner or in a small group. The judgment and cross-cultural questions call for an oral response, as does the debate section. Students generally tend to benefit from sharing their thoughts and perspectives in a spirited exchange, whether in small groups or in a broader class discussion.

A Exploring Themes

While reading the story a second time, students are asked to reflect on a single key question or aspect of the text. By the end of this reading they should be ready to tackle more demanding and substantive questions, which will expose the story's underlying meanings and universal truths.

B Analyzing Style

This section highlights salient literary devices and elements of style, such as metaphor, simile, symbol, personification, allusion, and alliteration. Students are required to analyze the ways in which an author uses language to reinforce themes and create a distinctive voice.

C Judging for Yourself

The questions in this section allow students to adopt a more flexible approach to the text and to move beyond the limits of the story. Students may be encouraged to speculate about events that have not been spelled out or to judge the wisdom of a character's actions. Sometimes they are asked to reflect on possible solutions to problems raised in the story. This offers classes the opportunity to engage in conflict-resolution activities as students assess how the problems they have analyzed in the story might best be resolved.

D Making Connections

If a class has a cross-cultural, multi-ethnic component, the questions in this section will encourage students to compare and contrast their views on controversial actions or standpoints in the story, using their own cultural and societal values as a touchstone. In a more homogeneous class, there are still rich opportunities to compare the group's common values with those expressed in the story, as well as to explore dissenting views within the class.

E Debate

Part 2 culminates with a debate. By this stage, students should have acquired the necessary vocabulary and command of English to enable them to present their oral arguments cogently and confidently. Debates can be conducted according to formal debating rules, or informally in groups or with a partner.

Part 3: Grammar in Context

Part 3 offers students a chance to review and practice a particular aspect of grammar that is well illustrated in the story. Structures covered include gerunds, participles, main and subordinate clauses, conditionals, tenses, agreement of pronoun and antecedent, participial and prepositional phrases, sentence fragments, dangling modifiers, appositives, indefinite and reflexive pronouns, coordinating conjunctions, and linking verbs.

Part 4: Vocabulary Building

Part 4 is new to the third edition. In this part, students are asked to focus on a particular aspect of vocabulary that arises in the chapter. The exercises in this section are varied. They have been designed to be as engaging as possible and discourage rote learning. The words, phrases, and idioms selected for instruction have been chosen with an eye to helping students express themselves with greater nuance and sophistication.

Part 5: Writing Activities

By the time students arrive at this section, they will have carefully considered the story and its related topics, acquired a richer vocabulary, and refreshed their understanding of one or more grammatical structures. They are now equipped to tackle the writing assignments, which range from paragraphs to complete essays. The questions include both expository and creative writing. Wherever feasible, one question encourages students to incorporate the language skills they have just practiced, thus reinforcing their learning in a different way. Another question is designed to get students to explore a work of art such as a novel, a movie, or a painting that connects to the theme of the story under discussion. Finally, students are sometimes asked to relate the story to other chapters in the anthology, offering them a chance to refine their ability to compare and contrast characters and themes.

Acknowledgments

We are deeply grateful to the following people, whose help has been invaluable in the writing of this book.

Bernard Seal, our project manager, who guided us through a major revamping of this edition with knowledge, judgment, forbearance, and humor. He was a trusted pillar of strength from start to finish.

Joe Chapple, our development editor, whose experience, encouragement, and meticulous approach to detail kept us honest until we found the right words.

The following people at Pearson, who contributed to the production of this book with expertise and care: Pietro Alongi, Tracey Cataldo, Rosa Chapinal, Amy McCormick, Liza Pleva, Massimo Rubini, and Jane Townsend.

The many teachers whose feedback over the years has helped us to revise and rethink the book. In particular, we thank Susan Stern and Tom McNichol, who have used the book since its inception, and whose incisive comments have been of particular value. Thanks also to Ellen Rosenfield and Patti Weissman, who graciously answered all grammar questions, large and small.

Margi Ward, who generously gave Sybil carte blanche to test her new material at the University of California at Berkeley Summer English Language Studies.

Ron Berman, who took the cover photograph, and who supported us in countless loving ways.

The many students from the University of California at Berkeley Extension and the University of California at Berkeley Summer English Language Studies, whose curiosity, openness, enthusiasm, and insights have been an inspiration for thirty years.

HUSBANDS, WIVES, AND LOVERS

Can-Can
The Cranes
The Kugelmass Episode
An Intruder

1 🖎 Can-Can

Arturo Vivante
(1923–2008)

Born in Italy, Arturo Vivante studied to be a doctor in Rome and practiced medicine for eight years. In 1958 he immigrated to the United States, where for the next fifty years he worked as a writer and teacher. He published three novels, *A Goodly Babe* (1966), *Doctor Giovanni* (1969), and *Truelove Knot* (2007), as well as several volumes of short stories, including *Run to the Waterfall* (1979), an autobiographical account of a half-Jewish family in Italy before and after World War II. Other works include *Writing Fiction* (1980), *Essays on Art and Ontology* (1980), and *The Tales of Arturo Vivante* (1990). The *New Yorker* published seventy of his short stories. In 2006 he received the Katherine Anne Porter award for fiction. He also translated into English the poems of Giacomo Leopardi, Italy's famous nineteenth-century lyric poet. Vivante is quoted as saying, "I write to know the mystery that even a small matter holds."

Can-Can[1]

A husband arranges a secret meeting with a woman and is surprised by the outcome.

"I'm going to go for a drive," he said to his wife. "I'll be back in an hour or two."

He didn't often leave the house for more than the few minutes it took him to go to the post office or to a store, but spent his time hanging around,[2] doing odd jobs—Mr. Fix-it, his wife called him—and also, though not nearly enough of it, painting—which he made his living[3] from.

"All right," his wife said brightly, as though he were doing her a favor. As a matter of fact, she didn't really like him to leave; she felt safer with him at home, and he helped look after the children, especially the baby.

"You're glad to be rid of[4] me, aren't you?" he said.

"Uh-huh," she said with a smile that suddenly made her look very pretty—someone to be missed.

She didn't ask him where he was going for his drive. She wasn't the least bit inquisitive,[5] though jealous she was in silent, subtle[6] ways.

As he put his coat on, he watched her. She was in the living room with their elder daughter. "Do the can-can, mother," the child said, at which she held up her skirt and did the can-can, kicking her legs up high in his direction.

He wasn't simply going out for a drive, as he had said, but going to a café, to meet Sarah, whom his wife knew but did not suspect, and with her go to a house on a lake his wife knew nothing about— a summer cottage to which he had the key.

"Well, goodbye," he said.

"Bye," she called back, still dancing.

This wasn't the way a husband expected his wife—whom he was about to leave at home to go to another woman—to behave at all, he thought. He expected her to be sewing or washing, not doing the can-can, for God's sake. Yes, doing something uninteresting and unattractive, like darning[7] children's clothes. She had no stockings on, no shoes, and her legs looked very white and smooth, secret, as though he had never touched them or come near them. Her feet, swinging up and down high in the air, seemed to be nodding to him. She held her skirt bunched up,[8] attractively. Why was she doing that of all times

---

1 **can-can** lively, sexy dance originating in France in the nineteenth century
2 **hanging around** not doing anything specific
3 **made his living** earned enough money to live on
4 **be rid of** be free of
5 **inquisitive** curious
6 **subtle** not obvious, complex
7 **darning** mending torn clothing
8 **bunched up** pulled together in folds

35 *now*? He lingered.[9] Her eyes had mockery[10] in them, and she laughed. The child laughed with her as she danced. She was still dancing as he left the house.

He thought of the difficulties he had had arranging this *rendezvous*[11]—
going out to a call box; phoning Sarah at her office (she was married,
40 too); her being out; his calling her again; the busy signal; the coin falling out of sight, his opening the door of the phone box in order to retrieve it; at last getting her on the line; her asking him to call again next week, finally setting a date.

Waiting for her at the café, he surprised himself hoping that she
45 wouldn't come. The appointment was at three. It was now ten past. Well, she was often late. He looked at the clock, and at the picture window for her car. A car like hers, and yet not hers—no luggage rack on it. The smooth hardtop gave him a peculiar pleasure. Why? It was 3:15 now. Perhaps she wouldn't come. No, if she was going to come at
50 all, this was the most likely time for her to arrive. Twenty past. Ah, now there was some hope. Hope? How strange he should be hoping for her absence. Why had he made the appointment if he was hoping she would miss it? He didn't know why, but simpler, simpler if she didn't come. Because all he wanted now was to smoke that cigarette,
55 drink that cup of coffee for the sake of them, and not to give himself something to do. And he wished he could go for a drive, free and easy,[12] as he had said he would. But he waited, and at 3:30 she arrived. "I had almost given up hope," he said.

They drove to the house on the lake. As he held her in his arms he
60 couldn't think of her; for the life of him[13] he couldn't.

"What are you thinking about?" she said afterwards, sensing his detachment.[14]

For a moment he didn't answer, then he said, "You really want to know what I was thinking of?"

65 "Yes," she said, a little anxiously.

He suppressed[15] a laugh, as though what he was going to tell her was too absurd or silly. "I was thinking of someone doing the can-can."

"Oh," she said, reassured. "For a moment I was afraid you were thinking of your wife."

---

9 **lingered** stayed behind
10 **mockery** making fun of someone (negatively)
11 **rendezvous** a meeting at a particular time and place

12 **free and easy** with a clear conscience
13 **for the life of him** even with great effort
14 **detachment** distance
15 **suppressed** restrained, held back

A Thinking About the Story

Discuss the following question with a partner.

> Which character do you sympathize with most—the husband, the wife, or the mistress? Explain your choice.

B Understanding the Plot

Be prepared to answer the following questions with a partner or the whole class.

1. What is the can-can?
2. What does the husband do for a living?
3. In the wife's view, is the husband a hard worker? Explain your answer.
4. Whom is the husband going to meet?
5. Does the wife suspect her husband of adultery?
6. Why was it so difficult for the husband and Sarah to arrange a meeting?
7. What is the husband's state of mind as he sits waiting for Sarah?
8. To whom or what does the pronoun *them* refer? (line 55)
9. What happens when the husband and Sarah reach their destination?
10. What is Sarah concerned about?
11. Is Sarah reassured by the husband's answer to her question?

PART 2 CRITICAL THINKING

A Exploring Themes

Reread "Can-Can." As you read, try to understand why the characters act as they do and what thoughts about life Arturo Vivante is attempting to convey.

1. What reasons are implied about why the husband has chosen to have an affair?
2. Does the wife do the can-can for her child or for her husband? Explain your answer.
3. What effect does the dance have on her husband?
4. What do the husband and wife expect from each other in marriage? Does each fulfill the other's expectations?

IRONY

Irony refers to a contrast between appearance and reality. This can be a contrast between what someone says and what he or she really means; or between what we would normally expect to happen in a situation and what really happens; or between what a character believes to be true and what we as readers actually know is true. For all three types of irony, what is important is that the contrast is meaningful to the story in a significant way.

Irony is crucial to both the humor and the poignancy of "Can-Can." For example, the scene where the husband waits for his lover's car is deeply ironic.

> *A car like hers, and yet not like hers—no luggage rack on it. The smooth hardtop gave him a peculiar pleasure.* (lines 47–48)

Here we have an ironic contrast between what we would normally expect—that a man would be excited about meeting his lover—and what really happens—that he feels a surprising feeling of relief that the car outside isn't hers. Later, in another moment of irony, the husband says to his lover, "I had almost given up hope" (lines 57–58). As readers, we experience the contrast between what she naturally thinks—that he is pleased to see her—and what we actually know—that he feels exactly the opposite.

Exercise 1

Explain the irony of the story's ending.

Exercise 2

Find and explain at least three more examples of irony in the story. Share your examples with a partner.

SYMBOL

A **symbol** is one thing that represents another. It can be a person, a place, an object, an action, or anything else with strong associations. Some symbols are general, meaning that most people in a culture will understand them—the lion is a symbol of courage and strength, the olive branch is a symbol of peace, Albert Einstein is a symbol of intelligence, and the red rose stands for romantic love. Other symbols are particular, meaning that they arise out of an individual story.

In "Can-Can," Vivante uses the dance as a central symbol.

Answer the following questions.

1. What associations do you have with the can-can? If necessary, research the dance online.
2. What does the can-can symbolize in the story? In your answer, pay attention to the detailed description of the wife dancing the can-can. How does it relate to the couple's marriage?

C Judging for Yourself

Express yourself as personally as you like in your answers to the following questions.

1. Do you think the expectations the couple have of each other are reasonable?
2. Do you think the husband will continue the affair?
3. Why do you think the husband doesn't leave the restaurant when he realizes he doesn't want to see his mistress?
4. Do you think the husband learns anything from the episode?
5. What do you imagine the couple's marriage will be like in the future?

D Making Connections

Answer the following questions with a classmate or in a small group.

1. How is adultery viewed in your culture?
2. Does the couple's marriage in "Can-Can" reflect the kind of marriage common in your culture?
3. In your country, would politicians or other public figures be denied or removed from office if they committed adultery? Do you think fidelity in marriage is relevant to public office?
4. Is honest communication between couples encouraged in your culture? If marriages run into difficulties, is family therapy an option?

E Debate

Decide whether you are for or against the following statement. Be prepared to argue your case in a class debate.

Adultery is a crime and should be punished by law.

FORMS ENDING IN –*ING*

In English, there are three forms ending in –*ing*: **gerunds**, **present participles**, and **verbs in the progressive**. Although these three forms share an -*ing* ending, their functions are quite different.

1. The **gerund** is related to a verb but acts as a noun. Like a noun, the gerund or gerund phrase can be the subject of a sentence or the object of a verb or preposition.

   The gerund can be the subject of a verb.

   > *Arranging this rendezvous was very difficult for him.*

   The gerund can be the object of a verb.

   > *He couldn't imagine arranging this rendezvous.*

   The gerund can also be the object of a preposition.

   > *He expected her to be doing something uninteresting and unattractive, like darning children's clothes.* (adapted from lines 28–30)

2. The **present participle** is related to a verb but acts as an adjective. As an adjective, the present participle or participial phrase must modify a noun or pronoun.

   > *Her feet, swinging up and down high in the air, seemed to be nodding to him.* (lines 32–33)

3. The present participle is also used to form a **verb in the progressive**. Progressive tenses show that an action is continuing over a period of time in the past, present, or future.

   > *Why was she doing that of all times now?* (lines 34–35)

Exercise 1

Find the paragraph in "Can-Can" that is composed mainly of gerunds and underline them.

Exercise 2

In each sentence that follows, decide if the italicized word is a gerund, present participle, or part of a verb in the progressive. Write your choice on the line.

1. "I'm *going* for a drive," he said to his wife. _____

2. She hated *sewing* for the family. _____

3. She held up her skirt and did the can-can, *kicking* her legs up high in his direction. _____

4. He objected to *seeing* her in this new role. _____

5. *Waiting* so long for his lover at the café made him feel nervous.

   _____

6. He looked at his watch, *hoping* she wouldn't come.

   _____

7. How strange he should be *hoping* for her absence.

   _____

8. *Smoking* a cigarette helped steady his nerves. _____

9. "What are you *thinking* about?" she said, sensing his detachment.

   _____

10. *Suppressing* a laugh, he answered her honestly.

    _____

Exercise 3

Write three sentences with *getting rid of* as a gerund, as a present participle, and as a verb in the progressive. Do the same with *lingering*.

PART 4 VOCABULARY BUILDING

FIXED EXPRESSIONS WITH *AND*

A **fixed expression** is a group of words that occur together to form a single unit. Some fixed expressions consist of two nouns, adjectives, adverbs, or verbs separated by *and*. Mastering these expressions will help you speak and write more naturally.

In "Can-Can" the husband *wished he could go for a drive, free and easy* (lines 56–57). The fixed expression *free and easy* means "with a clear conscience." The word order in this kind of expression is fixed: you cannot reverse the order and say *easy and free*.

Exercise 1

Write definitions for the following fixed expressions. If necessary, use a dictionary to help you. Then write sentences with each expression in a way that shows you understand how to use it correctly.

1. bread-and-butter _____

2. by and large _____

3. cut-and-dried   _____

4. give and take   _____

5. heart and soul   _____

6. ins and outs   _____

7. open-and-shut   _____

8. to and fro   _____

9. tried-and-true   _____

10. wheel and deal   _____

Exercise 2

What other similar fixed expressions can you think of? Share your fixed expressions with your class.

UNFAMILIAR WORDS

As you read literature in English, you will almost certainly come across words that you're unfamiliar with or have forgotten. Sometimes, you may be able to work out the meaning from how the word is used in context. Learning the meaning of these words will help you to expand your vocabulary.

Exercise 3

The following list of uncommon words are all glossed in the story. First try to guess the meaning of the word from its context. Check your answer using the glossary. Then write a sentence using the word in an appropriate new context.

1. subtle (line 15)   _____

2. linger (line 35)   _____

3. mockery (line 35)   _____

4. rendezvous (line 38)   _____

5. detachment (line 62)   _____

6. suppressed (line 66)   _____

Exercise 4

Complete the sentences that follow with the correct words from the list in Exercise 3. You will need to change the tense of the verb.

The husband barely _____ his astonishment as he watched his wife dancing the can-can. He looked at his watch and realized that he _____ too long, so he _____ his car keys and hurried out the door, hearing the _____ in her laugh. He knew he was losing his _____ and felt that the situation had become quite _____. As he made his way to his _____, he realized that his wife's unexpected dance was a _____ way of showing her true feelings.

PART 5 WRITING ACTIVITIES

1. Imagine a scene in which the wife in "Can-Can" is waiting for her husband to return. Write about her thoughts and feelings as the hours go by. Try to use gerunds and present participles in your writing.

2. In an essay of one to two pages, outline your views on what it takes to have an ideal marriage. Consider factors such as the pros and cons of having similar or opposite temperaments; of having one partner be more willing to compromise; and of sharing the same religious, educational, social, and economic background. Say whether you believe a perfect union is attainable.

3. *The Scarlet Letter* by Nathaniel Hawthorne and *Anna Karenina* by Leo Tolstoy are two famous novels that deal with adultery. In an essay of two to three pages, discuss any well-known work in your language that involves this subject. Outline the plot, explaining what drives the characters to adultery. Are the characters treated sympathetically?

2 ⬲ The Cranes

Peter Meinke
(b. 1932)

Born in Brooklyn, New York, Peter Meinke was determined to be a writer from an early age. After teaching high school English for two years, he went on to earn a Ph.D. in English Literature from the University of Minnesota in 1965. He and his wife, artist Jeanne Meinke, moved to Florida in 1966, where they have remained to this day. Meinke directed the Writing Workshop at Eckerd College for over twenty years, while simultaneously pursuing a distinguished career as a poet and fiction writer.

Meinke's first collection of short stories, *The Piano Tuner* (1986), received the Flannery O'Connor Award. In 2007 he published his second collection, *Unheard Music*. Meinke has also written seven books of poems, including *The Contracted World: New and Selected Poems* (2006). He has received many honors, including three prizes from the Poetry Society of America and two O. Henry Awards. In 2009 Meinke was appointed Poet Laureate of St. Petersburg, Florida. He has been described as a "skilled, wildly imaginative writer who loves the climactic epiphanies that terminate his terrifying situations."

The Cranes

A husband and wife embark on a mysterious outing.

"Oh!" She said, "what are those, the huge white ones?" Along the marshy shore two tall and stately[1] birds, staring motionless toward the Gulf,[2] towered above the bobbing egrets and scurrying plovers.[3]

5   "Well, I can't believe it," he said. "I've been coming here for years and never saw one…."

    "But what are they?" she persisted. "Don't make me guess or anything, it makes me feel dumb." They leaned forward in the car and the shower curtain spread over the front seat crackled and hissed.

10   "They've got to be whooping cranes,[4] nothing else so big!" One of the birds turned gracefully, as if to acknowledge the old Dodge[5] parked alone in the tall grasses. "See the black legs and black wingtips? Big! Why don't I have my binoculars?"[6] He looked at his wife and smiled.

    "Well," he continued after a while, "I've seen enough birds. But

15 whooping cranes, they're rare. Not many left."

    "They're lovely. They make the little birds look like clowns."

    "I could use a few clowns," he said. "A few laughs never hurt anybody."

    "Are you all right?" She put a hand on his thin arm. "Maybe this is

20 the wrong thing. I feel I'm responsible."

    "God, no!" His voice changed. "No way. I can't smoke, can't drink martinis,[7] no coffee, no candy. I not only can't leap buildings in a single bound,[8] I can hardly get up the goddamn stairs."

    She was smiling. "Do you remember the time you drank thirteen

25 martinis and asked that young priest to step outside and see whose side God was on?"

    "What a jerk[9] I was! How have you put up with me all this time?"

    "Oh no! I was proud of you! You were so funny, and that priest was a snot."[10]

---

1 **stately** dignified
2 **the Gulf** the Gulf of Mexico, a sea off the coast of Florida
3 **bobbing egrets and scurrying plovers** waterbirds moving their heads up and down and running with small steps
4 **whooping cranes** the tallest birds in North America, distinctive for their white bodies and unusual sound
5 **Dodge** an American car

6 **binoculars** instrument for seeing objects in the distance
7 **martinis** classic alcoholic drinks made with gin
8 **leap buildings in a single bound** jump easily over tall buildings; a reference to the comic-book hero Superman
9 **jerk** a mean, insensitive person (slang)
10 **snot** an arrogant, unpleasant person (outdated slang)

30　　　　"Now you tell me." The cranes were moving slowly over a small hillock, wings opening and closing like bellows.[11] "It's all right. It's enough," he said again. "How old am I, anyway, 130?"

　　　　"Really," she said, "it's me. Ever since the accident it's been one thing after the other. I'm just a lot of trouble to everybody."

35　　　　"Let's talk about something else," he said. "Do you want to listen to the radio? How about turning on that preacher station so we can throw up?"

　　　　"No," she said, "I just want to watch the birds. And listen to you."

　　　　"You must be pretty tired of that."

40　　　　She turned her head from the window and looked into his eyes. "I never got tired of listening to you. Never."

　　　　"Well, that's good," he said. "It's just that when my mouth opens, your eyes tend to close."

　　　　"They do not!" she said, and began to laugh, but the laugh turned
45　into a cough and he had to pat her back until she stopped. They leaned back in the silence and looked toward the Gulf stretching out beyond the horizon. In the distance, the water looked like metal, still and hard.

　　　　"I wish they'd court,"[12] he said. "I wish we could see them court, the cranes. They put on a show. He bows like Nijinsky[13] and jumps
50　straight up in the air."

　　　　"What does she do?"

　　　　"She lies down and he lands on her."

　　　　"No," she said, "I'm serious."

　　　　"Well, I forget. I've never seen it. But I do remember that they mate
55　for life and live a long time. They're probably older than we are! Their feathers are falling out and their kids never write."

　　　　She was quiet again. He turned in his seat, picked up an object wrapped in a plaid towel, and placed it between them in the front.

　　　　"Here's looking at *you*, kid,"[14] he said.

60　　　　"Do they really mate for life? I'm glad—they're so beautiful."

　　　　"Yep. Audubon[15] said that's why they're almost extinct: a failure of imagination."

　　　　"I don't believe that," she said. "I think there'll always be whooping cranes."

65　　　　"Why not?" he said.

　　　　"I wish the children were more settled. I keep thinking it's my fault."

11　**bellows** an instrument for blowing more air onto a fire

12　**court** try to attract an animal of the opposite sex for mating

13　**Nijinsky** Vaslav Nijinsky, a great twentieth-century Russian ballet dancer

14　**"Here's looking at *you*, kid."** a romantic line spoken by Humphrey Bogart in the classic film *Casablanca*

15　**Audubon** John James Audubon, a nineteenth-century expert on North American birds

"You think everything's your fault. Nicaragua,[16] ozone depletion.[17] Nothing is your fault. They'll be fine, and anyway, they're not children
70 anymore. Kids are different today, that's all. You were terrific." He paused. "You were terrific in ways I couldn't tell the kids about."

"I should hope not." She laughed and began coughing again, but held his hand when he reached over. When the cough subsided they sat quietly, looking down at their hands as if they were objects
75 in a museum.

"I used to have pretty hands," she said.

"I remember."

"Do you? Really?"

"I remember everything," he said.
80 "You always forgot everything."

"Well, now I remember."

"Did you bring something for your ears?"

"No, I can hardly hear anything, anyway!" But his head turned at a sudden squabble[18] among the smaller birds. The cranes were stepping
85 delicately away from the commotion.

"I'm tired," she said.

"Yes." He leaned over and kissed her, barely touching her lips. "Tell me," he said, "did I really drink thirteen martinis?"

But she had already closed her eyes and only smiled. Outside
90 the wind ruffled the bleached-out[19] grasses, and the birds in the white glare seemed almost transparent. The hull[20] of the car gleamed beetle-like—dull and somehow sinister[21] in its metallic isolation from the world around it.

Suddenly, the two cranes plunged[22] upward, their great wings
95 beating the air and their long slender necks pointed like arrows toward the sun.

---

16 **Nicaragua** reference to the American involvement in the Nicaraguan conflict in the 1980s
17 **ozone depletion** an environmental issue concerning destruction of the atmosphere
18 **squabble** a noisy, superficial conflict

19 **bleached-out** colorless, faded
20 **hull** outer covering
21 **sinister** threatening and evil-looking
22 **plunged** dived rapidly (usually into water)

A Thinking About the Story

Discuss the following question with a partner.

> Did the story have a positive or negative ending for you? Explain your answer.

B Understanding the Plot

Be prepared to answer the following questions with a partner or the whole class.

1. What has the couple brought with them in their car? List as many items as possible.

2. Why does the husband regret not having his binoculars? (line 13)

3. How would you describe the couple's state of health? Give as much evidence as you can.

4. Why did the husband invite the priest to go outside? (lines 28–29)

5. What is the significance of the wife's use of the past tense of *get* in line 41?

6. Why is the wife concerned about their children? Does her husband share her concerns?

7. Why couldn't the husband tell his children about the "ways" referred to in line 71?

8. Why does the wife ask her husband whether he has brought something for his ears? (line 82)

9. Why has the couple come to the Gulf Coast of Florida? Explain your answer fully.

A Exploring Themes

Reread "The Cranes." As you read, notice how Meinke uses subtle details to flesh out the couple's past life and their present situation in such a compact space. See how he brings together the various elements of the story like a jigsaw puzzle.

1. What do the cranes symbolize? Explain your answer with as many details as possible.

2. What is the couple's attitude toward religion? Does it help explain their actions?

3. How do the personalities of the husband and wife differ? Justify your answer.

4. Explain the ending as fully as possible, giving reasons for your interpretation.

B Analyzing Style

INFERENCE

When an author does not spell out exactly what is happening, the reader has to use **inference** to figure out what is being implied (indirectly expressed). Inference requires the reader to work hard at reading between the lines of the text. For example, when the husband in "The Cranes" compares the male crane to Nijinsky taking a bow, we can infer from the simile that he thinks the bird is exceptionally graceful and agile.

Exercise 1

Answer the following questions with a partner.

1. What is implied by the shower curtain in the front seat of the car?

2. What does *this* (line 19) refer to? How does it relate to the wife's comment that she feels *responsible*?

3. What is implied by the wife's comment that she is *just a lot of trouble to everybody*? (line 34)

4. What can we infer about the couple's relationship with their children?

5. What does the wife's anxiety about whether her husband has brought something for his ears (line 82) imply about the specifics of their plan?

6. What is the husband's final act? What can be inferred from this act about his relationship with his wife?

7. At the end of the story, why do the cranes suddenly take flight?

SETTING

The **setting** of a story refers to the time and place in which the action unfolds. It can also include the society being depicted as well as its values. Setting is crucial to "The Cranes." For example, Meinke uses a surprising simile to describe the waters of the Gulf as *look[ing] like metal, still and hard* (line 47). This description, with its cold, gray, unyielding associations, sets up a tension with the initial appearance of an innocent beach outing. In addition, Meinke heightens the expectation that something sinister is in the air by using loaded words like *crackled* and *hissed* (line 9) since *crackle* is frequently associated with fire and *hiss* with snakes.

Exercise 2

Answer the following questions.

1. Give as complete a description as you can of the car and its surrounding location, using details from the story.
2. How does the depiction of this setting foreshadow the couple's subsequent actions?
3. The action of the story takes place in the couple's car. There are a number of mysterious references that help to build an atmosphere of uncertainty. List three and explain them. Did you skip over any of these as you read the story the first time? Did you make any incorrect assumptions about them?
4. What do the images in lines 89–93 suggest?

SIMILE

A **simile** is an explicit comparison that contains the word *like* or *as*. Imaginative writers combine two unlikely components to make up the simile, giving readers the chance to appreciate the unexpectedness or aptness of the comparison. Meinke uses similes to great effect in "The Cranes." For example, the husband contrasts the stately behavior of the cranes on the shore with the less dignified actions of smaller, noisier birds that *look like clowns* (line 16). This comparison graphically reinforces the distinction between the cranes and the rest of the birds.

Exercise 3

Find at least six similes in the story and underline them. Then explain the two elements of the comparison for each one.

Exercise 4

Answer the following questions.

How do the similes relating to the cranes differ from the other similes in the story? How does this difference help illuminate a central theme of the story?

Exercise 5

Make up some similes of your own to describe the setting and the birds.

BLACK HUMOR

Black humor is a comic form in which serious topics like illness, injustice, and death are treated lightly. Some writers make fun of a terrible situation in order to relieve tension and make the situation more bearable. Meinke employs black humor throughout "The Cranes," particularly through the voice of the husband.

Exercise 6

In each example below, explain the humor of the husband's statement, paying particular attention to the underlying truth that is being obscured or made fun of.

1. "Why don't I have my binoculars?" (line 13)
2. "Now you tell me." (line 30)
3. "They're probably older than we are! Their feathers are falling out and their kids never write." (lines 55–56)
4. "Here's looking at *you*, kid." (line 59)

   Note: This line was made famous in the movie *Casablanca*. Research its significance in the movie before you connect it to "The Cranes."

C Judging for Yourself

Express yourself as personally as you like in your answers to the following questions.

1. Do you think the couple has the right to determine their fate?
2. In your view, was the couple cowardly or brave?
3. Would you say the couple has had a successful marriage?
4. What do you think about the couple's attitude toward organized religion?

D Making Connections

Answer the following questions with a classmate or in a small group.

1. How is suicide viewed in your culture? Among which sectors of society is it most frequent?
2. In your culture, do people respect the choice to end a life rather than endure a terminal illness? What do you think about this? Explain.
3. How easy is it to own a gun in your country? Do you agree with your country's gun policy? Explain your answer.
4. Do children have a responsibility to take care of their elderly or sick parents?

E Debate

Decide whether you are for or against the following statement. Be prepared to argue your case in a class debate.

Assisted suicide should be legal.

WISHES

When we make a **wish**, we express a desire for something to happen that is either unlikely or impossible. The verb tense depends on whether the wish is for an event in the future, present, or past. When a wish is followed by a noun clause, the word *that* can be omitted.

1. When we wish for something in the **future**, we use the **past modal**. The wish expresses a desire that is possible but unlikely to be fulfilled.

   *"I wish [that] they'd (they **would**) court," he said. "I wish [that] we **could** see them court, the cranes."* (lines 48–49)

2. When we wish for something in the **present**, we use the **simple past tense**. The wish expresses a desire for something to be different from how it really is.

   *"I wish the children **were** more settled. I keep thinking it's my fault."* (lines 66–67)

   In formal English, *were* is used even with a singular subject for wishes.

   *"I wish I **were** in better health."*

3. When we wish that something had happened in the **past**, we use the **past perfect tense**, which is formed by the auxiliary verb *had* plus the past participle. The wish expresses a desire that the past had gone differently.

   *"I wish we **had decided** to do this a year ago."*

Exercise 1

Look at the following sentences. Complete each sentence with the correct form of the verb in parentheses.

1. The couple wishes that they _____ to their children before going to the bay. (write)

2. "I wish I _____ a different kind of person," the husband sighs. (be)

3. She wishes he _____ their plan now. (carry out)

4. Their children wish their parents _____ them earlier about the state of their health. (inform)

The Cranes **21**

5. The husband wishes he _____ readier to act on their plan. (be)

6. They wish they _____ the cranes one more time. (see)

7. The wife wishes she _____ her children more when they were growing up. (teach)

8. "I wish I _____ the name of those birds." (know)

9. You wish you _____ the situation, but you can't. (change)

10. It's no good wishing that you _____ differently because you didn't. (act)

Exercise 2

Complete the following dialogue with your own verbs that fit the context and are in the appropriate tense. Compare your answers with a partner.

A. I wish we _____ the cranes courting yesterday. But at least we can see them now.

B. Yes, I bet our birdwatcher friends wish they _____ here today. Have you brought your binoculars?

A. Of course. I wish I _____ an expert on cranes. I know so little about their habits.

B. Did you remember to bring the bird book?

A. Oh dear, I wish I _____.

B. Well, it's my fault too. I wish I _____ you to bring it.

A. Well, I wish you _____ some good closeup photographs, but your camera doesn't have the right lens.

B. Yes, I wish I _____ a time machine and _____ to yesterday to see those magnificent birds dancing.

VOCABULARY BUILDING

PREPOSITIONS

A **preposition** is a part of speech that shows the connection or relationship between a noun or pronoun and another part of the sentence. Prepositions often relate to space and time, but not always. The most commonly used prepositions include *at, by, for, from, in, of, on, to,* and *with.* Even advanced nonnative speakers have problems with prepositions, as there is often no clear rule governing which one to use. The more you pay attention to how prepositions are used in context, the better you will develop your ability to choose the correct one.

"The Cranes" contains many different prepositions. For example: *"They make the little birds look **like** clowns."* (line 16)

Exercise 1

Complete each sentence with the correct preposition. All the expressions appear in the story. Try to do the exercise without looking back at the text.

1. An unidentified object was placed _____ them on the seat.

2. They both looked down _____ their hands, thinking about the changes in them.

3. There was a sudden squabble _____ the smaller birds, which caused the couple to look up.

4. The whooping cranes towered _____ the other birds.

5. They parked their car _____ the tall grasses.

6. The male whooping crane does not actually land _____ the female after the courting dance.

7. The birds caught _____ the white glare seemed almost transparent.

8. When the whooping cranes heard the other birds fighting, they delicately stepped away _____ them.

9. The husband joked that his wife was terrific _____ ways that were too private to be shared.

10. The wife was very happy to learn that cranes mate _____ life.

OXYMORON

An **oxymoron** is a literary device that yokes together two seemingly contradictory words in order to heighten the effect of the writing. For example, in "The Cranes," Meinke ends the story with the image of two cranes *plunging upward*. Since *plunge* usually means a rapid descent, the contradictory image of the birds diving up into the sky instead of down into the water reinforces the multi-layered effect of the ending. Some frequently used oxymorons include:

*At the height of her illness, she felt like a **living death**.*

*It would be a **cruel kindness** to demand that your alcoholic husband either seek help or leave home.*

Exercise 2

With a partner, discuss the contradictions contained in the following oxymorons.

benevolent despot   same difference

bittersweet   small fortune

controlled chaos   silent applause

honest crook   taped live

man child   virtual reality

old news   working vacation

PART 5 WRITING ACTIVITIES

1. Euthanasia or mercy killing is a highly controversial subject in most countries. Write an essay of two pages in which you consider the pros and cons of the issue. Include factors such as ethical, religious, and legal objections, and weigh them against the right of the individual to stop his or her suffering at a determined time. In your conclusion, say what your own beliefs are.

2. Imagine a telephone conversation involving the children of the couple when they hear the news about their parents. Write a dialogue of their reactions as they discuss what their parents have done. Try to include some wishes in your dialogue.

3. *The Sessions* (2012) and *Whose Life Is It Anyway?* (1981) are both films in which the protagonist is severely paralyzed, but the characters deal with their situations in very different ways. In the first movie, based on

a true story, the main character contracts polio as a child and must use a large machine in order to breathe. Despite this he becomes a writer and explores his sexuality with the help of a professional therapist. In the second movie, the patient goes to court, pleading his right to be released from treatment and allowed to die. In a short essay, discuss any movie, book, or newspaper article you've read that involves a similar situation. Describe the person's condition and what he or she chooses to do about it. Say whether you sympathize with the outcome.

4. Despite its subject, it could be argued that "The Cranes," with its uplifting final imagery, should not be read as a depressing story at all. Write a one- to two-page essay responding to this statement. Consider what we learn about the characters and their lives, and cite as many examples as possible to substantiate your position.

3 ☙ The Kugelmass Episode

Woody Allen
(b. 1935)

Born in Brooklyn, New York, to a lower-middle-class Jewish family, Woody Allen grew up shy and withdrawn. However, he quickly demonstrated a flair for writing and performing comedy. After writing the script for the movie *What's New Pussycat?* in 1965, he moved into the triple role of screenwriter, actor, and director of his own movie *Take the Money and Run* (1969), positions he has occupied with international fame and stature for almost half a century.

Allen's numerous movies range from comedies like *Annie Hall* (1977) and *Bullets Over Broadway* (1994) to the mixture of humor and drama found in *Hannah and Her Sisters* (1986) and *Husbands and Wives* (1992). His recent films include the travel romance *Vicky Christina Barcelona* (2008), the dark thriller *Match Point* (2005), the modern fairy tale *Midnight in Paris* (2011), and the psychological drama *Blue Jasmine* (2013). In addition to his many screenplays, he has written six plays and three collections of essays and short stories: *Getting Even* (1971), *Without Feathers* (1975), and *Side Effects* (1980). His stories, often satires and parodies of the anxieties associated with modern life, are filled with zany humor, surrealistic visions, and witty one-line jokes.

The Kugelmass Episode

When a New York professor has his deepest wish granted, his life takes an unexpected turn.

"The Kugelmass Episode" is a parody, or humorous imitation, of Gustave Flaubert's classic nineteenth-century novel Madame Bovary. *To appreciate the story, it is necessary to know the broad outline of the original novel: Emma Rouault attempts to escape from her boring existence on her father's farm by marrying a rural doctor, Charles Bovary. Emma quickly tires of her adoring husband's country ways and seeks excitement in two love affairs—with Leon, a young law student, and Rodolphe, a wealthy landowner. By the end of the book Emma has squandered all her husband's savings, is rejected by her two lovers, and commits suicide, appreciating only at the last minute Charles's faithful devotion to her.*

Kugelmass, a professor of humanities at City College, was unhappily married for the second time. Daphne Kugelmass was an oaf.[1] He also had two dull sons by his first wife, Flo, and was up to his neck in alimony[2] and child support.

5   "Did I know it would turn out so badly?" Kugelmass whined to his analyst[3] one day. "Daphne had promise.[4] Who suspected she'd let herself go and swell up like a beach ball? Plus she had a few bucks, which is not in itself a healthy reason to marry a person, but it doesn't hurt, with the kind of operating nut[5] I have. You see my point?"

10   Kugelmass was bald and as hairy as a bear, but he had soul.

"I need to meet a new woman," he went on. "I need to have an affair. I may not look the part, but I'm a man who needs romance. I need softness, I need flirtation. I'm not getting younger, so before it's too late I want to make love in Venice, trade quips at '21,'[6] and exchange coy

15 glances over red wine and candlelight. You see what I'm saying?"

Dr. Mandel shifted in his chair and said, "An affair will solve nothing. You're so unrealistic. Your problems run much deeper."

"And also this affair must be discreet," Kugelmass continued. "I can't afford a second divorce. Daphne would really sock it to me."[7]

20   "Mr. Kugelmass—"

---

1 **oaf** a stupid person
2 **alimony** money paid to a spouse after a divorce
3 **analyst** psychoanalyst, a therapist
4 **Daphne had promise** Daphne looked as if she would stay attractive.
5 **operating nut** ability to manage daily expenses (slang)

6 **trade quips at '21'** exchange witty remarks at 21, a well-known New York restaurant
7 **sock it to me** strongly attack me (by demanding more alimony) (slang)

"But it can't be anyone at City College, because Daphne also works there. Not that anyone on the faculty at C.C.N.Y. is any great shakes,[8] but some of those coeds...."[9]

"Mr. Kugelmass—"

25 "Help me. I had a dream last night. I was skipping through a meadow holding a picnic basket and the basket was marked 'Options.' And then I saw there was a hole in the basket."

"Mr. Kugelmass, the worst thing you could do is act out. You must simply express your feelings here, and together we'll analyze them.
30 You have been in treatment long enough to know there is no overnight cure. After all, I'm an analyst, not a magician."

"Then perhaps what I need is a magician," Kugelmass said, rising from his chair. And with that he terminated his therapy.

A couple of weeks later, while Kugelmass and Daphne were
35 moping around[10] in their apartment one night like two pieces of old furniture, the phone rang.

"I'll get it," Kugelmass said. "Hello."

"Kugelmass?" a voice said. "Kugelmass, this is Persky."

"Who?"

40 "Persky. Or should I say The Great Persky?"

"Pardon me?"

"I hear you're looking all over town for a magician to bring a little exotica[11] into your life? Yes or no?"

"Sh-h-h," Kugelmass whispered. "Don't hang up. Where are you
45 calling from, Persky?"

Early the following afternoon, Kugelmass climbed three flights of stairs in a broken-down apartment house in the Bushwick section of Brooklyn. Peering through the darkness of the hall, he found the door he was looking for and pressed the bell. I'm going to regret this, he
50 thought to himself.

Seconds later, he was greeted by a short, thin, waxy-looking man. "You're Persky the Great?" Kugelmass said. "The Great Persky. You want a tea?"

"No, I want romance. I want music. I want love and beauty."

55 "But not tea, eh? Amazing. O.K., sit down."

Persky went to the back room, and Kugelmass heard the sounds of boxes and furniture being moved around. Persky reappeared, pushing before him a large object on squeaky roller-skate wheels. He removed some old silk handkerchiefs that were lying on its top and blew away a
60 bit of dust. It was a cheap-looking Chinese cabinet, badly lacquered.[12]

"Persky," Kugelmass said, "what's your scam?"[13]

---

8 **is any great shakes** is exceptional (slang)
9 **coeds** female students (informal)
10 **moping around** doing nothing, in a depressed fashion

11 **exotica** exciting, unusual things
12 **lacquered** polished, coated with a shiny paint
13 **scam** a dishonest scheme

"Pay attention," Persky said. "This is some beautiful effect. I developed it for a Knights of Pythias[14] date last year, but the booking fell through.[15] Get into the cabinet."

65 "Why, so you can stick it full of swords or something?"

"You see any swords?"

Kugelmass made a face and, grunting, climbed into the cabinet. He couldn't help noticing a couple of ugly rhinestones[16] glued onto the raw plywood just in front of his face. "If this is a joke," he said.

70 "Some joke. Now, here's the point. If I throw any novel into this cabinet with you, shut the doors, and tap it three times, you will find yourself projected into that book."

Kugelmass made a grimace of disbelief.

"It's the *emess*,"[17] Persky said. "My hand to God. Not just a novel,
75 either. A short story, a play, a poem. You can meet any of the women created by the world's best writers. Whoever you dreamed of. You could carry on[18] all you like with a real winner. Then when you've had enough you give a yell, and I'll see you're back here in a split second."

"Persky, are you some kind of outpatient?"[19]

80 "I'm telling you it's on the level," Persky said.

Kugelmass remained skeptical. "What are you telling me—that this cheesy[20] homemade box can take me on a ride like you're describing?"

"For a double sawbuck."[21]

Kugelmass reached for his wallet. "I'll believe this when I see it,"
85 he said.

Persky tucked the bills in his pants pocket and turned toward his bookcase. "So who do you want to meet? Sister Carrie? Hester Prynne? Ophelia? Maybe someone by Saul Bellow? Hey, what about Temple Drake?[22] Although for a man your age she'd be a workout."

90 "French. I want to have an affair with a French lover."

"Nana?"[23]

"I don't want to have to pay for it."

"What about Natasha in 'War and Peace'?"

"I said French. I know! What about Emma Bovary? That sounds to
95 me perfect."

"You got it, Kugelmass. Give me a holler[24] when you've had enough." Persky tossed in a paperback copy of Flaubert's novel.

---

14 **Knights of Pythias** a group of men involved in charity work	21 **double sawbuck** twenty dollars (slang)
15 **the booking fell through** I was not hired in the end	22 **Sister Carrie, Hester Prynne, Ophelia, and Temple Drake** beautiful troubled heroines in works by Theodore Dreiser, Nathaniel Hawthorne, William Shakespeare, and William Faulkner, respectively
16 **rhinestones** cheap imitation diamonds	
17 *emess* truth (Yiddish)	
18 **carry on with** have a love affair with	23 **Nana** the prostitute in Emile Zola's novel *Nana*
19 **outpatient** a mentally disturbed person (slang)	
20 **cheesy** poorly made, tasteless (slang)	24 **give me a holler** shout to me (slang)

"You sure this is safe?" Kugelmass asked as Persky began shutting the cabinet doors.

"Safe. Is anything safe in this crazy world?" Persky rapped three times on the cabinet and then flung open the doors.

Kugelmass was gone. At the same moment, he appeared in the bedroom of Charles and Emma Bovary's house at Yonville. Before him was a beautiful woman, standing alone with her back turned to him as she folded some linen. I can't believe this, thought Kugelmass, staring at the doctor's ravishing[25] wife. This is uncanny. I'm here. It's her.

Emma turned in surprise. "Goodness, you startled me," she said. "Who are you?" She spoke in the same fine English translation as the paperback.

It's simply devastating, he thought. Then, realizing that it was he whom she had addressed, he said, "Excuse me. I'm Sidney Kugelmass. I'm from City College. A professor of humanities. C.C.N.Y.? Uptown. I—oh, boy?"

Emma Bovary smiled flirtatiously and said, "Would you like a drink? A glass of wine, perhaps?"

She is beautiful, Kugelmass thought. What a contrast with the troglodyte[26] who shared his bed! He felt a sudden impulse to take this vision into his arms and tell her she was the kind of woman he had dreamed of all his life.

"Yes, some wine," he said hoarsely. "White. No, red. No, white. Make it white."

"Charles is out for the day," Emma said, her voice full of playful implication.

After the wine, they went for a stroll in the lovely French countryside. "I've always dreamed that some mysterious stranger would appear and rescue me from the monotony of this crass[27] rural existence," Emma said, clasping his hand. They passed a small church. "I love what you have on," she murmured. "I've never seen anything like it around here. It's so … so modern."

"It's called a leisure suit,"[28] he said romantically. "It was marked down."[29] Suddenly he kissed her. For the next hour they reclined under a tree and whispered together and told each other deeply meaningful things with their eyes. Then Kugelmass sat up. He had just remembered he had to meet Daphne at Bloomingdale's.[30] "I must go," he told her. "But don't worry, I'll be back."

"I hope so," Emma said.

---

25 **ravishing** unusually beautiful
26 **troglodyte** an early cave dweller
27 **crass** vulgar, insensitive
28 **leisure suit** an unfashionable polyester suit
29 **marked down** on sale
30 **Bloomingdale's** a famous New York department store

He embraced her passionately, and the two walked back to the house. He held Emma's face cupped in his palms, kissed her again, and yelled, "O.K., Persky! I got to be at Bloomingdale's by three-thirty."

There was an audible pop, and Kugelmass was back in Brooklyn. "So? Did I lie?" Persky asked triumphantly.

"Look, Persky, I'm right now late to meet the ball and chain[31] at Lexington Avenue, but when can I go again? Tomorrow?"

"My pleasure. Just bring a twenty. And don't mention this to anybody."

"Yeah. I'm going to call Rupert Murdoch."[32]

Kugelmass hailed a cab and sped off to the city. His heart danced on point.[33] I am in love, he thought, I am the possessor of a wonderful secret. What he didn't realize was that at this very moment students in various classrooms across the country were saying to their teachers, "Who is this character on page 100? A bald Jew is kissing Madame Bovary?" A teacher in Sioux Falls, South Dakota, sighed and thought, Jesus, these kids, with their pot and acid.[34] What goes through their minds!

Daphne Kugelmass was in the bathroom-accessories department at Bloomingdale's when Kugelmass arrived breathlessly. "Where've you been?" she snapped. "It's four-thirty."

"I got held up in traffic," Kugelmass said.

Kugelmass visited Persky the next day, and in a few minutes was again passed magically to Yonville. Emma couldn't hide her excitement at seeing him. The two spent hours together, laughing and talking about their different backgrounds. Before Kugelmass left, they made love. "My God, I'm doing it with Madame Bovary!" Kugelmass whispered to himself. "Me, who failed freshman English."

As the months passed, Kugelmass saw Persky many times and developed a close and passionate relationship with Emma Bovary. "Make sure and always get me into the book before page 120," Kugelmass said to the magician one day. "I always have to meet her before she hooks up with this Rodolphe character."

"Why?" Persky asked. "You can't beat his time?"[35]

"Beat his time. He's landed gentry. Those guys have nothing better to do than flirt and ride horses. To me, he's one of those faces you see in the pages of *Women's Wear Daily*. With the Helmut Berger[36] hairdo. But to her he's hot stuff."

"And her husband suspects nothing?"

---

31 **the ball and chain** an insulting term for a wife, referring to shackles worn by a prisoner
32 **Rupert Murdoch** an international media owner known for his scandal-loving newspapers
33 **on point** like a ballet dancer in toe shoes
34 **pot and acid** marijuana and LSD (slang)
35 **beat his time** win out over a rival (slang)
36 **Helmut Berger** a handsome Austrian actor

"He's out of his depth. He's a lackluster little paramedic[37] who's thrown in his lot with a jitterbug.[38] He's ready to go to sleep by ten, and she's putting on her dancing shoes. Oh, well … See you later."

180   And once again Kugelmass entered the cabinet and passed instantly to the Bovary estate at Yonville. "How you doing, cupcake?" he said to Emma.

"Oh, Kugelmass," Emma sighed. "What I have to put up with. Last night at dinner, Mr. Personality dropped off to sleep in the middle of
185   the dessert course. I'm pouring my heart out about Maxim's[39] and the ballet, and out of the blue[40] I hear snoring."

"It's O.K., darling. I'm here now," Kugelmass said, embracing her. I've earned this, he thought, smelling Emma's French perfume and burying his nose in her hair. I've suffered enough. I've paid enough
190   analysts. I've searched till I'm weary. She's young and nubile,[41] and I'm here a few pages after Léon and just before Rodolphe. By showing up during the correct chapters, I've got the situation knocked.[42]

Emma, to be sure, was just as happy as Kugelmass. She had been starved for excitement, and his tales of Broadway night life, of fast cars
195   and Hollywood and TV stars, enthralled the young French beauty.

"Tell me again about O. J. Simpson,"[43] she implored that evening, as she and Kugelmass strolled past Abbé Bournisien's church.

"What can I say? The man is great. He sets all kinds of rushing[44] records. Such moves. They can't touch him."

200   "And the Academy Awards?" Emma said wistfully. "I'd give anything to win one."

"First you've got to be nominated."

"I know. You explained it. But I'm convinced I can act. Of course, I'd want to take a class or two. With Strasberg[45] maybe. Then, if I had
205   the right agent—"

"We'll see, we'll see. I'll speak to Persky."

That night, safely returned to Persky's flat, Kugelmass brought up the idea of having Emma visit him in the big city.

"Let me think about it," Persky said. "Maybe I could work it.
210   Stranger things have happened." Of course, neither of them could think of one.

---

37 **lackluster little paramedic** an insulting reference implying that Charles is boring and incompetent as a doctor
38 **thrown in his lot with a jitterbug** committed to someone who loves dancing and having fun
39 **Maxim's** a famous restaurant in Paris
40 **out of the blue** completely unexpectedly
41 **nubile** young and sexually attractive

42 **I've got the situation knocked.** I'm sure to win. (slang)
43 **O. J. Simpson** a former American football star, notorious for the murder trial in which he was acquitted of killing his wife
44 **rushing** a rapid move in American football
45 **Strasberg** Lee Strasberg, a famous acting teacher

"Where the hell do you go all the time?" Daphne Kugelmass barked at her husband as he returned home late that evening. "You got a chippie[46] stashed[47] somewhere?"

215 "Yeah, sure, I'm just the type," Kugelmass said wearily. "I was with Leonard Popkin. We were discussing Socialist agriculture in Poland. You know Popkin. He's a freak on the subject."

"Well, you've been very odd lately," Daphne said. "Distant. Just don't forget about my father's birthday. On Saturday?"

220 "Oh, sure, sure," Kugelmass said, heading for the bathroom.

"My whole family will be there. We can see the twins. And Cousin Hamish. You should be more polite to Cousin Hamish—he likes you."

"Right, the twins," Kugelmass said, closing the bathroom door and shutting out the sound of his wife's voice. He leaned against it and
225 took a deep breath. In a few hours, he told himself, he would be back in Yonville again, back with his beloved. And this time, if all went well, he would bring Emma back with him.

At three-fifteen the following afternoon, Persky worked his wizardry again. Kugelmass appeared before Emma, smiling and eager. The two
230 spent a few hours at Yonville with Binet[48] and then remounted the Bovary Carriage. Following Persky's instructions, they held each other tightly, closed their eyes, and counted to ten. When they opened them, the carriage was just drawing up at the side door of the Plaza Hotel, where Kugelmass had optimistically reserved a suite earlier in the day.

235 "I love it! It's everything I dreamed it would be," Emma said as she swirled joyously around the bedroom, surveying the city from their window. "There's F.A.O. Schwarz.[49] And there's Central Park, and the Sherry[50] is which one? Oh, there—I see. It's too divine."

On the bed there were boxes from Halston and Saint Laurent.[51]
240 Emma unwrapped a package and held up a pair of black velvet pants against her perfect body.

"The slacks suit is by Ralph Lauren," Kugelmass said. "You'll look like a million bucks in it. Come on, sugar, give us a kiss."

"I've never been so happy!" Emma squealed as she stood before the
245 mirror. "Let's go out on the town.[52] I want to see 'Chorus Line' and the Guggenheim and this Jack Nicholson character you always talk about. Are any of his flicks[53] showing?"

"I cannot get my mind around[54] this," a Stanford professor said. "First a strange character named Kugelmass, and now she's gone from
250 the book. Well, I guess the mark of a classic is that you can reread it a thousand times and always find something new."

---

46 **chippie** an immoral woman (slang)
47 **stashed** hidden away
48 **Binet** a minor character in *Madame Bovary*
49 **F.A.O. Schwarz** a large toy store
50 **the Sherry** an exclusive New York hotel
51 **Halston and Saint Laurent** designers
52 **Let's go out on the town.** Let's go out and enjoy ourselves.
53 **flicks** movies (slang)
54 **get my mind around** understand

The lovers passed a blissful weekend. Kugelmass had told Daphne he would be away at a symposium in Boston and would return Monday. Savoring each moment, he and Emma went to the movies, had dinner in Chinatown, passed two hours at a discothèque, and went to bed with a TV movie. They slept till noon on Sunday, visited SoHo, and ogled[55] celebrities at Elaine's.[56] They had caviar and champagne in their suite on Sunday night and talked until dawn. That morning, in the cab taking them to Persky's apartment, Kugelmass thought, It was hectic,[57] but worth it. I can't bring her here too often, but now and then it will be a charming contrast with Yonville.

At Persky's, Emma climbed into the cabinet, arranged her new boxes of clothes neatly around her, and kissed Kugelmass fondly. "My place next time," she said with a wink. Persky rapped three times on the cabinet. Nothing happened.

"Hmm," Persky said, scratching his head. He rapped again, but still no magic. "Something must be wrong," he mumbled.

"Persky, you're joking!" Kugelmass cried. "How can it not work?"

"Relax, relax. Are you still in the box, Emma?"

"Yes."

Persky rapped again—harder this time.

"I'm still here, Persky."

"I know, darling. Sit tight."

"Persky, we *have* to get her back," Kugelmass whispered. "I'm a married man, and I have a class in three hours. I'm not prepared for anything more than a cautious affair at this point."

"I can't understand it," Persky muttered. "It's such a reliable little trick."

But he could do nothing. "It's going to take a little while," he said to Kugelmass. "I'm going to have to strip it down.[58] I'll call you later."

Kugelmass bundled Emma into a cab and took her back to the Plaza. He barely made it to his class on time. He was on the phone all day, to Persky and to his mistress. The magician told him it might be several days before he got to the bottom of the trouble.

"How was the symposium?" Daphne asked him that night.

"Fine, fine," he said, lighting the filter end of a cigarette.

"What's wrong? You're as tense as a cat."

"Me? Ha, that's a laugh. I'm as calm as a summer night. I'm just going to take a walk." He eased out the door, hailed a cab, and flew to the Plaza.

"This is no good," Emma said. "Charles will miss me."

---

55 **ogled** stared rudely at
56 **Elaine's** a New York restaurant frequented by celebrities
57 **hectic** rushed and confused
58 **strip it down** take it apart

"Bear with me, sugar,"[59] Kugelmass said. He was pale and sweaty. He kissed her again, raced to the elevators, yelled at Persky over a pay phone in the Plaza lobby, and just made it home before midnight.

"According to Popkin, barley prices in Kraków have not been this stable since 1971," he said to Daphne, and smiled wanly as he climbed into bed.

The whole week went by like that. On Friday night, Kugelmass told Daphne there was another symposium he had to catch, this one in Syracuse. He hurried back to the Plaza, but the second weekend there was nothing like the first. "Get me back into the novel or marry me," Emma told Kugelmass. "Meanwhile, I want to get a job or go to class, because watching TV all day is the pits."[60]

"Fine. We can use the money," Kugelmass said. "You consume twice your weight in room service."

"I met an off-Broadway producer in Central Park yesterday, and he said I might be right for a project he's doing," Emma said.

"Who is this clown?" Kugelmass asked.

"He's not a clown. He's sensitive and kind and cute. His name's Jeff Something-or-Other, and he's up for a Tony."[61]

Later that afternoon, Kugelmass showed up at Persky's drunk.

"Relax," Persky told him. "You'll get a coronary."[62]

"Relax. The man says relax. I've got a fictional character stashed in a hotel room, and I think my wife is having me tailed by a private shamus."[63]

"O.K., O.K. We know there's a problem." Persky crawled under the cabinet and started banging on something with a large wrench.

"I'm like a wild animal," Kugelmass went on. "I'm sneaking around town, and Emma and I have had it up to here with each other.[64] Not to mention a hotel tab that reads like the defense budget."

"So what should I do? This is the world of magic," Persky said. "It's all nuance."[65]

"Nuance, my foot.[66] I'm pouring Dom Pérignon and black eggs into this little mouse, plus her wardrobe, plus she's enrolled at the Neighborhood Playhouse and suddenly needs professional photos. Also, Persky, Professor Fivish Kopkind, who teaches Comp Lit[67] and who has always been jealous of me, has identified me as the sporadically

---

59 **Bear with me, sugar.** Be patient with me, darling.
60 **the pits** the worst situation imaginable (slang)
61 **he's up for a Tony** he's been nominated for a Broadway theater award
62 **You'll get a coronary.** You'll have a heart attack.
63 **shamus** detective (Yiddish slang)

64 **Emma and I have had it up to here with each other.** Emma and I are sick of each other.
65 **It's all nuance.** It's hard to understand and can't be rushed.
66 **my foot** expression of disagreement (slang)
67 **Comp Lit** Comparative Literature

appearing character in the Flaubert book. He's threatened to go to
330 Daphne. I see ruin and alimony, jail. For adultery with Madame Bovary,
my wife will reduce me to beggary."

"What do you want me to say? I'm working on it night and day.
As far as your personal anxiety goes, that I can't help you with. I'm a
magician, not an analyst."

335 By Sunday afternoon, Emma had locked herself in the bathroom
and refused to respond to Kugelmass's entreaties. Kugelmass stared
out the window at the Wollman Rink[68] and contemplated suicide.
Too bad this is a low floor, he thought, or I'd do it right now. Maybe
if I ran away to Europe and started life over.... Maybe I could sell the
340 *International Herald Tribune*, like those young girls used to.

The phone rang. Kugelmass lifted it to his ear mechanically.

"Bring her over," Persky said. "I think I got the bugs[69] out of it."

Kugelmass's heart leaped. "You're serious?" he said. "You got it
licked?"[70]

345 "It was something in the transmission. Go figure."[71]

"Persky, you're a genius. We'll be there in a minute. Less than a
minute."

Again the lovers hurried to the magician's apartment, and again
Emma Bovary climbed into the cabinet with her boxes. This time there
350 was no kiss. Persky shut the doors, took a deep breath, and tapped the
box three times. There was the reassuring popping noise, and when
Persky peered inside, the box was empty. Madame Bovary was back
in her novel. Kugelmass heaved a great sigh of relief and pumped the
magician's hand.

355 "It's over," he said. "I learned my lesson. I'll never cheat again, I
swear it." He pumped Persky's hand again and made a mental note to
send him a necktie.

Three weeks later, at the end of a beautiful spring afternoon, Persky
answered his doorbell. It was Kugelmass, with a sheepish expression
360 on his face.

"O.K., Kugelmass," the magician said. "Where to this time?"

"It's just this once," Kugelmass said. "The weather is so lovely,
and I'm not getting any younger. Listen, you've read *Portnoy's
Complaint*?[72] Remember The Monkey?"[73]

365 "The price is now twenty-five dollars, because the cost of living is
up, but I'll start you off with one freebie, due to all the trouble I caused
you."

---

68 **Wollman Rink** an outdoor skating rink in
New York's Central Park
69 **bugs** errors, problems (slang)
70 **You got it licked?** You've solved it? (slang)
71 **Go figure.** Can you believe it? (slang)

72 *Portnoy's Complaint* an erotic novel by
Philip Roth
73 **The Monkey** a female character in *Portnoy's Complaint*, skillful at fulfilling the main
character's sexual fantasies

"You're good people," Kugelmass said, combing his few remaining hairs as he climbed into the cabinet again, "This'll work all right?"

370 "I hope. But I haven't tried it much since all that unpleasantness."

"Sex and romance," Kugelmass said from inside the box. "What we go through for a pretty face."

Persky tossed in a copy of "Portnoy's Complaint" and rapped three times on the box. This time, instead of a popping noise there was a

375 dull explosion, followed by a series of crackling noises and a shower of sparks. Persky leaped back, was seized by a heart attack, and dropped dead. The cabinet burst into flames, and eventually the entire house burned down.

Kugelmass, unaware of this catastrophe, had his own problems.

380 He had not been thrust into "Portnoy's Complaint," or into any other novel, for that matter. He had been projected into an old textbook, "Remedial Spanish,"[74] and was running for his life over a barren, rocky terrain as the word "tener" ("to have")—a large and hairy irregular verb—raced after him on its spindly[75] legs.

---

74 **Remedial Spanish** Spanish for slow learners   75 **spindly** thin

---

PART 1 **FIRST READING**

A Thinking About the Story

Discuss the following question with a partner.

Did you find the story funny? Explain your answer.

B Understanding the Plot

Be prepared to answer the following questions with a partner or the whole class.

1. Why did Kugelmass marry Daphne? Why won't he divorce her?
2. Why is Kugelmass's analyst against his having an affair?
3. What does Kugelmass's dream mean?
4. What are the disadvantages of Temple Drake and Nana as potential lovers for Kugelmass?
5. Why does Kugelmass fear his "rival" Rodolphe?

6. What does Kugelmass think of Emma's husband, Charles?

7. What is Emma's main complaint against Charles?

8. What does Kugelmass criticize Emma for during her prolonged stay at the Plaza Hotel?

9. What are Emma's ambitions for herself during her New York visit?

10. Does Kugelmass's wife suspect that he is having an affair? Explain your answer.

11. What is different about the last time Emma and Kugelmass say goodbye?

12. What happens to Kugelmass at the end?

CRITICAL THINKING

A Exploring Themes

Reread "The Kugelmass Episode." As you read, look at how Woody Allen exposes his characters' weaknesses through dialogue peppered with jokes.

1. How is Kugelmass's relationship with his wife, Daphne, presented? Illustrate your answer with details.

2. What attitudes toward women are reflected in the story?

3. What are Emma's values? Explain your answer.

4. How does the story make fun of literature teachers and their students?

5. What is ironic about the ending of the story?

B Analyzing Style

DIALOGUE

Stories can vary widely in their use of **dialogue**, or conversation. When there is a great deal of dialogue, it can reveal much about the characters and push the plot along rapidly. "The Kugelmass Episode" is composed almost entirely of dialogue, with virtually no descriptive writing. The dialogue is informal, slangy, and unmistakably from the New York of the 1970s. The short, snappy lines serve as a showcase for Woody Allen's famous one-line jokes.

The following dialogue from the story is representative of Allen's style:

"Did I know it would turn out so badly?" Kugelmass whined to his analyst one day. "Daphne had promise. Who suspected she'd let herself go and swell up like a beach ball? Plus she had a few bucks, which is not in itself a healthy reason to marry a person, but it doesn't hurt, with the kind of operating nut I have. You see my point?" (lines 5–9)

Answer the following questions.

1. What is the effect of using dialogue in this fashion?

2. Which verbal jokes in the story appealed to you the most? Why?

3. How do you imagine a professor of humanities to speak? Does Kugelmass come up to your expectations or not? Explain your answer.

4. Can you tell the characters apart from the way they speak? If you can, how? If not, how would you describe the way they sound?

FLAT CHARACTERS

The English novelist and critic E. M. Forster divided characters into the categories of **round** and **flat**. Round characters are fully formed, complex people who may act unpredictably and who struggle and change over the course of a story, finally achieving greater self-knowledge. Flat characters, in contrast, are one-dimensional, predictable people who do not change or increase their self-awareness. "The Kugelmass Episode" is peopled with flat characters, who remain essentially unaware and unchanged in the course of the story.

For more about *round characters*, see "Everyday Use" (pages 157–176).

Exercise 2

Answer the following questions.

1. In what ways are Kugelmass, Emma, and Daphne flat characters?

2. How does the flat nature of the characters affect your sympathy for their predicament? Does this increase the humor of the situation for you?

3. How does telling the story primarily through dialogue influence the way we see Kugelmass and Emma? Explain your answer.

4. Choose a flat character from another story in this anthology. Say what gives the character its one-dimensional aspect.

ANACHRONISM

Anachronism refers to something that doesn't belong in the historical time period of the story. It can be anything that is out of place, such as a person, an object, an event, or an expression. The effect is to create a striking inconsistency that readers will immediately notice. In "The Kugelmass Episode," both Kugelmass and Emma are transported out of their own century and country, giving rise to many anachronisms, which are one of the main sources of humor in the story. For example, when Emma and Kugelmass are strolling past the church in Yonville, she begs him to tell her more about the American football star O. J. Simpson—a person not yet born who played a sport not yet invented. Similarly, Emma's comment that an off-Broadway producer is *up for a Tony* (line 311) is funny because of how casually she says it, as if it were normal for a nineteenth-century French woman to be talking about modern American theater.

Exercise 3

Work with a partner to find examples of anachronism in the story. Say whether you feel these anachronisms are humorous and explain why.

ALLUSION

An **allusion** is a brief reference to something that an author assumes will be familiar to the reader, making it unnecessary for the reference to be explained explicitly. Allusions are frequently made to people or stories from literature, history, religion, and popular culture. "The Kugelmass Episode" has many allusions to the worlds of sports, theater, fashion, and literature. For example, when Emma and Kugelmass talk about O. J. Simpson (line 196), it is taken for granted that the reader will know about his legendary football record.

Exercise 4

Answer the following questions.

1. Persky alludes to various literary heroines in lines 86–93. Why did Persky choose these fictional women? What do we learn about Kugelmass from his reactions to Persky's list?

2. Why does Kugelmass allude to Emma's literary lover Rodolphe? (lines 170–175)

3. What do the allusions to F.A.O. Schwartz, the Sherry, Halston, Saint Laurent, and Ralph Lauren tell us about Emma's character? (lines 237–242)

4. Pick out Emma's allusions to acting and actors during her first two stays in New York.

5. What does Kugelmass's wish to be in *Portnoy's Complaint* reveal about him?

6. Find at least one more allusion in the story and explain it.

C   Judging for Yourself

Express yourself as personally as you like in your answers to the following questions.

1. Do you think Kugelmass deserved his fate at the end of the story? Justify your answer.

2. In your opinion, might further psychoanalysis have helped Kugelmass?

3. Do you sympathize with Daphne Kugelmass? Why or why not?

4. If it were possible, would you be interested in meeting Emma Bovary? Explain your answer. Are there other characters in fiction whom you would like to meet? If so, which ones?

D   Making Connections

Answer the following questions with a classmate or in a small group.

1. Is divorce common in your culture? When a couple splits up, is it customary to award alimony?

2. Are Woody Allen's movies shown in your country? Which ones have you seen? Do you find his comedies funny? Why or why not?

3. In your culture, is it common to seek help for personal problems from an analyst or psychologist? If not, to whom do people usually turn for help in personal matters?

4. Celebrities such as athletes, politicians, royalty, or movie stars are frequently the object of people's fantasies. In your country, whom do people dream about being or meeting? Is there someone you dream about?

E   Debate

Decide whether you are for or against the following statement. Be prepared to argue your case in a class debate.

Physical attraction is not a good basis for marriage.

THE PASSIVE VOICE

Verbs can be in two voices: **active** and **passive**. Only transitive verbs can be used in the passive voice.

In the active voice the subject of the sentence is the **agent** that performs the action and is the focus of our attention.

> *Kugelmass **hailed** a cab.* (line 148)

This sentence can be changed from the active voice to the passive voice. The passive is constructed using a form of the verb *to be* plus a past participle.

> *A cab **was hailed** by Kugelmass.*

The cab has become the focus of the sentence, along with the action that is done to it. Kugelmass (the agent) is no longer the focus. The agent is moved to a position after the verb and is introduced by the preposition *by.*

If the agent is unknown or unimportant, it can be left out.

> *The stage **was prepared** carefully before the magician's performance.*

The passive voice can also be used when the subject of the sentence is the impersonal pronoun *it.*

> *It **is known** that New York has many psychoanalysts.*

Note: Try not to overuse the passive voice in your writing. Relying on passive verbs will slow your narrative flow and sound awkward. Exceptions to this rule include academic papers and technical writing, where the passive voice is sometimes the preferred form.

Exercise 1

Change the following sentences from the active voice to the passive voice. Keep the tenses consistent. The first is done for you as an example.

1. Most people consider magic to be a dangerous art.

   Magic is considered by most people to be a dangerous art.

2. Everybody in New York knows the Plaza Hotel.
3. Many people wearing Yves Saint Laurent dresses will attend the party.
4. All French literature students read *Madame Bovary*.
5. Only Persky understands the magic box.
6. Emma may bankrupt Kugelmass if he isn't careful.
7. A large, hairy spider has caught Kugelmass.
8. The sudden changes in *Madame Bovary* confused many literature professors.

9. In nineteenth-century France, rich people rode horses every day.

10. Emma's beauty and youth attracted Kugelmass instantly.

Exercise 2

Underline all the verbs in the following sentences from the story. For each verb, indicate whether it is active or passive by writing the letter A or P above it.

1. Kugelmass was gone. At the same moment, he appeared in the bedroom of Charles and Emma Bovary's house at Yonville. (lines 102–103)

2. "I got held up in traffic," Kugelmass said. (line 159)

3. Kugelmass visited Persky the next day, and in a few minutes was again passed magically to Yonville. (lines 160–161)

4. "And her husband suspects nothing?" (line 176)

5. Kugelmass's heart leaped. "You're serious?" he said. (line 343)

6. Persky leaped back, was seized by a heart attack, and dropped dead. (lines 376–377)

7. He had not been thrust into "Portnoy's Complaint," or into any other novel, for that matter. (lines 380–381)

8. He had been projected into an old textbook. (line 381)

Exercise 3

Write five sentences using the passive voice. Three sentences should have an identifiable agent. The fourth sentence should start with the impersonal pronoun *it*. The fifth sentence should have an unknown agent.

PART 4 VOCABULARY BUILDING

VERBS THAT INTRODUCE DIALOGUE

Dialogue is the spoken conversation between two or more characters. The verb *say* is most commonly used to introduce dialogue. However, there are many other verbs that can be used for variety and effect, depending on the context. These verbs include *argue, babble, cheer, disagree, explain, inquire, observe, respond,* and *sob.* Since "The Kugelmass Episode" is composed mainly of dialogue, Woody Allen employs a variety of verbs to describe the way the characters speak.

Exercise 1

Make sure you understand the meaning of each verb below. Complete the sentences with the most appropriate verb from the list.

whined (line 5)   sighed (line 183)

whispered (line 44)   implored (line 196)

yelled (line 140)   squealed (line 244)

snapped (line 158)   mumbled (line 267)

1. "Please, please can't I go to the party on Saturday night?" _____ the teenager.

2. "Where are you?" _____ the mountaineer, peering anxiously down the slope.

3. "Don't bother me now. I'm far too busy,"_____ the boss to his employee.

4. "Pass me your opera glasses," the wife _____ to her husband during the performance.

5. The judge requested the witness to speak more clearly after she _____, "I'm not sure I can positively identify that man."

6. "I wish I could afford to go with you to Greece this summer," _____ my friend.

7. "Do we really have homework on the weekend?" _____ the students to their teacher.

8. "Thank you for the cookies!" _____ the boy in delight.

IDIOMS

An **idiom** is an expression containing two or more words with a figurative or hidden meaning. Its meaning is not a literal translation of its separate parts, but rather something quite different. For example, one could say that Kugelmass *jumped the gun* when he made the decision to enter Persky's magic box. The idiom *jump the gun* means to do something quickly without thinking about the consequences. It is impossible to deduce this meaning from the three words that constitute the idiom. Instead, one has to learn its definition separately.

Exercise 2

The idioms in the left-hand column below appear in the story. Use the context to help you match each idiom to its definition in the right-hand column.

Idioms

_____ **1.** up to one's neck (line 4)

_____ **2.** in a split second (line 78)

_____ **3.** let oneself go (lines 6–7)

_____ **4.** on the level (line 80)

_____ **5.** out of one's depth (line 177)

_____ **6.** throw in one's lot with (line 178)

_____ **7.** pour one's heart out (line 185)

_____ **8.** get to the bottom of (line 284)

_____ **9.** have it up to here with (line 320)

Definitions

a. ally oneself with a person or group

b. be sick of

c. discover the truth about something

d. seriously burdened

e. very quickly

f. not care about one's appearance

g. express one's feelings

h. legitimate

i. unable to cope

Exercise 3

Write sentences using the idioms in Exercise 2 to show you understand their meaning. For example: "He was *up to his neck in debt*, so he declared bankruptcy."

PART 5 WRITING ACTIVITIES

1. In an essay of two to three pages, consider this question: If you had the opportunity to go back in time, what aspects of twenty-first-century life would you willingly leave behind and which would you most like to take with you? Explain the reasons for your decisions.

2. Using "The Kugelmass Episode" as a model, create an extended dialogue of about two pages between one of the following pairs: an unhappily married couple, an analyst and his or her patient, or you and your favorite movie star. Keep the dialogue naturally conversational. You may include some descriptive sentences, but keep them to a minimum. In your writing, try to incorporate some of the new idioms you have learned from the story.

3. Many books, movies, and paintings center on fantasy and magic. Fantasy is crucial to Gabriel García Márquez's *One Hundred Years of Solitude*, and it is the basis for popular stories like *The Lord of the Rings* and *Harry Potter*. Almost all of Salvador Dalí's paintings are also rooted in the fantastic imagination. Write a one- or two-page essay describing the fantasy elements of a book, movie, or painting you are familiar with. Say how the work integrates the fantastic with the real. Conclude your piece with a paragraph expressing your opinion on fantasy and magic in the arts.

4. In an essay of one to two pages, compare the story "Can-Can" on pages 4–5 with "The Kugelmass Episode." What similarities do you see in the two stories? Which story do you prefer? Why?

4 ≈ An Intruder

Nadine Gordimer
(b. 1923)

Born in South Africa, Nadine Gordimer has consistently portrayed the tragic consequences of apartheid, or racial separation, on both blacks and whites. Unlike many of her white literary compatriots, Gordimer has chosen to remain in South Africa, and her more recent work covers the dramatic changes in the country's political landscape since the fall of apartheid in 1994. Over the years she has been recognized as a moral force for change in her country. She won the Nobel Prize for Literature in 1991.

Gordimer's novels include *The Lying Days* (1953), *Occasion for Loving* (1963), *The Conservationist* (1974), *A Sport of Nature* (1987), *None to Accompany Me* (1994), and *No Time Like the Present* (2012). In addition, she has written numerous volumes of short stories, among which are *Livingstone's Companions* (1971), *Crimes of Conscience* (1991), *Loot* (2003), and *Beethoven Was One-Sixteenth Black* (2007). Her latest collection of essays is *Telling Times: Writing and Living, 1954–2008*. She has been showered with literary awards, including Scotland's James Tait Black Memorial Prize in 1972 and England's Booker Prize in 1974. In 2007 she was the recipient of the French Legion of Honor.

An Intruder[1]

*A home is invaded under mysterious circumstances, changing the
lives of its occupants.*

Someone had brought her along; she sat looking out of the rest
of the noisy party in the nightclub like a bush-baby[2] between
trees. He was one of them, there was no party without him, but
under the cross-fire of private jokes, the anecdotes and the drinking
5 he cornered her, from the beginning, with the hush of an even more
private gentleness and tenderness: 'The smoke will brown those ears
like gardenia petals.' She drank anything so long as it was soft.[3] He
touched her warm hand on the glass of lemonade; 'Pass the water,'
he called, and dipping his folded handkerchief in among the ice cubes,
10 wrung it out[4] and drew the damp cloth like cool lips across the inside
of her wrists. She was not a giggler despite her extreme youth, and she
smiled the small slow smile that men brought to her face without her
knowing why. When one of the others took her to dance, he said
seriously, 'For God's sake don't breathe your damned brandy on her,
15 Carl, she'll wilt.'[5] He himself led her to the dark crowded circle in
shelter, his arms folded round her and his handsome face pressed back
at the chin, so that his eyes looked down on her in reassurance even
while the din of bouzouki[6] and drum stomped out speech,[7] stomped
through bones and flesh in one beat pumped by a single bursting heart.
20   He was between marriages, then (the second or third had just
broken up—nobody really knew which), and this was always a high
time,[8] for him. They said, Seago's back in circulation;[9] it meant that
he was discovering his same old world anew, as good as new. But
while he was setting off for the parties, the weekend dashes here and
25 there, the pub-crawls,[10] he was already saying to her mother as he sat
in the garden drinking coffee, 'Look at the mother and see what you're
getting in the daughter. Lucky man that I am.'
    Marie and her mother couldn't help laughing and at the same time
being made to feel a little excited and worldly.[11] His frail little
30 marmoset[12]—as he called her—was an only child, they were mother-and-
daughter, the sort of pair with whom a father couldn't be imagined,
even if he hadn't happened to have been dispensed with[13] before he

---

1 **intruder** uninvited and unwelcome person
2 **bush-baby** a small nocturnal primate found in
   Africa
3 **soft** nonalcoholic
4 **wrung it out** squeezed it out well
5 **wilt** lose freshness
6 **bouzouki** a stringed instrument from Greece
7 **stomped out speech** made it impossible to
   hear someone speaking (figurative language)

8 **a high time** a very exciting time (unusual
   usage)
9 **back in circulation** out in society again
10 **pub-crawls** going from bar to bar
11 **worldly** sophisticated
12 **marmoset** a small monkey found in South
   America
13 **dispensed with** gotten rid of

could cast the reminder of a male embrace between them in the form of a likeness or gesture they didn't share. Mrs. Clegg had earned a living

35 for them both, doing very pale pastels of the children of the horsey set,[14] and very dark pastels of African women for the tourist shops.

She was an artist and therefore must not be too conventional:[15] she knew James Seago had been married before, but he was so attractive—so charming, so considerate of Marie and her and such

40 a contrast to the boys of Marie's own age who didn't even bother to open a car door for a woman—there was something touching[16] about this man, whose place was in a dinner-jacket among the smart set, appreciating the delicacy of the girl. 'You don't mind if I take her out with my ruffian[17] friends? You'll let me look after her?'—In the face of

45 this almost wistful candour[18] and understanding, who could find any reality in his 'reputation' with women? He came for Marie night after night in his old black Lancia.[19] His ruddy, clear-skinned face and lively eyes blotted out the man her mother heard talked about, the creation of gossip. He was—no, not like a son to her, but an equal. When he said

50 something nice, he was not just being kind to an older woman. And his photograph was often on the social page.[20]

In the nightclubs and restaurants he liked to go to, he drank bottle after bottle of wine with friends and told his mimicking stories, all the time caressing Marie like a kitten. Sometimes he insisted that she

55 literally sit on his knees. She spoke little, and when she did it was to utter slow, sensible things that commanded a few seconds' polite attention before the voices broke out at one another again. But on his knees she did not speak at all, for while he was gesturing, talking, in response to the whole cave of voices and music and movement, she

60 felt his voice through his chest rather than heard him and was filled, like a child bottling up tears, with appalling sexual desire. He never knew this and when he made love to her—in his bed, in the afternoons, because he kept the evenings for his friends—she was as timid and rigid as if she had never been warmed by lust. He had to coax her: 'My

65 little marmoset, my rabbit-nose, little teenage-doll, you will learn to like this, really you will....' And in time, always using the simple words with which some shy pet is persuaded to drink a saucer of milk, he taught her to do all the strange things she would not have guessed were love-making at all, and that he seemed to enjoy so much. Afterwards,

70 they would go home and have tea with her mother in the garden.

With his usual upper-class candour, he constantly remarked that he hadn't a bean;[21] but this, like his reputation with women, didn't match

---

14 **horsey set** upper-class families who can afford expensive hobbies like riding horses
15 **conventional** having traditional values
16 **touching** moving, sympathetic
17 **ruffian** a rough person
18 **wistful candour** sad and dreamy honesty
19 **Lancia** an Italian car
20 **social page** gossip section of a newspaper
21 **he hadn't a bean** he didn't have any money (British slang)

the facts of his life as Marie and her mother knew them. He had
enough money for the luxuries of bachelor life, if not for necessities.
75 There was the old but elegant Lancia and there were always notes
in the expensive crocodile-skin wallet (an inscription on a silver
plate, from a former wife, inside) to pay the hotel managers and
restaurateurs he was so friendly with, though he lived in a shabby
room in an abandoned-looking old house rented by a couple who
80 were his close friends. His English public school accent got him a
number of vague jobs on the periphery of influential business groups,
where the crude-speaking experts felt themselves hampered[22] in public
relations by their South African inarticulateness;[23] these jobs never
lasted long. Wifeless and jobless after many wives and jobs, he still
85 appeared to be one of those desirable men who can take anything they
want of life if they think it worth the bother.

Marie, gravely fluffing out her dark hair in the ladies' rooms of
nightclubs where old attendants watched from their saucers of small
change, wondered what she would say when her mother found out
90 about the afternoons in James's room. But before this could happen,
one day in the garden when she was out of earshot,[24] he said to her
mother, 'You know, I've been making love to her, I know one shouldn't
…? But we'll be able to get married very soon. Perhaps next year.'

He was looking after Marie, as she walked into the house, with
95 the rueful,[25] affectionate gaze with which one marks a child growing
up. Mrs. Clegg was irresistibly tempted to fit the assumption that
she took sexual freedom for granted: after all, she was an artist, not
a bourgeois[26] housewife. She decided, again, his frankness was
endearingly admirable; he was human, Marie was beautiful, what
100 else could you expect?

The marriage was put off several times—there was some business
of his trying to get back his furniture from his divorced wife, and then
there was a job connected with an Angolan diamond-mining company
that didn't come off.[27] At last he simply walked in one morning with
105 the licence and they were married without Marie or her mother
going to the hairdresser or any friends being told. That night there
was a surprise for his bride: apparently two of his best friends were
arriving on a visit from England, and all their old friends were to meet
them at the airport and go straight to their favourite nightclub, the
110 place where, incidentally, he and Marie had met. The bouzouki player
was persuaded to carry on until nearly five in the morning, and then
they went to someone's house where the champagne was produced
as the sky pinkened and the houseboy came in with his dust-pan and

---

22 **hampered** hindered, blocked
23 **inarticulateness** inability to express oneself well
24 **out of earshot** out of hearing distance

25 **rueful** regretful
26 **bourgeois** typically middle class
27 **come off** happen

brush. Marie did not drink and she repaired her perfect makeup every
hour; though pale, she was as fresh and circumspect[28] among their
puffy faces and burning eyes at the end of the night as she was at the
beginning. He slept all next day and she lay contentedly beside him
in the room in the old house, watching the sun behind the curtains try
first this window and then the next. But no one could get in; he and she
were alone together.

They found a flat, not a very pleasant one, but it was only temporary.
It was also cheap. He was so amusing about its disadvantages, and it
was such fun to bob in and out of each other's way in the high dark
cell of a bathroom every morning, that after the dismay of her first look
at the place, she really ceased to see the things she disliked about it so
much—the fake marble fireplace and the thick mesh burglar-proofing
over all the windows. 'What are these people afraid of?' Her tiny nostrils
stiffened in disdain.[29]

'Angel … your world is so pink and white and sweet-smelling …
there are stale women with mildew between their breasts[30] who daren't
open doors.'

She put up white gauzy curtains everywhere, and she went about
in short cotton dressing-gowns that smelt of the warm iron. She got
a part-time job and saved to buy a scrubbed white wood dining table
and chairs, and a rose silk sari to make up as a divan cover. 'Damned
lawyers twiddling their thumbs.[31] When'll I see my furniture from
that freckled bitch,' he said. The wife-before-the-last, a Catholic, was
referred to as 'Bloody-minded Mary, Our Lady of the Plastic Peonies'[32]
because, looking back on it, what he really couldn't stand about her
was the habit she had of putting artificial flowers on the table among
real leaves. He seemed to have parted from these women on the worst
of terms and to dismiss his association with them—a large part of his
life—as a series of grotesque[33] jokes.

'What do you think you'd call me if we were divorced?'

'You …' He took Marie's head between his hands and smoothed
back the hair from her temples, kissing her as if trying with his lips
the feel of a piece of velvet. 'What could anyone say about you.' When
he released her she said, going deep pink from the ledges of her small
collar-bones to her black eyes, all pupil: 'That sugar-tit tart.'[34] The
vocabulary was his all right, coming out in her soft, slow voice. He was
enchanted, picked her up, carried her round the room. 'Teenage-doll!
Marmoset-angel! I'll have to wash your mouth out with soap and water!'

---

28 **circumspect** prudent, careful
29 **disdain** contempt
30 **stale women with mildew between their breasts** insulting reference to aging women
31 **twiddling their thumbs** doing nothing (idiom)

32 **'Bloody-minded Mary, Our Lady of the Plastic Peonies'** insulting reference to James's Catholic ex-wife
33 **grotesque** unnaturally ugly
34 **sugar-tit tart** vulgar reference to Marie's body and morals

They continued to spend a lot of time at nightclubs and drinking places. Sometimes at eleven o'clock on a weekday night, when lights were going out in bedrooms all over the suburb, he would take the old Lancia scrunching over the dark drive of someone's house, and while Marie waited in the car, stand throwing gravel[35] at a window until his friends appeared and could be persuaded to get dressed and come out. He and his friends were well known in the places they went to and they stayed until they were swept out. Manolis or Giovanni, the Greek or Italian owner, would sit deep in the shadows, his gaze far back in fatigue that ringed his eyes like a natural marking, and watch these people who were good business and would not go to bed: these South Africans who did not know any better. Sometimes she and the proprietor in whose blood the memory of Dionysiac pleasures[36] ran were the only spectators left. James, her husband, did not appear drunk during these sessions, but next day he would remember nothing of what he had said or done the night before. She realized that she, too, sitting on his lap while he murmured loving things into her ear under the talk, was blacked out along with the rest. But she had seen envy behind the expressions of other women that suggested they wouldn't care for such an exhibition of affection.

There were people who seemed to know him whom he didn't remember at all, either; a man who came up to them as they were getting out of the car in town one day and laid a hand on his shoulder—'James....'

He had looked round at the man, casual, edgy, with the patient smile of someone accosted by a stranger.

'James ... What's the matter? Colin—'

'Look, old man, I'm sorry, but I'm afraid—'

'Colin. Colin. The Golden Horn Inn, Basutoland.'

He continued to look into the man's face as if at an amiable lunatic, while the man's expression slowly changed to a strange, coquettish[37] smile. 'Oh I see. Well, that's all right, James.'

She supposed they must have been drinking together once.

Sometimes she wondered if perhaps he had been as crazy about those other women, his wives, as he was about her, and did not remember: had forgotten other wild nights in the wine that washed them all out. But that was not possible; she enjoyed the slight twinge of jealousy she induced in herself with the thought. She was going to have a baby, and he had never had a child with anyone else. She said, 'You haven't a child somewhere?'

'Breed from those gorgons?[38] Are you mad?'

---

35 **gravel** small stones
36 **Dionysiac pleasures** wild, drink-filled parties named after the Greek god Dionysus
37 **coquettish** flirtatious
38 **gorgons** hideous women (Greek mythology)

But coarse words were not for her; he said to her mother, 'Do you think I should have given her a child? She's a little girl herself.' He kissed and petted her more than ever, the signs of her womanhood saddened and delighted him, like precocity.[39] She did not talk to him about after the baby was born, about a bigger flat—a little house, perhaps, with a garden?—and where to dry napkins[40] and not being able to leave a baby at night. In the meantime, they had a good time, just as before.

And then one night—or rather one early morning—something awful happened that made it suddenly possible for her to speak up for a move, napkins, the baby as a creature with needs rather than as a miraculous function of her body. They had been at Giovanni's until the small hours, as usual, there had been some occasion for celebration. She drove home and they had gone to bed and into a sleep like a death—his from drink, hers from exhaustion. Pregnancy made her hungry and she woke at eight o'clock to the church bells of Sunday morning and slid out of bed to go to the kitchen. She bumped into a chair askew[41] in the passage, but in her sleepy state it was nothing more significant than an obstacle, and when she reached the kitchen she stood there deeply puzzled as if she had arrived somewhere in sleep and would wake in the presence of familiar order in a moment.

For the kitchen was wrecked; flour had been strewn, syrup had been thrown at the walls, soap powder, milk, cocoa, salad oil were upset over everything. The white muslin curtains were ripped to shreds. She began to shake; and suddenly ran stumbling back to the bedroom.

He lay fast asleep, as she had lain, as they both had lain while this—Thing—happened. While Someone. Something. In the flat with them.

'James,' she screamed hoarsely whispering, and flung herself on him. His head came up from under his arm, the beard strong-textured in the pink firm skin; he frowned at her a moment, and then he was holding her in a kind of terror of tenderness. 'Marmoset. Rabbit.' She buried her head in the sleep-heat between his shoulder and neck and gestured fiercely back at the door.

'Christ almighty! What's wrong?'

'The kitchen! The kitchen!'

He struggled to get up.

'Don't go there.'

'Sweetling, tell me, what happened?'

She wouldn't let him leave her. He put his two hands round her stone-hard belly while she controlled shuddering breaths. Then they

---

39 **precocity** unusually early development

40 **napkins** diapers (British English)

41 **askew** out of position

went together into the other rooms of the flat, the kitchen, the living room, and the dark hole of a bathroom, her bare feet twitching distastefully like a cat's at each step. 'Just look at it.' They stood at the kitchen door. But in the living room she said, *'What is it?'* Neither of them spoke. On each of the three divisions of the sofa cushions there was a little pile, an offering. One was a slime of contraceptive jelly with hair-combings—hers—that must have been taken from the wastepaper basket in the bedroom; the other was toothpaste and razor blades; the third was a mucous of half-rotted vegetable matter—peelings, tea leaves, dregs—the intestines of the dustbin.

In the bathroom there were more horrors; cosmetics were spilt, and the underwear she had left there was arranged in an obscene collage[42] with intimate objects of toilet.[43] Two of her pretty cotton gowns lay in the bath with a bottle of liqueur emptied on them. They went again from room to room in silence. But the mess spoke secretly, in the chaos there was a jeering[44] pattern, a logic outside sense that was at the same time *recognizable*, as a familiar object turned inside-out draws a blank and yet signals. There was something related only to them in this arrangement without values of disrelated objects and substances; it was, after all, the components of their daily existence and its symbols. It was all horrible; horribly familiar, even while they were puzzled and aghast.[45]

'This flat. The light has to be on in the bathroom all day. There's no balcony where the baby could sleep. The washing will never dry. I've never been able to get rid of the black beetles in the kitchen, whatever I put down.'

'All right, angel, poor angel.'

'We can't live here. It's not a place for a baby.'

He wanted to phone for the police but it did not seem to occur to her that there could be a rational explanation for what had happened, a malicious[46] and wicked intruder who had scrawled contempt on the passionate rites of their intimacy[47], smeared filth on the cosy contemporary home-making of the living room, and made rags of the rose silk cover and the white muslin curtains. To her, evil had come out of the walls, as the black beetles did in the kitchen.

It was not until some days had passed and she had calmed down—they found another flat—that the extraordinariness of the whole business began to mean something to her: she and James had gone round the flat together, that morning, and there wasn't a door or

---

42 **obscene collage** a vulgar composition
43 **intimate objects of toilet** personal bathroom and bedroom items
44 **jeering** mocking, ridiculing
45 **aghast** horrified

46 **malicious** hateful
47 **scrawled contempt on the passionate rites of their intimacy** openly disrespected their private relationship (figurative language)

275 window by which anyone could have got in. Not a pane was broken and there was that ugly burglar-proofing, anyway. There was only one outer door to the flat, and she had locked it when they came home and put the key, as usual, on the bedside table; if someone had somehow managed to steal the key, how could they have put it back on the table

280 after leaving the flat, and how could the door have been left bolted on the inside? But more amazing than how the intruder got in, why had he done so? Not a penny or a piece of clothing had been stolen.

They discussed it over and over again, as he kept saying, 'There must be an explanation, something so simple we've missed it.

285 Poltergeists[48] won't do. Are you sure there couldn't have been someone hiding in the flat when we came home, marmoset-baby? Did either of us go into the living room before we went to bed?' —For of course he didn't remember a thing until he woke and found she had flung herself on him terrified.

290 'No. I told you. I went into the living room to get a bottle of lime juice, I went into all the rooms,' she repeated in her soft, slow, reasonable voice; and this time, while she was speaking, she began to know what else he would never remember, something so simple that she had missed it.

295 She stood there wan,[49] almost ugly, really like some wretched pet monkey shivering in a cold climate. But she was going to have a child, and—yes, looking at him, she was grown-up, now, suddenly, as some people are said to turn white-haired overnight.

---

48 **poltergeists** ghosts that move objects around

49 **wan** unnaturally pale

A Thinking About the Story

Discuss the following questions with a partner.

How would you describe James? What sort of person is he?

B Understanding the Plot

Be prepared to answer the following questions with a partner or the whole class.

1. How does James treat Marie when he first meets her in the nightclub?
2. What are the major differences between James and Marie? List as many as possible.
3. Where is Marie's father?
4. Why does Marie's mother like James? Explain your answer.
5. What makes James so attractive to Marie?
6. What are James's economic circumstances? Explain your answer.
7. In what way does James's British accent help him in South African society?
8. How does Marie's mother react to the information that James has been making love to her daughter?
9. What is unusual about Marie's wedding day?
10. What is the relationship between James and his ex-wives?
11. Explain what is meant by "these South Africans who did not know any better." (lines 163–164)
12. Why, in your opinion, does James not recognize Colin? (lines 173–184)
13. What connects the destruction in the kitchen, living room, and bathroom?
14. How does Marie's attitude toward their flat change the morning after the intrusion?
15. What do you think Marie comes to understand at the end?

CRITICAL THINKING

A Exploring Themes

Reread "An Intruder." As you read, consider carefully the psychological portrait Nadine Gordimer paints of James, Marie, and Marie's mother.

1. What is James's attitude toward women? Substantiate your answer with examples from the story.

2. What observations does Gordimer make regarding the social circle James moves in? Give as many details as possible.

3. Who do you think the intruder was? Why did he or she act in this way? Explain your answer in detail.

4. How does Marie change in the course of the story?

5. "An Intruder" was initially titled "Out of the Walls." How does Marie's reaction that "evil had come out of the walls" reflect a major theme in the story? (lines 269–270)

B Analyzing Style

SIMILE AND METAPHOR

Writers use imagery to create vivid pictures that appeal to our senses (sight, touch, smell, hearing, and taste). The most effective writing contains striking and fresh images and avoids commonly used comparisons. Nadine Gordimer's writing in "An Intruder" abounds in imagery. She makes especially full and imaginative use of **similes**, which are direct comparisons using *like* or *as*, and **metaphors**, which are implied comparisons in which one element is described in terms of another to create a connection. Gordimer uses simile and metaphor to present both the appearance and personality of her characters, as well as their surroundings and actions. Marie is introduced with a simile:

> … *she sat looking out of the rest of the noisy party in the nightclub like a bush-baby between trees.* (lines 1–3)

Gordimer immediately evokes Marie as a small, furry wild animal with big brown eyes, out of its natural environment, the nocturnal forest. In this example, *like* directly unites the two elements of the comparison.

In less direct fashion, Gordimer uses a metaphor to intensify the horror left behind by the intruder: the half-rotted vegetable matter on the sofa is described as *the intestines of the dustbin* (line 245). With this disturbing image, Gordimer compares the exposed contents of the trash can with the insides of an animal.

Exercise 1

Answer the following questions.

1. In the first paragraph, the conversation at the party where James meets Marie is described in terms of a military metaphor. What is the metaphor? Explain its two components. What is the effect of the metaphor?

2. In the first paragraph, which simile reinforces Marie's fragility? Explain the simile. In what way is this simile extended into a metaphor in lines 14–15?

3. Explain the simile … *[he] drew the damp cloth like cool lips across the inside of her wrists* (lines 10–11). How does this simile help heighten the erotic atmosphere in the nightclub?

4. With what are the drum and the bouzouki compared in lines 18–19? Explain the metaphor as fully as possible.

5. In lines 52–70, what simile conveys Marie's petlike image in James's eyes? What other imagery conveys Marie's extreme youthfulness in these lines?

6. What metaphors underline the unpleasant smallness and darkness of the couple's apartment? (lines 123–124 and 237)

7. At the end of the story, Marie is described in new animal terms. What is the animal? How does this image reflect how she has changed?

Exercise 2

Find and explain one more simile and one more metaphor in the story. Explain how each contributes to our understanding of the themes.

C Judging for Yourself

Express yourself as personally as you like in your answers to the following questions.

1. Do you think Marie's mother behaved responsibly toward her daughter?

2. In your opinion, is the couple's marriage likely to survive? Explain your answer fully.

3. Do you think James has the capacity to be a good father? Why or why not?

4. Why, in your opinion, did Marie marry James?

D Making Connections

Answer the following questions with a classmate or in a small group.

1. In your culture, what is the attitude toward the marriage of an older man and a younger woman? Is there a difference if the situation is reversed?

2. Is there a minimum age for marriage in your country? If so, what is it? If not, should there be?

3. Does the way you speak—for example, your accent or dialect—influence the way people regard you in your country?

4. How do young people spend their leisure time in your country? For example, is drinking and dancing at clubs a popular activity? If not, what are the main ways in which young people enjoy themselves?

E Debate

Decide whether you are for or against the following statement. Be prepared to argue your case in a class debate.

A person's character is determined at birth.

PART 3 GRAMMAR IN CONTEXT

ADJECTIVE CLAUSES

An **adjective clause** is a dependent or subordinate clause, which means it cannot be a sentence on its own. It must be attached to a main clause. Adjective clauses modify (describe) nouns or pronouns. They have a subject and a verb, and they are introduced by the relative pronouns *who, whom, whose, which,* and *that* and the relative adverbs *when* and *where*. The noun referred to by the relative pronoun or relative adverb is called the **antecedent**. In the following examples, the adjective clause is in **bold** and its antecedent is <u>underlined</u>.

1. The relative pronouns *who, whom, whose,* and *that* are used to refer to people.

   - *Who* is used when the pronoun is the subject of an adjective clause.

     *… there are stale <u>women</u> with mildew between their breasts **who daren't open doors**.* (lines 130–131)

   - *Whom* and *that* are used when the pronoun is the object of a relative clause. They may also be omitted. Note that in informal English *who* is frequently used instead of *whom*.

     *There were <u>people</u> **whom he didn't remember at all** …* (adapted from lines 173–174)

     *There were <u>people</u> **he didn't remember at all**.*

- *Whom* is used after a preposition.

  *James was <u>a man</u> **to whom party lovers were immediately drawn**.*
- *Whose* is possessive.

  *Sometimes <u>the proprietor</u>, **whose blood contained the memory of Dionysiac pleasures,** was the only spectator left.*

2. The relative pronouns *which, that,* and *whose* are used to refer to animals or things.

   - *That* and *which* can both be used as the subject of an adjective clause.

     *… she went about in short cotton <u>dressing-gowns</u> **that smelt of the warm iron**.* (lines 132–133)

     *<u>The apartment</u>, **which was small and dark**, was no place for a baby.*

   - *That* and *which* can also both be used as the object of an adjective clause. When used as the object, they may be omitted.

     *… and she smiled the small slow <u>smile</u> **that men brought to her face**.* (lines 11–12)

     *… she enjoyed the slight twinge of <u>jealousy</u> **she induced in herself with the thought**.* (lines 189–190)

   - When the relative pronoun is the object of a preposition, the pronoun *which* must be used.

     *There wasn't <u>a door or window</u> **by which anyone could have got in**.* (lines 274–275)

   - The possessive relative pronoun *whose* is used for things as well as for people.

     *Marie was like a small <u>animal</u> **whose den has been invaded**.*

3. The relative adverbs *when* and *where* refer to nouns of time and place.

   - *When* modifies a noun representing a time. It may be omitted, or *that* may be used instead.

     *Marie remembered clearly <u>the moment</u> **when she first saw James at the nightclub**.*

   - *Where* modifies a noun representing a place. It may also be omitted, or *that* may be used instead.

     *… and all their old friends were to meet them at the airport and go straight to their favorite nightclub, <u>the place</u> **where, incidentally, he and Marie had met**.* (lines 108–110)

Exercise 1

Follow the instructions below concerning lines 28–86 in "An Intruder."

1. Underline all the adjective clauses with a single line. Put a double line under the relative pronoun or relative adverb that begins each clause. Circle its antecedent.

2. How many adjective clauses did you find?

3. Do any of the adjective clauses begin with a relative adverb? If so, which one(s)?

4. In which adjective clauses is the relative pronoun omitted? Name the omitted pronoun. Is the relative pronoun the subject or the object of the verb?

5. Is the clause *that she literally sit on his knees* (lines 54–55) an adjective clause? How about the clause *that he hadn't a bean* (line 72)? Explain your answers.

RESTRICTIVE AND NONRESTRICTIVE ADJECTIVE CLAUSES

There are two kinds of adjective clauses: restrictive and nonrestrictive. A restrictive adjective clause is essential to the meaning of the noun it modifies, while a nonrestrictive adjective clause is not essential in this way. In the following sentences the adjective clause is in **bold** and the antecedent is underlined.

1. A **restrictive clause** identifies and limits the noun it modifies. It cannot be omitted without changing the meaning of the sentence. Since it is essential to the noun it modifies, it is not set off by commas from its antecedent. In a restrictive clause, *who* and *that* are interchangeable, as are *which* and *that*.

    Marie looked for an <u>apartment</u> **that/which would be suitable for her new baby**.

    In this sentence, the emphasis is not on apartments in general but rather on an apartment that is baby-friendly.

    Marie's mother was a <u>woman</u> **who/that was easily flattered**.

    In this sentence, the emphasis is not on women in general but rather on a woman who is susceptible to flattery.

2. A **nonrestrictive clause** is not essential to defining the antecedent. It gives additional details or information. It is set off by commas from its antecedent.

    - In nonrestrictive clauses, always use *who* or *whom* when referring to people. Do not use the relative pronoun *that*.

        Marie's <u>husband</u>, **who spoke with an upper-class British accent**, *settled quickly into South African society.*

    - In nonrestrictive clauses, always use *which* when referring to things. Do not use the relative pronoun *that*.

        The <u>parties</u>, **which were always filled with drinking and noise**, *soon bored her.*

Find two restrictive and two nonrestrictive adjective clauses in lines 28–86.

Complete the following sentences with the correct relative pronoun or relative adverb. Punctuate each sentence according to whether the relative clause is restrictive or nonrestrictive.

1. Mrs. Clegg _____ thought of herself as a bohemian was easily charmed by James.

2. James saw himself as a man to _____ the world owed a living.

3. She rushed out of the house _____ had suddenly lost all its charm for her.

4. He picked up their clothes from the floor _____ they'd been thrown.

5. James smiled blankly at the man _____ face he couldn't remember.

6. The wine _____ the bartender served was chilled just right.

7. James compared Marie to a marmoset _____ is a small, furry animal.

8. She realized that her husband _____ she relied on had let her down.

9. His head _____ was throbbing horribly felt as if it would burst open.

10. Marie never forgot the morning _____ she woke up and saw the mess.

Write five sentences relating to the story, using an adjective clause in each one. Try to vary the relative pronouns and relative adverbs that introduce your clauses. Make sure you follow the punctuation rules for restrictive and nonrestrictive clauses.

VOCABULARY BUILDING

ADJECTIVES

In addition to metaphor and simile, **adjectives** are used to flesh out descriptions. They serve to intensify atmosphere, heighten comparisons, and sharpen images. For example, Gordimer uses a few well-chosen adjectives to contrast dainty Marie with her coarse wedding guests: *Marie did not drink and she repaired her **perfect** makeup every hour; though **pale**, she was as **fresh** and **circumspect** among their **puffy** faces and **burning** eyes at the end of the night as she was at the beginning.* (lines 114–117)

Exercise 1

Match each adjective from the story in the left-hand column to the appropriate context in the right-hand column below.

ADJECTIVE

_____ **1.** touching (line 41)

_____ **2.** wistful (line 45)

_____ **3.** rigid (line 64)

_____ **4.** shabby (line 78)

_____ **5.** circumspect (line 115)

_____ **6.** intimate (line 248)

_____ **7.** jeering (line 251)

_____ **8.** aghast (line 257)

_____ **9.** malicious (line 266)

_____ **10.** wan (line 295)

CONTEXT

a. expression on hearing news of a plane crash

b. advice from a lawyer to his client

c. gossip intended to hurt the subject

d. plot of a sad movie

e. response of a hostile audience

f. appearance after the flu

g. army regulations at all times

h. furniture after years of hard use

i. knowledge of someone close

j. longing of a poet for his lost love

Exercise 2

Write sentences using the adjectives in Exercise 1 to show you understand their meaning. For example: "The movie was so *touching* that I cried long after it was over."

1. Look at the editorial page of a large daily newspaper. Read the editorials carefully, paying special attention to their format and style. Write your own one-page editorial in which you take up the subject of drinking among young people. You might include issues such as the excessive drinking of high school and college students, the consequences of driving while drunk, and the advantages of raising or lowering the legal drinking age. Your editorial should persuade the reader of the soundness of your point of view. Give your editorial an apt heading.

2. Romance between an older man and a younger woman has been a recurring theme in books and movies over the years. Two examples are Charlotte Bronte's classic nineteenth-century novel *Jane Eyre*, in which a young governess falls in love with her older employer, and the contemporary television drama *Mad Men*, in which a powerful, married, middle-aged advertising executive weds his very young secretary. Choose a movie or television series you've seen or a book you've read that revolves around this kind of relationship or its reverse (an older woman and a younger man), and describe the plot and characters. Consider what sparked the romance, and say whether it worked out in the end. Try to use some similes and/or metaphors when you describe the characters.

3. Nadine Gordimer makes full use of evocative imagery as she creates the nightclub scene at the start of the story. Select a public place where you can closely observe the people who are there. It could, for example, be a college campus, a park, or a restaurant. Then, using the lively pictorial writing in lines 1–19 as a model, write three paragraphs describing the place, the people in it, and what the people are wearing, doing, and saying. Try to make your scene come alive on the page.

PARENT AND CHILD

Powder
Mother
Eveline
My Oedipus Complex

5 ⮀ Powder

Tobias Wolff

(b. 1945)

Born in Birmingham, Alabama, Tobias Wolff was a child of a broken marriage. After his parents' divorce, he traveled around the country with his mother, ending up in the Pacific Northwest, where his mother married an abusive man. Wolff chronicled his traumatic childhood in the groundbreaking memoir *This Boy's Life* (1989), which was later made into a movie starring Leonardo DiCaprio and Robert De Niro. His second memoir, *Pharaoh's Army: Memories of the Lost War* (1994), described his tour of duty in Vietnam as a member of the Green Berets. Today, he is a professor at Stanford University.

An accomplished short-story writer, Wolff has published several collections: *In the Garden of the North American Martyrs* (1981), *Back in the World* (1985), *The Night in Question* (1996), and *Our Story Begins* (2008). His spare, elegant prose has been compared to the writing of Raymond Carver and Richard Ford. In 2003 he published his first novel, *Old School*. He has won numerous writing awards, including the PEN/Faulkner Award for his novella *The Barracks Thief* (1984), several O. Henry Awards, the *Los Angeles Times* Book Prize, and the American Academy of Arts and Letters Award in Literature (2001).

Powder

A boy and his father bond in an unusual way.

Just before Christmas my father took me skiing at Mount Baker. He'd had to fight for the privilege of my company, because my mother was still angry with him for sneaking me into a nightclub during our last visit, to see Thelonious Monk.[1]

5   He wouldn't give up. He promised, hand on heart, to take good care of me and have me home for dinner on Christmas Eve, and she relented. But as we were checking out of the lodge that morning it began to snow, and in this snow he observed some quality that made it necessary for us to get in one last run.[2] We got in several last runs.

10   He was indifferent to[3] my fretting.[4] Snow whirled around us in bitter, blinding squalls,[5] hissing like sand, and still we skied. As the lift bore us to the peak yet again, my father looked at his watch and said, "Criminey.[6] This'll have to be a fast one."

    By now I couldn't see the trail. There was no point in trying. I stuck
15 to him like white on rice and did what he did and somehow made it[7] to the bottom without sailing off a cliff. We returned our skis and my father put chains on the Austin-Healy[8] while I swayed from foot to foot, clapping my mittens and wishing I were home. I could see everything. The green tablecloth, the plates with the holly pattern,
20 the red candles waiting to be lit.

    We passed a diner on our way out. "You want some soup?" my father asked. I shook my head. "Buck up,"[9] he said. "I'll get you there. Right, doctor?"

    I was supposed to say, "Right, doctor," but I didn't say anything.
25   A state trooper[10] waved us down[11] outside the resort. A pair of sawhorses were blocking the road. The trooper came up to our car and bent down to my father's window. His face was bleached by the cold. Snowflakes clung to his eyebrows and to the fur trim of his jacket and cap.

30   "Don't tell me," my father said.

    The trooper told him. The road was closed. It might get cleared, it might not. Storm took everyone by surprise. So much, so fast. Hard to get people moving. Christmas Eve. What can you do?

---

1 **Thelonious Monk** American jazz pianist and composer (1917–1982)
2 **one last run** a final time skiing down the mountain
3 **indifferent to** unconcerned with
4 **fretting** worrying
5 **squalls** brief, violent storms

6 **Criminey** an old-fashioned exclamation of surprise
7 **made it** reached (informal)
8 **Austin-Healy** a British sports car
9 **Buck up** Cheer up
10 **state trooper** police officer
11 **waved us down** signaled us to stop

My father said, "Look. We're talking about four, five inches. I've
taken this car through worse than that."

The trooper straightened up, boots creaking. His face was out of
sight but I could hear him. "The road is closed."

My father sat with both hands on the wheel, rubbing the wood
with his thumbs. He looked at the barricade for a long time. He seemed
to be trying to master the idea of it. Then he thanked the trooper, and
with a weird, old-maidy show of caution turned the car around. "Your
mother will never forgive me for this," he said.

"We should have left before," I said. "Doctor."

He didn't speak to me again until we were both in a booth at the
diner, waiting for our burgers. "She won't forgive me," he said. "Do
you understand? Never."

"I guess," I said, but no guesswork was required; she wouldn't
forgive him.

"I can't let that happen." He bent toward me. "I'll tell you what
I want. I want us to be together again. Is that what you want?"

I wasn't sure, but I said, "Yes, sir."

He bumped my chin with his knuckles. "That's all I needed
to hear."

When we finished eating he went to the pay phone in the back of
the diner, then joined me in the booth again. I figured he'd called my
mother, but he didn't give a report. He sipped at his coffee and stared
out the window at the empty road. "Come on!" When the trooper's car
went past, lights flashing, he got up and dropped some money on the
check. "Okay. *Vamanos.*"[12]

The wind had died. The snow was falling straight down, less of it
now; lighter. We drove away from the resort, right up to the barricade.
"Move it," my father told me. When I looked at him he said, "What are
you waiting for?" I got out and dragged one of the sawhorses aside,
then pushed it back after he drove through. When I got inside the car
he said, "Now you're an accomplice.[13] We go down[14] together." He put
the car in gear and looked at me. "Joke, doctor."

"Funny, doctor."

Down the first long stretch I watched the road behind us, to see
if the trooper was on our tail.[15] The barricade vanished. Then there
was nothing but snow: snow on the road, snow kicking up from the
chains, snow on the trees, snow in the sky; and our trail in the snow. I
faced around and had a shock. The lie of the road behind us had been

---

12 *Vamanos.* Let's go. (Spanish)
13 **accomplice** a partner in crime

14 **go down** experience defeat
15 **on our tail** following us

marked by our own tracks, but there were no tracks ahead of us. My father was breaking virgin snow between a line of tall trees. He
75 was humming "Stars Fell on Alabama." I felt snow brush along the floorboards under my feet. To keep my hands from shaking I clamped them between my knees.

My father grunted in a thoughtful way and said, "Don't ever try this yourself."

80 "I won't."

"That's what you say now, but someday you'll get your license and then you'll think you can do anything. Only you won't be able to do this. You need, I don't know—a certain instinct."

"Maybe I have it."

85 "You don't. You have your strong points, but not … you know. I only mention it because I don't want you to get the idea this is something just anybody can do. I'm a great driver. That's not a virtue, okay? It's just a fact, and one you should be aware of. Of course you have to give the old heap[16] some credit, too—there aren't many cars
90 I'd try this with. Listen!"

I listened. I heard the slap of the chains, the stiff, jerky rasp of the wipers, the purr of the engine. It really did purr. The car was almost new. My father couldn't afford it, and kept promising to sell it, but here it was.

95 I said, "Where do you think that policeman went to?"

"Are you warm enough?" He reached over and cranked up the blower.[17] Then he turned off the wipers. We didn't need them. The clouds had brightened. A few sparse, feathery flakes drifted into our slipstream and were swept away. We left the trees and entered a
100 broad field of snow that ran level for a while and then tilted sharply downward. Orange stakes had been planted at intervals in two parallel lines and my father ran a course[18] between them, though they were far enough apart to leave considerable doubt in my mind as to where exactly the road lay. He was humming again, doing little scat riffs[19]
105 around the melody.

"Okay then. What are my strong points?"

"Don't get me started," he said. "It'd take all day."

"Oh, right. Name one."

"Easy. You always think ahead."

110 True. I always thought ahead. I was a boy who kept his clothes on numbered hangers to ensure proper rotation. I bothered my teachers

---

16 **the old heap** an old, rundown car (slang)
17 **cranked up the blower** turned up the heater
18 **ran a course** created a path
19 **scat riffs** improvised jazz tunes

for homework assignments far ahead of their due dates so I could make
up schedules. I thought ahead, and that was why I knew that there
would be other troopers waiting for us at the end of our ride, if we got
115 there. What I did not know was that my father would wheedle[20] and
plead his way past them—he didn't sing "O Tannenbaum"[21] but just
about—and get me home for dinner, buying a little more time before
my mother decided to make the split final. I knew we'd get caught;
I was resigned to it. And maybe for this reason I stopped moping[22] and
120 began to enjoy myself.

Why not? This was one for the books.[23] Like being in a speedboat,
only better. You can't go downhill in a boat. And it was all ours. And it
kept coming, the laden trees, the unbroken surface of snow, the sudden
white vistas. Here and there I saw hints of the road, ditches, fences,
125 stakes, but not so many that I could have found my way. But then I
didn't have to. My father in his forty-eighth year, rumpled,[24] kind,
bankrupt of honor, flushed with certainty. He was a great driver. All
persuasion, no coercion.[25] Such subtlety[26] at the wheel, such tactful
pedalwork. I actually trusted him. And the best was yet to come—
130 switchbacks and hairpins[27] impossible to describe. Except maybe to say
this: If you haven't driven fresh powder, you haven't driven.

---

20 **wheedle** persuade through flattery
21 **"O Tannenbaum"** a song traditionally sung
    at Christmas
22 **moping** feeling and acting sad
23 **This was one for the books.** This was
    something to be remembered.

24 **rumpled** having a wrinkled and untidy
    appearance
25 **coercion** force
26 **subtlety** delicate skill
27 **switchbacks and hairpins** very sharp turns
    on a steep road

PART 1 FIRST READING

A **Thinking About the Story**

Discuss the following questions with a partner.

What qualities do you usually associate with a father? How many of
these qualities apply to the father in the story?

B Understanding the Plot

Be prepared to answer the following questions with a partner or the whole class.

1. Why is the narrator's mother reluctant to let him go skiing with his father?
2. What is the boy fretting about in line 10?
3. Why does the boy refuse the soup?
4. What will the consequences for the father be if he brings the boy home late?
5. Why does the father wait for the trooper's car to go past?
6. Why does the father choose to call his son "an accomplice"? (lines 65–66)
7. What are the boy's feelings as they leave the road and plow through the snow? List them in detail.
8. Why doesn't the boy's father answer his son's question as to where the trooper has gone? (line 95)
9. What is the main difference between the son and his father?
10. Do the boy and his father encounter the troopers again? If so, what happens?
11. Does the boy ultimately enjoy the experience? Explain your answer.

CRITICAL THINKING

A Exploring Themes

Reread "Powder." As you read, think about how Wolff depicts the evolving father/son bond. Do you view the father differently the second time you read the story?

1. In what ways does the boy draw closer to his father during their adventure together?
2. What is the state of the parents' relationship? Give as many details as possible to support your answer.
3. In what ways does the story invert the traditional father/son relationship?
4. How does the boy change in the course of the story?

REPETITION

Repetition can be an effective device for creating atmosphere or for indicating the significance of a theme. It can take the form of repetitive language or of parallel events that occur multiple times. In "Powder," Wolff uses repetition in several ways.

Exercise 1

Examine carefully the various ways in which Wolff describes snow in lines 10–11, 70–76, 98–99, and 122–131. Show how each description echoes the narrator's state of mind at that moment.

Exercise 2

The father and son address each other as "doctor" several times in the story. Explain the different ways that they use this nickname.

ALLITERATION

Alliteration is similar to repetition except that, instead of a repeated phrase or event, alliteration involves the repetition of consonant sounds to produce a certain effect. Wolff uses alliteration to evoke the experience of falling powder. For example, as the snowstorm diminishes, the narrator refers to *a few ... feathery flakes* (line 98). The repetition of the soft "f" sound reinforces the insubstantiality of the flakes, which are compared to light, fluffy feathers in distinct contrast to the earlier blizzard-like conditions.

Exercise 3

Answer the following questions.

1. What consonant sounds that refer to the snowstorm are repeated in line 11? How do they help evoke the storm?
2. What alliteration other than *feathery flakes* can you find in lines 98–99? What is the effect of this alliteration?

C Judging for Yourself

Express yourself as personally as you like in your answers to the following questions.

1. How old do you think the boy is? Give reasons for your answer.
2. Do you sympathize with the boy's mother? Explain your answer fully.
3. What do you think of the father's risk-taking? Is he reckless, or is he brave? Should he be punished?
4. Do you find the father an endearing character? Why or why not?
5. In your view, does the boy fundamentally benefit from this experience? If so, how? If not, why not?

D Making Connections

Answer the following questions in a small group.

1. In your culture, is there a typical role model for fathers? If yes, what is it? If no, why not?
2. Skiing is a popular winter sport in the United States. What are some popular winter sports in your country?
3. Are the police generally looked on as a positive or negative force in your country? Explain your answer.
4. How is divorce regarded in your country? Is it easy or difficult to get a divorce? Is there any shame attached to divorce?

E Debate

Decide whether you are for or against the following statement. Be prepared to argue your case in a class debate.

Divorce should be avoided for the sake of the children.

PART 3 GRAMMAR IN CONTEXT

PARTICIPIAL PHRASES

Writers use **participial phrases** to add variety and economy to their sentences. Participial phrases begin with a present or past participle and, like adjectives, are used to give more information about the noun or pronoun they modify. Present participles end in -*ing*, while most past participles end in -*ed, -d,* or -*t.*

The participial phrase may be placed next to or away from the noun or pronoun it modifies. In the following examples, the participial phrase is in **bold** and the noun it modifies is <u>underlined</u>.

- The participial phrase can be placed next to the noun it modifies.

  *… the red <u>candles</u> **waiting to be lit**.* (line 20)

  *The trooper bent his <u>face</u> **bleached by the cold** to the car window.*

- Sometimes the participial phrase is separated from the noun or pronoun it modifies. When this happens, a comma is needed.

  *My <u>father</u> sat with both hands on the wheel, **rubbing the wood with his thumbs**.* (lines 38–39)

- The participial phrase can sometimes be placed at the beginning of the sentence, before the noun it modifies. For example, the previous sentence from the story could have been written:

  ***Rubbing the wood with his thumbs**, my <u>father</u> sat with both hands on the wheel.*

Exercise 1

In the following sentences from the story, underline each participial phrase and circle the noun or pronoun it modifies.

1. Snow whirled around us in bitter, blinding squalls, hissing like sand, and still we skied. (lines 10–11)
2. We returned our skis and my father put chains on the Austin-Healy while I swayed from foot to foot, clapping my mittens and wishing I were home. (lines 16–18)
3. I thought ahead, and that was why I knew that there would be other troopers waiting for us at the end of our ride, if we got there. (lines 113–115)
4. What I did not know was that my father would wheedle and plead his way past them … and get me home for dinner, buying a little more time before my mother decided to make the split final. (lines 115–118)
5. My father in his forty-eighth year, rumpled, kind, bankrupt of honor, flushed with certainty. (lines 126–127)

Exercise 2

Combine the following sentence pairs by reducing one of the clauses in each pair to a participial phrase. You may use either a present or a past participle. The first one has been done for you.

1. A state trooper waved us down outside the resort. The trooper came up to our car and bent down to my father's window. (lines 25–27)

   Waving us down outside the resort, the trooper came up to our car and bent down to my father's window.

2. My father drove away. He promised hand on heart to take good care of me.

3. I stuck to him like white on rice. I somehow made it to the bottom without sailing off a cliff.

4. Snow covered the car. The car slid through the trees.

5. I knew we would get caught. I was resigned to the consequences.

6. I looked at my father at the end of the ride. I actually trusted him.

DANGLING MODIFIERS

When a participial phrase is placed at the beginning of a sentence, it needs to modify the subject. If a participial phrase that is not meant to modify the subject is placed at the beginning of a sentence, the meaning will be unclear or distorted.

> **Skiing down the mountain,** *snow fell in my eyes.*

As written, the participial phrase *skiing down the mountain* modifies *snow*, which doesn't make any sense. Instead, the sentence could be written: **Skiing down the mountain,** *I had snow in my eyes.*

> **Waiting for his plan to work,** *the trooper didn't notice my father.*

In "Powder," it is the father who comes up with a plan to distract the trooper, but the placement of the participial phrase makes it seem as if the policeman were planning something instead. The sentence could be rewritten: *The trooper didn't notice my father* **waiting for his plan to work.** Now, the participial phrase correctly modifies the father. By making sure that your participial phrases are placed correctly, you will avoid confusion in your writing.

Exercise 3

Rewrite the following sentences to eliminate the dangling modifiers. Change only the independent clause, adding or altering words as necessary. You may need to change your independent clause from the active to the passive or vice versa.

1. Fretting horribly, the snow blinded the boy.

   _____

2. Watching him take out his notebook, the trooper scared me.

   _____

3. Sipping his coffee, the trooper's car was observed by my father.

   _____

4. Skiing through the trees, dense snow surrounded us.

_____

5. After finishing the meal, the car engine was turned on.

_____

SENTENCE FRAGMENTS

In formal writing, every sentence requires a main clause. If a sentence is made up of a phrase or if it contains only a dependent clause, it is called a **sentence fragment**. It should be noted that writers frequently ignore strict grammar rules and use sentence fragments in their creative work.

In "Powder," Wolff writes:

> _So much, so fast._ (line 32)

In this instance, the subject and verb are missing. A grammatically correct sentence would read: _The snow fell hard and fast._

> _Hard to get people moving._ (lines 32–33)

Once again, the subject and verb are missing. A grammatically correct sentence would read: _**It was** hard to get people moving._

> _Because we were so late._

Here we have a dependent clause only; the main clause is missing. A grammatically correct sentence would read: _**I was getting increasingly anxious** because we were so late._

Exercise 4

Rewrite the last paragraph of the story (lines 121–131). Take out all the sentence fragments and substitute complete sentences. Then compare what you have written with the original text and discuss the effect of the difference in style.

PART 4   VOCABULARY BUILDING

ALLITERATIVE EXPRESSIONS

We have seen how writers use alliteration—repetition of sounds within and across words—to create special effects. However, some words and phrases in English come "ready-made" with alliteration. For example, the father promises _hand on heart_ (line 5) to bring his son home in time for dinner on Christmas Eve.

Exercise 1

Use a dictionary if necessary to find the meaning of these words and phrases and then write a definition on each line.

1. aid and abet _____
2. cold comfort _____
3. bag of bones _____
4. double-dealing _____
5. far-fetched _____
6. highhanded _____
7. life and limb _____
8. mind over matter _____
9. shipshape _____
10. wishy-washy _____

Exercise 2

Complete the sentences with an appropriate word or expression from the list in Exercise 1.

1. After her illness, she was nothing but a _____.

2. "I wish you would learn to keep your room _____," sighed the mother to her teenage child.

3. There is a lot of _____ in the criminal world.

4. The soldiers risked _____ when confronting the overwhelming enemy numbers.

5. It is a serious offense to _____ a criminal.

6. If managers are _____, they will alienate their employees.

7. This is no time for _____ actions, but rather for courage and determination.

8. The professor rejected the student's _____ excuse about an alien snatching his homework.

9. It was _____ to the boy to hear he'd failed the exam by only one point.

10. Don't allow yourself to give up now since it's definitely a case of _____.

PREPOSITIONS

Prepositions are a vital part of sentence construction. They show the relationship of a noun or pronoun to other parts of a sentence. Knowing the correct preposition to use is often difficult since there are few set rules. Sometimes prepositions are part of fixed expressions and sometimes they depend on the context. It is helpful to work on recognizing them in a reading and then to practice using them.

Exercise 3

Complete the paragraph with the correct prepositions. All the expressions appear in the story. Try to do the exercise without referring to the story. Compare your answers with a partner.

   As the boy and his father left the restaurant, the snow was whirling _____ them, but his father seemed indifferent _____ the bad weather. While the boy swayed _____ foot _____ foot, his father, flushed _____ determination, urged his son into the car. Hand _____ heart he promised his son that they would arrive home in time for Christmas Eve dinner, since he'd had to fight _____ the right to see him that day. After a while, the boy drifted _____ a dreamy state, and remembered how he had stuck _____ his dad as they skied in the blizzard. He hunched over with his hands clamped tightly _____ his knees and stared _____ the scenery. His father revved up the engine, and the car ran a course _____ the trees. The boy sat up straight, smiled, and decided that this journey would be one _____ the books.

PART 5   WRITING ACTIVITIES

1. Write a two-page essay on a memorable trip you have taken with a member of your family. In your essay, depict the surroundings, describe the relationship with your relative, and say whether the experience changed you in any way. Try to use participial phrases in your description.

2. Close to 50 percent of marriages in the United States end in divorce. In an essay of two to three pages, examine the issue of divorce in your country. Give the divorce-rate statistics, analyze the major reasons couples split up, and say what the effect frequently is on the family.

In your conclusion, explain what measures might be taken to lower the divorce rate.

3. John Le Carré's spy novel *A Perfect Spy* and Steven Spielberg's movie *Catch Me If You Can* both feature charming, irresponsible, dishonest fathers whose behavior has a profound effect on their sons. Write an essay on a book you've read or movie or play that you've seen that deals with the effect of an unusual parent on his or her children. Say whether the ending left you feeling uplifted or depressed.

6 ~ Mother

Grace Paley
(1922–2007)

Born in New York City to Russian-Jewish immigrants, Grace Paley heard English, Russian, and Yiddish spoken at her childhood home in the Bronx. As a result, she developed an acute ear for reproducing dialect, and her stories are full of Jewish, African-American, Irish, and other ethnic accents. Paley taught literature and creative writing at Sarah Lawrence, Columbia, and Dartmouth. In addition to her writing and academic career, she led a politically active life that included taking a vocal position against the Vietnam War, fighting for women's rights, and promoting pacifism.

Paley's stories often employ first-person narration and are peopled with vulnerable, ordinary characters who endure the ups and downs of their lives with love, humor, and patience. She published four collections of short stories: *The Little Disturbances of Man* (1959), *Enormous Changes at the Last Minute* (1974), *Later the Same Day* (1985), and *Collected Stories* (1994). She also published several volumes of poetry, including *Begin Again: Collected Poems* (1992) and *Fidelity* (published posthumously in 2008). In 1986 she was made New York's first State Author, and she was named Vermont State Poet in 2003.

Mother

Years after her death, a mother is remembered by her child.

One day I was listening to the AM radio. I heard a song: "Oh, I Long[1] to See My Mother in the Doorway." By God! I said, I understand that song. I have often longed to see my mother in the doorway. As a matter of fact, she did stand frequently in various

5 doorways looking at me. She stood one day, just so, at the front door, the darkness of the hallway behind her. It was New Year's Day. She said sadly, If you come home at 4 A.M. when you're seventeen, what time will you come home when you're twenty? She asked this question without humor or meanness. She had begun her worried preparations

10 for death. She would not be present, she thought, when I was twenty. So she wondered.

Another time she stood in the doorway of my room. I had just issued a political manifesto[2] attacking the family's position on the Soviet Union. She said, Go to sleep for godsakes, you damn fool, you

15 and your Communist ideas. We saw them already, Papa and me, in 1905. We guessed it all.

At the door of the kitchen she said, You never finish your lunch. You run around senselessly. What will become of you?

Then she died.

20 Naturally for the rest of my life I longed to see her, not only in doorways, in a great number of places—in the dining room with my aunts, at the window looking up and down the block, in the country garden among zinnias and marigolds,[3] in the living room with my father.

25 They sat in comfortable leather chairs. They were listening to Mozart. They looked at one another amazed. It seemed to them that they'd just come over on the boat. They'd just learned the first English words. It seemed to them that he had just proudly handed in a 100 percent correct exam to the American anatomy[4] professor. It seemed as

30 though she'd just quit the shop[5] for the kitchen.

I wish I could see her in the doorway of the living room.

---

1 **long** want badly
2 **manifesto** a declaration of intentions or principles
3 **zinnias and marigolds** brightly colored summer flowers

4 **anatomy** the study of the parts of the body
5 **the shop** short for sweatshop, a factory with long hours and difficult working conditions

She stood there a minute. Then she sat beside him. They owned an expensive record player. They were listening to Bach. She said to him, Talk to me a little. We don't talk so much anymore.

35   I'm tired, he said. Can't you see? I saw maybe thirty people today. All sick, all talk talk talk talk. Listen to the music, he said. I believe you once had perfect pitch.[6] I'm tired, he said.

Then she died.

---

6 **perfect pitch** the ability to recognize and reproduce a musical note exactly

FIRST READING

A Thinking About the Story

Discuss the following question with a partner.

> Did you sympathize more with the mother or the child in the story? Explain your answer.

B Understanding the Plot

Be prepared to answer the following questions with a partner or your class.

1. Through whose eyes is the story told?
2. What were the mother's concerns regarding her teenage child?
3. What country were the parents born in? How do we know?
4. What were the political beliefs of the narrator as a teenager?
5. What profession was the father studying for?
6. Why was the father particularly proud of his examination results?
7. Explain the expression: "She'd just quit the shop for the kitchen" (lines 30). Why was this a positive event to recall?
8. Later in life, what was the father's attitude toward his work?
9. What leisure-time activity did the narrator's parents share? How did this change over time?

A   Exploring Themes

Reread "Mother." As you read, look at how Paley has packed so much information and such a range of feeling and time into such a small space. This gives "Mother" the density of a poem.

1. How would you characterize the mother's relationship with her child?

2. How does the relationship between the parents change?

3. How did the economic circumstances of the family change? Give examples to illustrate your answer.

4. What does the narrator's mother imply happened to them in 1905? How did these events shape her political views?

   Note: You may have to do some research to answer this question.

5. In what ways have the adult narrator's feelings toward his or her mother changed over time? How would you describe the mood of the narrator looking back?

B   Analyzing Style

FLASHBACK

Flashback is a narrative technique in which the story in the present is interrupted by scenes set in the past. Through this device, some aspect of character or plot is illuminated. Along with literature, films also commonly employ flashbacks to highlight the significance of certain events.

Most of the information essential to an understanding of "Mother" is conveyed through flashbacks. For example, at the start of the story the narrator is listening to the radio; then in the next moment the reader is transported back to a much earlier event that occurred one New Year's Day when the narrator was seventeen.

Exercise 1

Answer the following questions with a partner.

1. How many flashbacks does "Mother" contain? Where does each flashback begin and end?

2. What word links several of the flashbacks? What is the thematic significance of this word?

3. How do the flashbacks in the first half of the story differ from those in the second half?

4. What is the effect of telling this story in a rapid series of flashbacks?

5. What sentence is repeated in the story? Why is it repeated? Explain your answer as fully as possible.

TONE

Tone refers to the attitude of the writer toward the characters and themes of the story. For example, the tone may be humorous, sarcastic, ironic, cheerful, pessimistic, angry, unfeeling, compassionate, or satirical.

Exercise 2

Answer the following questions.

1. How would you characterize the tone of "Mother"?

2. What are some of the ways in which the author conveys this tone?

3. How does the tone add to our understanding of the narrator and our feelings toward him or her?

4. Choose another story in the Parent and Child section of this book. Compare and contrast the tone in "Mother" with the tone in that story and say how it affects our view of the characters in each case.

C Judging for Yourself

Express yourself as personally as you like in your answers to the following questions.

1. Do you feel the mother was overprotective of her child?

2. What role do you think the father played in his child's upbringing?

3. Do you think the narrator is male or female? Justify your answer.

4. In your view, does the narrator have reason to regret his or her behavior toward the mother?

5. About how old do you estimate the narrator to be when listening to the radio at the start of the story? Give reasons for your answer.

D Making Connections

Answer the following questions in a small group.

1. Are male teenagers in your culture given more freedom by their parents than female teenagers?

2. Do teenagers in your country tend to be politically more radical than their parents?

3. Do teenagers feel a need to express their individuality in your country? If so, how? If not, why not?

4. Would you say that you had a closer relationship with your mother or your father when you were a teenager? Explain your answer.

5. Do you think being a child of immigrants affects the parent/child relationship? If so, in what ways?

E Debate

Decide whether you are for or against the following statement. Be prepared to argue your case in a class debate.

Teenagers should be allowed to make their own mistakes.

PAST TENSES

In English, there are many tenses that can be used to refer to past events. Some of these tenses refer to events in the past that are completely finished, and some refer to events that started in the past and continue into the present. Some tenses are used for single, complete events; others are used for events that continue or "progress" over a period of time in the past.

1. The **simple past** is used for an event that began and ended at a certain time in the past.

    *She **stood** one day, just so, at the front door, the darkness of the hallway behind her.* (lines 5–6)

2. The **past progressive** is used to show that an action was in progress when something else occurred. It takes the form of the past tense of *to be* plus the present participle.

    *One day I **was listening** to the AM radio. I heard a song: "Oh, I Long to See My Mother in the Doorway."* (lines 1–2)

3. The **present perfect** can be used in several situations. We often use it when we are more concerned with the effect of an action at the present moment and less interested in when the action started. It takes the form of the present tense of *to have* plus the past participle.

    • It can be used to indicate that an action began in the past and continues or recurs into the present.

    *I **have** often **longed** to see my mother in the doorway.* (lines 3–4)

- It can be used to show that something occurred at an unspecified time in the past.

  *I **have seen** my mother in the doorway.*

- It can also be used to suggest that an action has very recently been completed.

  *My mother is here. I **have** just **seen** her in the doorway.*

4. The **present perfect progressive** is used to talk about an action or a situation that began in the past and continues to the present. The action or situation is usually not finished. It is continuing, and it will probably continue into the future. It takes the form of *have/has been* plus the present participle.

   *For months I **have been longing** to see my mother in the doorway.*

5. The **past perfect** is used to show that something had already been completed before another action began in the past. It takes the form of the past tense of *to have* plus the past participle.

   *I **had** just **issued** a political manifesto attacking the family's position on the Soviet Union. She said, Go to sleep for godsakes, you damn fool …. (lines 12–14)*

6. The **past perfect progressive** is used to talk about an action that was in progress when another action in the past interrupted it. It takes the form of *had been* plus the present participle.

   *I **had been working on** my political manifesto for weeks when she ordered me to stop.*

Exercise

Complete the sentences with a correct tense of the verb in parentheses. The verb in parentheses applies to both sentences in the pair. Although it may be possible, do not use the same tense in each pair. The first answer is done for you.

1. (behave) When I was a teenager, I frequently <u>behaved</u> badly toward my mother.

   I knew that I <u>had been behaving</u> badly, so I promised I would stop.

2. (achieve) It amazed my parents that they _____ so much in such a short time. "We _____ so much in such a short time," said my father in amazement to my mother.

3. (listen) My mother _____ to music when I burst into the room after school.
   My mother _____ to music every day of my school life.

4. (talk) "I _____ to you for the past ten minutes and you haven't heard a word!" said my mother in exasperation.

"I _____ to you for at least ten minutes before I realized you hadn't heard a word!" said my mother in exasperation.

5. (return) My parents _____ to Russia only once since they arrived in this country.

My parents _____ to Russia for the first time last year.

6. (worry) Although my mother constantly _____ about dying, she didn't express her fears to me.

Although my mother _____ about dying for years, she expressed her fears to me only last week.

7. (hand in) You _____ your exam, so it is too late to request extra time.

You _____ your exam, so it was too late to request extra time.

8. (run around) When I was young, I _____ senselessly.

When I was young, I _____ senselessly before I was stopped by the death of my mother.

9. (quit) After my father graduated, my mother _____ working.

"I didn't know you _____ working!" exclaimed my father to my mother.

10. (look for) Before dinner was served, I _____ my mother in the garden.

Although I _____ my mother for nearly ten minutes, I still hadn't found her by the time dinner was served.

11. (study) My father and mother _____

English soon after they arrived in the United States.

My father and mother _____ English

for the past three months.

VOCABULARY BUILDING

WORDS IN CONTEXT

"Mother" doesn't have much unfamiliar vocabulary. As a result, you can take the time to think through each new word in its context. This will reduce your dependence on a dictionary.

Exercise 1

With a partner, replace each of the italicized words or expressions with appropriate vocabulary from the text. Try to do this exercise from memory, referring to the story only if necessary.

1. I read your *declaration of principles* last night and have decided to vote for you.

2. Teenagers frequently act *thoughtlessly* and suffer the consequences.

3. Surprisingly, not all great musicians have *a totally accurate ear*.

4. After immigrating to a new country, it is not uncommon to *yearn* for one's place of birth.

5. Any student who *submits* his or her essay late will be penalized.

6. If you act with *malice* toward your spouse, you will probably

regret it.

7. The government *gave out* a pamphlet explaining its policy toward immigration.

8. The lessons involving *the study of the body* were my father's favorite classes at the university.

Exercise 2

Compose eight new sentences using your answers from Exercise 1 in a new context.

1. Write a memory piece of two to three pages, focusing on an event in your teenage years. As in "Mother," start in the present and use something unexpected like a sound, a smell, or a gesture to trigger your memory and send you back into the past. Use past and present tenses appropriately.

2. Write a two-page essay analyzing the roots of teenage rebellion against parental and other types of authority. Begin your essay by considering why adolescents traditionally feel the need to challenge the rules of adult society. Think about the positive and negative aspects of this confrontation, and say what steps you would advocate to improve the situation.

3. Marcel Proust's *Remembrance of Things Past* is one of the most famous works of fiction centering on memory. Write a review for a newspaper or magazine on a book you have read in which a character looks back on events that occurred in the past. Briefly explain its contents and say why you recommend it.

4. "Mother" and "Powder" (pages 68–71) are both told by a narrator who relates a problematic relationship with a parent. In an essay, compare and contrast these relationships. Consider the ending of each story and say how it influences the tone of the narration.

7 ∾ Eveline

James Joyce
(1882–1941)

Born in Dublin, Ireland, James Joyce was one of the most influential writers of the twentieth century. He was a brilliant student, attending a famous Jesuit boarding school until his father's bankruptcy forced him to leave. In 1904 he left the Catholic Church and departed from Ireland for good. Joyce married and lived with his family in Trieste, Zurich, and Paris, where he taught English and wrote the works that made him famous.

In 1914, Joyce published the short story collection *Dubliners*, which he described as representing "a chapter of the moral history" of Ireland. Then came the novel *A Portrait of the Artist as a Young Man* (1916), which fictionalized Joyce's break with the Catholic Church and his new identity as a writer. In his great novel *Ulysses* (1922), Joyce perfected the technique of stream of consciousness, creating interior monologues in which time is disrupted to capture the inner thought processes of the characters. This novel established Joyce as a major voice who would influence the work of many writers to come, including Virginia Woolf and William Faulkner.

Eveline

A young woman is faced with a life-changing decision.

She sat at the window watching the evening invade the avenue. Her head was leaned against the window curtains, and in her nostrils was the odour of dusty cretonne.[1] She was tired.

Few people passed. The man out of the last house passed on his way home; she heard his footsteps clacking along the concrete pavement and afterwards crunching on the cinder path before the new red houses. One time there used to be a field there in which they used to play every evening with other people's children. Then a man from Belfast bought the field and built houses in it—not like their little brown houses, but bright brick houses with shining roofs. The children of the avenue used to play together in that field—the Devines, the Waters, the Dunns, little Keogh the cripple,[2] she and her brothers and sisters. Ernest, however, never played: he was too grown up. Her father used often to hunt them in out of the field[3] with his blackthorn stick; but usually little Keogh used to keep *nix*[4] and call out when he saw her father coming. Still they seemed to have been rather happy then. Her father was not so bad then; and besides, her mother was alive. That was a long time ago; she and her brothers and sisters were all grown up; her mother was dead. Tizzie Dunn was dead, too, and the Waters had gone back to England. Everything changes. Now she was going to go away like the others, to leave her home.

Home! She looked round the room, reviewing all its familiar objects which she had dusted once a week for so many years, wondering where on earth[5] all the dust came from. Perhaps she would never see again those familiar objects from which she had never dreamed of[6] being divided. And yet during all those years she had never found out the name of the priest whose yellowing photograph hung on the wall above the broken harmonium[7] beside the coloured print of the promises made to Blessed Margaret Mary Alacoque.[8] He had been a school friend of her father. Whenever he showed the photograph to a visitor her father used to pass it with a casual word:

'He is in Melbourne[9] now.'

---

1 **cretonne** a type of fabric
2 **cripple** a physically handicapped person (term no longer used in North America)
3 **hunt them in out of the field** chase them out of the field into the house (unusual usage)
4 **keep *nix*** keep watch (old British slang)
5 **where on earth** expression used to emphasize a question

6 **never dreamed of** never thought it possible
7 **harmonium** musical instrument similar to an organ
8 **Margaret Mary Alacoque** a Catholic saint
9 **Melbourne** city in Australia

She had consented to go away, to leave her home. Was that wise? She tried to weigh each side of the question. In her home anyway she
35 had shelter and food; she had those whom she had known all her life about her. Of course she had to work hard, both in the house and at business. What would they say of her in the Stores when they found out that she had run away with a fellow? Say she was a fool, perhaps; and her place would be filled up by advertisement. Miss Gavan would
40 be glad. She had always had an edge on her,[10] especially whenever there were people listening.

'Miss Hill, don't you see these ladies are waiting?'

'Look lively,[11] Miss Hill, please.'

She would not cry many tears at leaving the Stores.

45 But in her new home, in a distant unknown country, it would not be like that. Then she would be married—she, Eveline. People would treat her with respect then. She would not be treated as her mother had been. Even now, though she was over nineteen, she sometimes felt herself in danger of her father's violence. She knew it was that that
50 had given her the palpitations.[12] When they were growing up he had never gone for her,[13] like he used to go for Harry and Ernest, because she was a girl; but latterly[14] he had begun to threaten her and say what he would do to her only for her dead mother's sake. And now she had nobody to protect her, Ernest was dead and Harry, who was in the
55 church decorating business, was nearly always down somewhere in the country. Besides, the invariable squabble[15] for money on Saturday nights had begun to weary her unspeakably.[16] She always gave her entire wages—seven shillings—and Harry always sent up what he could, but the trouble was to get any money from her father. He said
60 she used to squander[17] the money, that she had no head,[18] that he wasn't going to give her his hard-earned money to throw about the streets, and much more, for he was usually fairly bad on Saturday night. In the end he would give her the money and ask her had she any intention of buying Sunday's dinner. Then she had to rush out as
65 quickly as she could and do her marketing, holding her black leather purse tightly in her hand as she elbowed[19] her way through the crowds and returning home late under her load of provisions. She had to

---

10 **She (Miss Gavan) had always had an edge on her** Miss Gavan was always particularly sharp toward her (unusual usage)

11 **Look lively** Hurry up (informal, old-fashioned English)

12 **palpitations** rapid heartbeats

13 **gone for her** attacked her

14 **latterly** recently

15 **invariable squabble** constant argument over something unimportant

16 **unspeakably** horribly

17 **squander** waste

18 **she had no head** she had no ability (to deal with money)

19 **elbowed** pushed through the crowd

work hard to keep the house together[20] and to see that the two young
children who had been left to her charge[21] went to school regularly and
70 got their meals regularly. It was hard work—a hard life—but now that
she was about to leave it she did not find it a wholly undesirable life.

She was about to explore another life with Frank. Frank was very
kind, manly, open-hearted. She was to go away with him by the
night-boat to be his wife and to live with him in Buenos Ayres,[22]
75 where he had a home waiting for her. How well she remembered the
first time she had seen him; he was lodging in a house on the main road
where she used to visit. It seemed a few weeks ago. He was standing
at the gate, his peaked cap pushed back on his head and his hair
tumbled forward over a face of bronze. Then they had come to know
80 each other. He used to meet her outside the Stores every evening and
see her home. He took her to see *The Bohemian Girl*[23] and she felt elated
as she sat in an unaccustomed part of the theatre with him. He was
awfully fond of music and sang a little. People knew that they were
courting,[24] and, when he sang about the lass that loves a sailor, she
85 always felt pleasantly confused. He used to call her Poppens out of fun.
First of all it had been an excitement for her to have a fellow and then
she had begun to like him. He had tales of distant countries. He had
started as a deck boy at a pound a month[25] on a ship of the Allan Line
going out of Canada. He told her the names of the ships he had been
90 on and the names of the different services. He had sailed through the
Straits of Magellan and he told her stories of the terrible Patagonians.
He had fallen on his feet[26] in Buenos Ayres, he said, and had come over
to the old country[27] just for a holiday. Of course, her father had found
out the affair and had forbidden her to have anything to say to him.
95 'I know these sailor chaps,' he said.

One day he had quarrelled with Frank, and after that she had to
meet her lover secretly.

The evening deepened in the avenue. The white of two letters in
her lap grew indistinct. One was to Harry; the other was to her father.
100 Ernest had been her favourite, but she liked Harry too. Her father was
becoming old lately, she noticed; he would miss her. Sometimes he
could be very nice. Not long before, when she had been laid up[28] for a
day, he had read her out of a ghost story and made toast for her at the

---

20 **keep the house together** prevent the family
   from breaking up
21 **left to her charge** left in her care
22 **Buenos Ayres** the capital of Argentina
   (usually spelled Buenos Aires)
23 **The Bohemian Girl** a nineteenth-century
   opera
24 **courting** romantically involved

25 **a deck boy at a pound a month** a low
   position on a ship at a small salary
26 **had fallen on his feet** had overcome
   problems and succeeded
27 **the old country** the country of a person's
   birth
28 **laid up** sick

fire. Another day, when their mother was alive, they had all gone for a
105 picnic to the Hill of Howth. She remembered her father putting on her
mother's bonnet[29] to make the children laugh.

Her time was running out, but she continued to sit by the window,
leaning her head against the window curtain, inhaling the odour of
dusty cretonne. Down far in the avenue she could hear a street organ
110 playing. She knew the air.[30] Strange that it should come that very night
to remind her of the promise to her mother, her promise to keep the
home together as long as she could. She remembered the last night
of her mother's illness; she was again in the close,[31] dark room at the
other side of the hall and outside she heard a melancholy air of Italy.
115 The organ-player had been ordered to go away and given sixpence. She
remembered her father strutting back into the sick-room saying:

'Damned Italians! coming over here!'

As she mused the pitiful vision of her mother's life laid its spell
on the very quick of her being[32]—that life of common-place sacrifices
120 closing in final craziness. She trembled as she heard again her mother's
voice saying constantly with foolish insistence:

'Derevaun Seraun! Derevaun Seraun!'[33]

She stood up in a sudden impulse of terror. Escape! She must
escape! Frank would save her. He would give her life, perhaps love,
125 too. But she wanted to live. Why should she be unhappy? She had a
right to happiness. Frank would take her in his arms, fold her in his
arms. He would save her.

She stood among the swaying crowd in the station at the North
Wall. He held her hand and she knew that he was speaking to her,
130 saying something about the passage over and over again. The station
was full of soldiers with brown baggages. Through the wide doors
of the sheds she caught a glimpse of the black mass of the boat, lying
in beside the quay wall, with illumined portholes.[34] She answered
nothing. She felt her cheek pale and cold and, out of a maze of distress,
135 she prayed to God to direct her, to show her what was her duty. The
boat blew a long mournful whistle into the mist. If she went, tomorrow
she would be on the sea with Frank, steaming towards Buenos Ayres.
Their passage had been booked.[35] Could she still draw back after all
he had done for her? Her distress awoke a nausea in her body and she
140 kept moving her lips in silent fervent[36] prayer.

---

29 **bonnet** woman's hat
30 **air** tune
31 **close** airless, stuffy
32 **laid its spell on the very quick of her
     being** affected her very deeply (figurative
     language)
33 **"Derevaun Seraun!"** probably meaningless
     words
34 **illumined portholes** lighted windows on a
     ship
35 **Their passage had been booked.** Their
     tickets had been paid for.
36 **fervent** intense

A bell clanged upon her heart. She felt him seize her hand:

'Come!'

All the seas of the world tumbled about her heart. He was drawing her into them: he would drown her. She gripped with both hands at the
145 iron railing.

'Come!'

No! No! No! It was impossible. Her hands clutched the iron in frenzy. Amid the seas she sent a cry of anguish.

'Eveline! Evvy!'

150 He rushed beyond the barrier and called to her to follow. He was shouted at to go on, but he still called to her. She set her white face to him,[37] passive, like a helpless animal. Her eyes gave him no sign of love or farewell or recognition.

---

37 **set her white face to him** resisted him
(usually written *set one's face against*)

FIRST READING

A Thinking About the Story

Discuss the following questions with a partner.

How did you expect the story to end? What influenced your prediction?

B Understanding the Plot

Be prepared to answer the following questions with a partner or your class.

1. Did Eveline have a happy childhood? Explain your answer.
2. What kind of man is Eveline's father? Give details to support your answer.
3. What is Eveline's situation at work?
4. In what way does Eveline want to be different from her mother?
5. Why does Eveline miss the presence of her brothers Harry and Ernest?
6. What does Eveline mean when she says her father "was usually fairly bad on Saturday night"? (lines 62–63)
7. What does Eveline's father expect from her on a daily basis?
8. What do we learn about Frank? Give as many details as possible.
9. What does Evelyn's father mean by the statement "I know these sailor chaps"? (line 95)

10. What were the circumstances surrounding the death of Eveline's mother?

11. What are the pros and cons that influence Eveline as she considers what to do? List as many as possible.

CRITICAL THINKING

A Exploring Themes

Reread "Eveline." As you read, try to feel the sense of loneliness and claustrophobia that Joyce builds around Eveline's life.

1. Why do Eveline's thoughts keep returning to her past as she sits at the window?

2. What do we learn about the values of the Dublin society in which Eveline lives and works?

3. Why does Eveline have such a strong sense of duty and need for self-sacrifice?

4. What does Frank represent in the story?

5. What is the significance of the priest in the photograph? (lines 26–32)

6. What can we infer about why Eveline changed her mind at the last minute?

B Analyzing Style

IMAGERY

Joyce uses **imagery** throughout "Eveline" to portray the protagonist's exterior and interior life. His evocative verbal pictures include adjectives that appeal to the senses, as well as metaphor and personification.

A **metaphor** is an implied comparison in which one thing is described as something else without using the words *like* or *as*. For example: *Eveline's life is an empty desert.* **Personification** means giving human characteristics to something nonhuman. For example: *The ocean called out to Eveline.*

Exercise 1

Answer the following questions about lines 1–3.

1. Find the example of personification and explain its effect.

2. Explain how the imagery in the opening paragraph establishes Eveline's brooding mood and suffocating surroundings.

3. How does this imagery foreshadow Eveline's decision to stay?

4. Where in the story is this imagery repeated? What is the effect of this repetition?

Exercise 2

Answer the following questions about lines 128–153.

1. How does the scene in lines 128–131 provide a contrast with Eveline's home life?

2. How is the boat described in line 132? How does the imagery reflect Eveline's mood?

3. How do the descriptions of Eveline in lines 134–140 indicate what she is feeling? Whom does she remind you of when she is "moving her lips in silent fervent prayer"?

4. There are two metaphors in lines 141–144. Explain them and show how they help convey the intensity of Eveline's feelings.

Exercise 3

Find more adjectives in the story that create vivid pictures for the reader and enhance the atmosphere. Explain your choices.

FLASHBACK

In "Eveline," Joyce uses **flashback** to interrupt the story in the present and depict scenes set in the past. By exploring Eveline's memories, Joyce paints a remarkably full portrait of his protagonist. We get a deep insight into Eveline's personality in just a few pages, as we follow her thoughts and feelings about the events that have shaped her life.

Exercise 4

Answer the following questions.

1. What is the significance of the flashback in lines 7–20?

2. What is the point of the flashback to Eveline's workplace?

3. How does the flashback to her mother's death influence Eveline?

4. In what ways do the flashbacks containing Frank contrast with the rest of Eveline's life?

5. How do all the flashbacks taken together help us understand Eveline's final decision?

C Judging for Yourself

Express yourself as personally as you like in your answers to the following questions.

1. Do you think Eveline will regret her decision to stay?
2. In your view, would her father have approved of any man that Eveline met? Explain your answer.
3. Do you think Eveline's mother had the right to make her promise to keep the home together for as long as possible?
4. To what extent is Eveline responsible for her situation?
5. Do you see "Eveline" as a love story?

D Making Connections

Answer the following questions in a small group.

1. In your country, do women often feel trapped in roles they don't want? Discuss the economic, cultural, religious, or other factors that might limit women's choices.
2. Is there a feminist movement in your country? If there is, do you support its goals? Give reasons for your answer.
3. In your culture, what are some of the reasons people have for getting married? Consider both practical and romantic reasons.
4. Do many people emigrate from your country? Where do they go? Why?
5. Is alcoholism a problem where you live? If so, which groups of people are most likely to drink excessively? Are there organizations to help people stop drinking?

E Debate

Decide whether you are for or against the following statement. Be prepared to argue your case in a class debate.

The pursuit of happiness is a basic human right.

PART 3 GRAMMAR IN CONTEXT

PARALLEL STRUCTURE: COORDINATING CONJUNCTIONS

When two or more elements in a sentence are joined by a **coordinating conjunction** (*and, but, or, nor*) the rules of **parallel structure** apply. This means that the linked parts must have the same grammatical form. A coordinating conjunction can link two words, two phrases, or two clauses. The more complex a sentence, the harder it can be to maintain parallel structure. Following these rules is especially important in writing.

1. Coordinating conjunctions can link two or more of the same part of speech.

*She felt her cheek <u>pale</u> **and** <u>cold</u>.* (line 134)

*Her eyes gave him no sign of <u>love</u> **or** <u>farewell</u> **or** <u>recognition</u>.* (lines 152–153)

2. Coordinating conjunctions can link two or more of the same type of phrase.

*She heard his footsteps <u>clacking along the concrete pavement</u> **and** afterwards <u>crunching on the cinder path</u>.* (adapted from lines 5–6)

3. Coordinating conjunctions can link two or more clauses.

*<u>Ernest had been her favourite</u>, **but** <u>she liked Harry too</u>.* (line 100)

When the subject of the two clauses joined by a coordinating conjunction is the same, it is possible to omit the second subject.

*He <u>rushed beyond the barrier</u> **and** <u>called to her to follow</u>.* (line 150)

It is easy to make the mistake of linking unmatched elements with a coordinating conjunction.

Incorrect: *Eveline loves <u>her father</u> **and** <u>to go out with Frank</u>.* [noun and infinitive]

Correct: *Eveline loves <u>to be with her father</u> **and** <u>to go out with Frank</u>.* [two infinitives]

Incorrect: *Frank hoped <u>to marry Eveline</u> **and** <u>that she would come with him to Argentina</u>.* [infinitive and noun clause]

Correct: *Frank hoped <u>that Eveline would marry him</u> **and** <u>that she would come with him to Argentina</u>.* [two noun clauses]

Exercise 1

Rewrite the following sentences with correct parallel structure. There may be more than one way to fix the sentence. Compare your answers with a partner.

1. Eveline loved to sit by the window and watching the passersby.
2. Eveline needed freedom, but not to hurt her brothers.
3. Eveline's father didn't see Frank approaching or to stop by the house.
4. The children loved playing together in the neighborhood and to throw the ball to each other.
5. Eveline heard the sailors shouting to each other and who were swearing loudly.
6. Miss Gavan wanted to run the whole store and more control.
7. Eveline knew that she could stay home or leaving for a new life in Buenos Aires.
8. Eveline's mother listened to someone playing the street organ and who was talking loudly.

9. Her father accused Eveline of squandering the money he gave her and that she was totally irresponsible.

10. Frank saw the ship getting ready to leave but which still had people boarding.

Exercise 2

Write three sentences in which coordinating conjunctions join two or more nouns, adverbs, or adjectives. Then write two more sentences in which coordinating conjunctions join two phrases and two clauses.

PARALLEL STRUCTURE: CORRELATIVE CONJUNCTIONS

The rules of parallel structure apply to the **correlative conjunctions** *either ... or, neither ... nor, both ... and,* and *not only ... but also.*

1. Like coordinating conjunctions, correlative conjunctions can link two parts of speech, two phrases, or two clauses.

   *Eveline had to take care of **both** <u>her father</u> **and** <u>her siblings</u>.* [nouns]

   *She had to work hard, **both** <u>at home</u> **and** <u>in the shop</u>.* [prepositional phrases]

   *She had to work hard **both** <u>when she was at home</u> **and** <u>when she was at work</u>.* [clauses]

2. With correlative conjunctions, it is important to keep the verb in agreement with its subject.

   * When you connect two subjects with *both ... and,* use a plural verb.

     ***Both** Eveline **and** Frank <u>are</u> happy at first.*

   * When you connect two subjects with the correlative conjunctions *either ... or, not only ... but also,* or *neither ... nor,* the verb should agree with the noun that is closest to it.

     ***Either** music **or** theater <u>is</u> enough to make Eveline happy with Frank.*

     ***Either** dinner **or** drinks <u>are</u> enough to make Eveline happy with Frank.*

     ***Neither** riches **nor** love <u>persuades</u> Eveline to leave.*

     ***Neither** love **nor** riches <u>persuade</u> Eveline to leave.*

     ***Not only** Harry **but also** Ernest <u>protects</u> Eveline.*

     ***Not only** Frank **but also** Eveline's brothers <u>protect</u> her.*

Exercise 3

Complete the following sentences with the appropriate form of the verb in parentheses. Pay attention to subject/verb agreement.

1. Both she and Frank _____ the boat in the distance (see/s)

2. Her father not only _____ her to work, but also _____ that she manage the house. (expect/s, demand/s)

3. Neither Frank nor her friends _____ how to handle her father. (know/knows)

4. Either the shop assistants or their manager _____ there to serve the customers. (is/are)

5. Both Eveline's friends and her brother _____ her to leave with Frank. (encourage/s)

6. Either Eveline or her father _____ to compromise. (need/s)

7. Not only Eveline but also her brothers _____ of escape. (dream/s)

8. Neither little Keogh nor Tizzie Dunn _____ to this day. (survive/s)

PART 4 VOCABULARY BUILDING

DESCRIPTIVE VERBS

It is common to associate adjectives with language that can help us see, feel, hear, smell, and taste the details that an author is describing. However, many verbs have the same power to evoke the senses.

In "Eveline," Joyce uses such **descriptive verbs** to compelling effect. For example, when he writes that Eveline *elbowed her way through the crowds* (line 66), Joyce creates a picture of the harried young woman pushing through a mass of people as she tries to do her shopping. The verb *elbowed* highlights how stressful the outing is for Eveline, as we feel the pressure of her arms against the bodies of the people around her.

Exercise 1

With a partner, find the following verbs in the story. Look at their context, and with the help of a dictionary take turns explaining to each other what the verbs mean.

clack (line 5)   tremble (line 120)

crunch (line 6)   clang (line 141)

tumble (lines 79)   seize (line 141)

strut (line 116)   clutch (line 147)

Like imagery involving adjectives, all the verbs in Exercise 1 appeal to our senses (sight, hearing, taste, touch, and smell). Decide which sense is most closely associated with each verb and explain why.

IDIOMATIC EXPRESSIONS

An **idiomatic expression** contains two or more words of which at least one word has a figurative or hidden meaning. Therefore, by analyzing the separate parts of the expression, it may not be possible to understand the whole. A good learner dictionary might be needed to help you understand precisely what an idiomatic expression means and how it is used. Increasing your knowledge of idiomatic expressions is a significant way to broaden your vocabulary skills.

Exercise 3

Find the following idiomatic expressions in the story. The wording of some of them has been changed slightly. Use the context to help you understand their meaning. Write a brief definition on each line.

1. on one's way (lines 4–5) _____

2. keep watch (line 15) _____

3. weigh each side of the question (line 34) _____

4. have a head for (line 60) _____

5. see someone home (line 81) _____

6. fall on one's feet (line 92) _____

7. run out of time (line 107) _____

8. catch a glimpse of (line 132) _____

Exercise 4

Use the expressions in Exercise 3 to complete the following sentences. Note that you may need to change the pronoun or the tense of the verb.

1. Before making any decision Eveline would always carefully

   _____.

2. Frank insisted that he _____ after the performance.

3. Eveline understood that she had to _____ over her younger siblings.

4. Frank tried to _____ Eveline through the crowd of soldiers.

5. Eveline's father didn't believe she would _____ if things went wrong with Frank.

6. Eveline knew that she would _____ if she didn't make a move soon.

7. Her father wanted Eveline to believe that she didn't _____ figures so he could justify taking her money.

8. Eveline had to elbow through the crowd _____ to the market.

PART 5 WRITING ACTIVITIES

1. The decision to emigrate is usually very difficult. Write an essay of about two pages centering on emigration from your country. Look at the sectors that most frequently emigrate, say what their reasons are, and note whether these groups have changed noticeably over the last fifty years. Include the country or countries that are the most popular destinations. In your conclusion, say whether you would consider emigrating. If your answer is yes, say where you would like to go and why. If your answer is no, explain your reasons.

   Note: With the help of a dictionary, make sure you understand the difference between *immigrate* and *emigrate*.

2. Write an imaginary letter from Eveline to a personal advice columnist (for example, "Dear Abby"), asking for help in her predicament. Include the columnist's reply to her.

3. "Eveline" comes from a collection of short stories called *Dubliners*, in which James Joyce uses the city of Dublin, Ireland, as a physical and symbolic setting for the lives of people from many different walks of life. Write an essay of two pages about a book you have read or a movie you have seen in which a city plays a major role in the work. In your essay, describe the aspects of the city that stand out and explain how the setting serves to influence the actions and lives of the characters.

4. Both "Eveline" and "Mother" (pages 82–83) are parent/child stories written in a series of flashbacks. Compare the ways in which memory plays an important role in each story. Show how the children's memories of their past continue to affect them as adults.

8 ⋙ My Oedipus Complex

Frank O'Connor
(1903–1966)

Born in Cork, Ireland, Frank O'Connor was the only child of very poor, working-class parents. An Irish nationalist, he joined the Irish Republican Army (IRA), fought actively for an Ireland independent of Britain, and was imprisoned for two years. Later he spent many years in the United States, teaching at a number of prestigious universities, including Harvard and Stanford. A prolific writer, O'Connor achieved greatest recognition for his short-story collections, such as *Guests of the Nation* (1931), *My Oedipus Complex and Other Stories* (1963), and *A Life of Your Own and Other Stories* (1969). He also published two novels, *The Saint and Mary Kate* (1932) and *Dutch Interior* (1940); two autobiographies; poetry anthologies; plays; and books of literary criticism.

O'Connor's short stories reflect the realities of Irish life as he knew it. The naturalistic language of his writing seeks to capture the flavor of the Irish tongue, and many of his stories are infused with humor. "My Oedipus Complex" is a semiautobiographical story in which O'Connor depicts his childhood relationship with his parents.

My Oedipus Complex[1]

A small boy's world is turned upside down when his father returns home from the First World War.

Father was in the army all through the war—the first war, I mean—so, up to the age of five, I never saw much of him, and what I saw did not worry me. Sometimes I woke and there was a big figure in khaki[2] peering down at me in the candlelight. Sometimes in the
5 early morning I heard the slamming of the front door and the clatter of nailed boots down the cobbles[3] of the lane. These were Father's entrances and exits. Like Santa Claus he came and went mysteriously.

In fact, I rather liked his visits, though it was an uncomfortable squeeze between Mother and him when I got into the big bed in the
10 early morning. He smoked, which gave him a pleasant musty smell,[4] and shaved, an operation of astounding interest. Each time he left a trail of souvenirs—model tanks and Gurkha[5] knives with handles made of bullet cases, and German helmets and cap badges and button sticks, and all sorts of military equipment—carefully stowed away in
15 a long box on top of the wardrobe, in case they ever came in handy.[6] There was a bit of the magpie[7] about Father; he expected everything to come in handy. When his back was turned, Mother let me get a chair and rummage through his treasures. She didn't seem to think so highly of them as he did.

20 The war was the most peaceful period of my life. The window of my attic faced southeast. My mother had curtained it, but that had small effect. I always woke with the first light and, with all the responsibilities of the previous day melted, feeling myself rather like the sun, ready to illumine and rejoice. Life never seemed so simple
25 and clear and full of possibilities as then. I put my feet out from under the clothes[8]—I called them Mrs. Left and Mrs. Right—and invented dramatic situations for them in which they discussed the problems of the day. At least Mrs. Right did; she was very demonstrative, but I hadn't the same control of Mrs. Left, so she mostly contented herself
30 with nodding agreement.

---

1 **Oedipus Complex** Sigmund Freud developed the theory of the Oedipus complex to explain the jealous attachment of a young boy to his mother. According to Freud, young boys want to take their father's place in their mother's sexual affections.
2 **khaki** material used for military uniforms
3 **cobbles** cobblestones, round stones for paving streets

4 **musty smell** a damp, stale odor
5 **Gurkha knives** knives with sharp, curved blades carried by Nepalese soldiers who served in the British army
6 **came in handy** were useful
7 **magpie** a bird that collects small shiny objects for its nest
8 **clothes** bedclothes (sheets and blankets)

They discussed what Mother and I should do during the day, what Santa Claus should give a fellow for Christmas, and what steps should be taken to brighten the home. There was that little matter of the baby, for instance. Mother and I could never agree about that. Ours was the
35 only house in the terrace without a new baby, and Mother said we couldn't afford one till Father came back from the war because they cost seventeen and six.[9]

That showed how simple she was. The Geneys up the road had a baby, and everyone knew they couldn't afford seventeen and six.
40 It was probably a cheap baby, and Mother wanted something really good, but I felt she was too exclusive.[10] The Geneys' baby would have done us fine.

Having settled my plans for the day, I got up, put a chair under the attic window, and lifted the frame high enough to stick out my head.
45 The window overlooked the front gardens of the terrace behind ours, and beyond these it looked over a deep valley to the tall, red brick houses terraced up the opposite hillside, which were all still in shadow, while those at our side of the valley were all lit up, though with long strange shadows that made them seem unfamiliar; rigid[11] and painted.
50 After that I went into Mother's room and climbed into the big bed. She woke and I began to tell her of my schemes. By this time, though I never seemed to have noticed it, I was petrified[12] in my nightshirt, and I thawed as I talked until, the last frost melted, I fell asleep beside her and woke again only when I heard her below in the kitchen, making
55 the breakfast.

After breakfast we went into town; heard Mass at St. Augustine's[13] and said a prayer for Father, and did the shopping. If the afternoon was fine[14] we either went for a walk in the country or a visit to Mother's great friend in the convent, Mother Saint Dominic. Mother had them all
60 praying for Father, and every night, going to bed, I asked God to send him back safe from the war to us. Little, indeed, did I know what I was praying for!

One morning, I got into the big bed, and there, sure enough, was Father in his usual Santa Claus manner, but later, instead of uniform,
65 he put on his best blue suit, and Mother was as pleased as anything. I saw nothing to be pleased about, because, out of uniform, Father was altogether less interesting, but she only beamed, and explained that our prayers had been answered, and off we went to Mass to thank God for having brought Father safely home.

---

9 **seventeen and six** seventeen shillings and sixpence (old British currency)
10 **exclusive** demanding
11 **rigid** stiff

12 **petrified** frozen (unusual use)
13 **heard Mass at St. Augustine's** attended a church service
14 **fine** sunny (British English)

70　　The irony of it! That very day when he came in to dinner he took off his boots and put on his slippers, donned the dirty old cap he wore about the house to save him from colds, crossed his legs, and began to talk gravely to Mother, who looked anxious. Naturally, I disliked her looking anxious, because it destroyed her good looks, so I interrupted

75　him.

"Just a moment, Larry!" she said gently.

This was only what she said when we had boring visitors, so I attached no importance to it and went on talking.

"Do be quiet, Larry!" she said impatiently. "Don't you hear me

80　talking to Daddy?"

This was the first time I heard those ominous[15] words, "talking to Daddy," and I couldn't help feeling that if this was how God answered prayers, he couldn't listen to them very attentively.

"Why are you talking to Daddy?" I asked with as great a show of

85　indifference[16] as I could muster.[17]

"Because Daddy and I have business to discuss. Now, don't interrupt again!"

In the afternoon, at Mother's request, Father took me for a walk. This time we went into town instead of out in the country,

90　and I thought at first, in my usual optimistic way, that it might be an improvement. It was nothing of the sort. Father and I had quite different notions of a walk in town. He had no proper interest in trams, ships, and horses, and the only thing that seemed to divert him was talking to fellows as old as himself. When I wanted to stop he simply

95　went on, dragging me behind him by the hand; when he wanted to stop I had no alternative but to do the same. I noticed that it seemed to be a sign that he wanted to stop for a long time whenever he leaned against a wall. The second time I saw him do it I got wild. He seemed to be settling himself forever. I pulled him by the coat and trousers, but,

100　unlike Mother who, if you were too persistent, got into a wax[18] and said: "Larry, if you don't behave yourself, I'll give you a good slap," Father had an extraordinary capacity for amiable inattention. I sized him up[19] and wondered would I cry, but he seemed to be too remote to be annoyed even by that. Really, it was like going for a walk with a

105　mountain! He either ignored the wrenching and pummeling[20] entirely, or else glanced down with a grin of amusement from his peak. I had never met anyone so absorbed in himself as he seemed.

15　**ominous** threatening
16　**show of indifference** appearance of not caring
17　**muster** gather
18　**got into a wax** got angry (old British slang)
19　**sized him up** judged him
20　**wrenching and pummeling** pulling and hitting

At teatime, "talking to Daddy" began again, complicated this time by the fact that he had an evening paper, and every few minutes he put it down and told Mother something new out of it. I felt this was foul play.[21] Man for man, I was prepared to compete with him any time for Mother's attention, but when he had it all made up for him by other people it left me no chance. Several times I tried to change the subject without success.

"You must be quiet while Daddy is reading, Larry," Mother said impatiently.

It was clear that she either genuinely liked talking to Father better than talking to me, or else that he had some terrible hold on her[22] which made her afraid to admit the truth.

"Mummy," I said that night when she was tucking me up,[23] "do you think if I prayed hard God would send Daddy back to the war?"

She seemed to think about that for a moment.

"No, dear," she said with a smile. "I don't think He would."

"Why wouldn't He, Mummy?"

"Because there isn't a war any longer, dear."

"But, Mummy, couldn't God make another war, if He liked?"

"He wouldn't like to, dear. It's not God who makes wars, but bad people."

"Oh!" I said.

I was disappointed about that. I began to think that God wasn't quite what He was cracked up to be.[24]

Next morning I woke at my usual hour, feeling like a bottle of champagne. I put out my feet and invented a long conversation in which Mrs. Right talked of the trouble she had with her own father till she put him in the Home.[25] I didn't quite know what the Home was but it sounded the right place for Father. Then I got my chair and stuck my head out of the attic window. Dawn was just breaking, with a guilty air that made me feel I had caught it in the act.[26] My head bursting with stories and schemes, I stumbled in next door, and in the half-darkness scrambled into the big bed. There was no room at Mother's side so I had to get between her and Father. For the time being I had forgotten about him, and for several minutes I sat bolt upright,[27] racking my brains[28] to know what I could do with him. He was taking up more than his fair share of the bed, and I couldn't get comfortable, so I gave him several kicks that made him grunt and stretch. He made room all

---

21 **foul play** not fair
22 **he had some terrible hold on her** he had a frightening control over her
23 **when she was tucking me up** when she was helping me get comfortable in bed (British)
24 **God wasn't quite what He was cracked up to be** God didn't live up to His reputation

25 **the Home** an institution for old people
26 **caught it in the act** caught it doing something bad
27 **sat bolt upright** sat very straight
28 **racking my brains** thinking as hard as I could

right, though. Mother waked and felt for me. I settled back comfortably in the warmth of the bed with my thumb in my mouth.

"Mummy!" I hummed, loudly and contentedly.

"Sssh! dear," she whispered. "Don't wake Daddy!"

150   This was a new development, which threatened to be even more serious than "talking to Daddy." Life without my early-morning conferences was unthinkable.

"Why?" I asked severely.

"Because poor Daddy is tired."

155   This seemed to me a quite inadequate reason, and I was sickened by the sentimentality of her "poor Daddy." I never liked that sort of gush,[29] it always struck me as insincere.

"Oh!" I said lightly. Then in my most winning tone:[30] "Do you know where I want to go with you today, Mummy?"

160   "No, dear," she sighed.

"I want to go down the Glen and fish for thornybacks with my new net, and then I want to go out to the Fox and Hounds, and—"

"Don't-wake-Daddy!" she hissed angrily, clapping her hand across my mouth.

165   But it was too late. He was awake, or nearly so. He grunted and reached for the matches. Then he stared incredulously at his watch.

"Like a cup of tea, dear?" asked Mother in a meek, hushed voice I had never heard her use before. It sounded almost as though she were afraid.

170   "Tea?" he exclaimed indignantly. "Do you know what the time is?"

"And after that I want to go up the Rathcooney Road," I said loudly, afraid I'd forget something in all those interruptions.

"Go to sleep at once, Larry!" she said sharply.

I began to snivel.[31] I couldn't concentrate, the way that pair went
175 on, and smothering my early-morning schemes was like burying a family from the cradle.[32]

    Father said nothing, but lit his pipe and sucked it, looking out into the shadows without minding[33] Mother or me. I knew he was mad. Every time I made a remark Mother hushed me irritably. I was
180 mortified.[34] I felt it wasn't fair, there was even something sinister in it. Every time I had pointed out to her the waste of making two beds when we could both sleep in one, she had told me it was healthier

---

29 **gush** sentimentality
30 **winning tone** charming voice
31 **snivel** whine, complain weakly
32 **smothering my early-morning schemes was like burying a family from the cradle** destroying or suffocating my early-morning plans was like burying babies before they had a chance to grow up
33 **minding** paying attention to
34 **mortified** very embarrassed

like that, and now here was this man, this stranger, sleeping with her without the least regard for her health!

185 He got up early and made tea, but though he brought Mother a cup he brought none for me.

"Mummy," I shouted, "I want a cup of tea, too."

"Yes, dear," she said patiently. "You can drink from Mummy's saucer."

190 That settled it. Either Father or I would have to leave the house. I didn't want to drink from Mother's saucer; I wanted to be treated as an equal in my own home, so, just to spite her, I drank it all and left none for her. She took that quietly, too.

But that night when she was putting me to bed she said gently:
195 "Larry, I want you to promise me something."

"What is it?" I asked.

"Not to come in and disturb poor Daddy in the morning. Promise?"

"Poor Daddy" again! I was becoming suspicious of everything involving that quite impossible man.

200 "Why?" I asked.

"Because poor Daddy is worried and tired and he doesn't sleep well."

"Why doesn't he, Mummy?"

"Well, you know, don't you, that while he was at the war Mummy
205 got the pennies from the post office?"

"From Miss MacCarthy?"

"That's right. But now, you see, Miss MacCarthy hasn't any more pennies, so Daddy must go out and find us some. You know what would happen if he couldn't?"

210 "No," I said, "tell us."

"Well, I think we might have to go out and beg for them like the poor old woman on Fridays. We wouldn't like that, would we?"

"No," I agreed. "We wouldn't."

"So you'll promise not to come in and wake him?"

215 "Promise."

Mind you,[35] I meant that. I knew pennies were a serious matter, and I was all against having to go out and beg like the old woman on Fridays. Mother laid out all my toys in a complete ring round the bed so that, whatever way I got out, I was bound to fall over one of them.

220 When I woke I remembered my promise all right. I got up and sat on the floor and played—for hours, it seemed to me. Then I got my chair and looked out the attic window for more hours. I wished it was time for Father to wake; I wished someone would make me a cup of tea. I didn't feel in the least like the sun; instead, I was bored and so

---

35 **mind you** an expression used for emphasis

225 very, very cold! I simply longed for the warmth and depth of the big feather bed.

At last I could stand it no longer. I went into the next room. As there was still no room at Mother's side I climbed over her and she woke with a start.

230 "Larry," she whispered, gripping my arm very tightly, "what did you promise?"

"But I did, Mummy," I wailed, caught in the very act. "I was quiet for ever so long."

"Oh, dear, and you're perished!"[36] she said sadly, feeling me all 235 over. "Now, if I let you stay will you promise not to talk?"

"But I want to talk, Mummy," I wailed.

"That has nothing to do with it," she said with a firmness that was new to me. "Daddy wants to sleep. Now, do you understand that?"

I understood it only too well. I wanted to talk, he wanted to sleep, 240 whose house was it, anyway?

"Mummy," I said with equal firmness, "I think it would be healthier for Daddy to sleep in his own bed."

That seemed to stagger[37] her, because she said nothing for a while.

"Now, once for all," she went on, "you're to be perfectly quiet or go 245 back to your own bed. Which is it to be?"

The injustice of it got me down.[38] I had convicted her out of her own mouth of inconsistency and unreasonableness, and she hadn't even attempted to reply. Full of spite, I gave Father a kick, which she didn't notice but which made him grunt and open his eyes in alarm.

250 "What time is it?" he asked in a panic-stricken voice, not looking at mother but at the door, as if he saw someone there.

"It's early yet," she replied soothingly. "It's only the child. Go to sleep again. … Now, Larry," she added, getting out of bed, "you've wakened Daddy and you must go back."

255 This time, for all her quiet air, I knew she meant it, and knew that my principal rights and privileges were as good as lost[39] unless I asserted them at once. As she lifted me, I gave a screech, enough to wake the dead, not to mind Father.[40] He groaned.

"That damn child! Doesn't he ever sleep?"

260 "It's only a habit, dear," she said quietly, though I could see she was vexed.[41]

---

36 **perished** frozen (unusual use)
37 **stagger** amaze
38 **got me down** depressed me
39 **were as good as lost** were just about lost

40 **I gave a screech, enough to wake the dead, not to mind Father.** I yelled loudly enough to wake the dead, not to mention Father.
41 **vexed** annoyed, irritated

"Well, it's time he got out of it," shouted Father, beginning to heave in the bed. He suddenly gathered all the bedclothes about him, turned to the wall, and then looked back over his shoulder with nothing showing,
265 only two small, spiteful, dark eyes. The man looked very wicked.

To open the bedroom door, Mother had to let me down, and I broke free and dashed for the farthest corner, screeching. Father sat bolt upright in bed.

"Shut up, you little puppy!" he said in a choking voice.
270 I was so astonished that I stopped screeching. Never, never had anyone spoken to me in that tone before. I looked at him incredulously and saw his face convulsed with rage. It was only then that I fully realized how God had codded[42] me, listening to my prayers for the safe return of this monster.
275 "Shut up, you!" I bawled, beside myself.

"What's that you said?" shouted Father, making a wild leap out of the bed.

"Mick, Mick!" cried Mother. "Don't you see the child isn't used to you?"
280 "I see he's better fed than taught," snarled Father, waving his arms wildly. "He wants his bottom smacked."[43]

All his previous shouting was as nothing to these obscene words referring to my person. They really made my blood boil.

"Smack your own!" I screamed hysterically. "Smack your own!
285 Shut up! Shut up!"

At this he lost his patience and let fly at me.[44] He did it with the lack of conviction you'd expect of a man under Mother's horrified eyes, and it ended up as a mere tap, but the sheer indignity of being struck at all by a stranger, a total stranger who had cajoled[45] his way back from
290 the war into our big bed as a result of my innocent intercession,[46] made me completely dotty.[47] I shrieked and shrieked, and danced in my bare feet, and Father, looking awkward and hairy in nothing but a short gray army shirt, glared down at me like a mountain out for murder. I think it must have been then that I realized he was jealous too. And
295 there stood Mother in her nightdress, looking as if her heart was broken between us. I hoped she felt as she looked. It seemed to me that she deserved it all.

From that morning out my life was a hell. Father and I were enemies, open and avowed. We conducted a series of skirmishes[48]
300 against one another, he trying to steal my time with Mother and I

---

42 **codded** played a joke on, tricked (unconventional use)
43 **He wants his bottom smacked.** He deserves to be punished with a spanking.
44 **let fly at me** attacked me suddenly

45 **cajoled** persuaded unfairly, coaxed
46 **intercession** prayer
47 **dotty** crazy
48 **skirmishes** small battles

his. When she was sitting on my bed, telling me a story, he took to[49] looking for some pair of old boots which he alleged he had left behind him at the beginning of the war. While he talked to Mother I played loudly with my toys to show my total lack of concern. He created a

305 terrible scene one evening when he came in from work and found me at his box, playing with his regimental badges, Gurkha knives and button sticks. Mother got up and took the box from me.

"You mustn't play with Daddy's toys unless he lets you, Larry," she said severely. "Daddy doesn't play with yours."

310 For some reason Father looked at her as if she had struck him and then turned away with a scowl.

"Those are not toys," he growled, taking down the box again to see had I lifted[50] anything. "Some of those curios are very rare and valuable."

315 But as time went on I saw more and more how he managed to alienate[51] Mother and me. What made it worse was that I couldn't grasp his method or see what attraction he had for Mother. In every possible way he was less winning than I. He had a common accent[52] and made noises at his tea. I thought for a while that it might be the

320 newspapers she was interested in, so I made up bits of news of my own to read to her. Then I thought it might be the smoking, which I personally thought attractive, and took his pipes and went round the house dribbling[53] into them till he caught me. I even made noises at my tea, but Mother only told me I was disgusting. It all seemed to hinge

325 round[54] that unhealthy habit of sleeping together, so I made a point of dropping into their bedroom and nosing round, talking to myself, so that they wouldn't know I was watching them, but they were never up to anything[55] that I could see. In the end it beat me. It seemed to depend on being grown-up and giving people rings, and I realized I'd

330 have to wait.

But at the same time I wanted him to see that I was only waiting, not giving up the fight. One evening when he was being particularly obnoxious,[56] chattering away well above my head,[57] I let him have it.[58] "Mummy," I said, "do you know what I'm going to do when I

335 grow up?"

"No, dear," she replied. "What?"

"I'm going to marry you," I said quietly.

---

49 **took to** developed the habit of
50 **lifted** taken, stolen
51 **alienate** put a distance between
52 **common accent** lower-class accent
53 **dribbling** dropping saliva
54 **hinge round** depend on

55 **were never up to anything** were never misbehaving
56 **obnoxious** very unpleasant, offensive
57 **above my head** too difficult for me to understand
58 **I let him have it** I attacked him (slang)

Father gave a great guffaw[59] out of him, but he didn't take me in.[60] I knew it must only be pretense. And Mother, in spite of everything,
340 was pleased. I felt she was probably relieved to know that one day Father's hold on her would be broken. "Won't that be nice?" she said with a smile.

"It'll be very nice," I said confidently. "Because we're going to have lots and lots of babies."

345 "That's right, dear," she said placidly. "I think we'll have one soon, and then you'll have plenty of company."

I was no end pleased about that because it showed that in spite of the way she gave in to Father she still considered my wishes. Besides, it would put the Geneys in their place.[61]

350 It didn't turn out like that, though. To begin with, she was very preoccupied[62]—I supposed about where she would get the seventeen and six—and though Father took to staying out late in the evenings it did me no particular good. She stopped taking me for walks, became as touchy as blazes,[63] and smacked me for nothing at all. Sometimes I
355 wished I'd never mentioned the confounded baby—I seemed to have a genius for bringing calamity on myself.

And calamity it was! Sonny arrived in the most appalling hullabaloo[64]—even that much he couldn't do without a fuss—and from the first moment I disliked him. He was a difficult child—so far
360 as I was concerned he was always difficult—and demanded far too much attention.

Mother was simply silly about him, and couldn't see when he was only showing off. As company he was worse than useless. He slept all day, and I had to go round the house on tiptoe to avoid waking
365 him. It wasn't any longer a question of not waking Father. The slogan now was "Don't-wake-Sonny!" I couldn't understand why the child wouldn't sleep at the proper time, so whenever Mother's back was turned I woke him. Sometimes to keep him awake I pinched him as well. Mother caught me at it one day and gave me a most unmerciful
370 flaking.[65]

One evening, when Father was coming in from work, I was playing trains in the front garden.

I let on[66] not to notice him; instead, I pretended to be talking to myself, and said in a loud voice: "If another bloody[67] baby comes into
375 this house, I'm going out."

Father stopped dead and looked at me over his shoulder.

---

59 **guffaw** a loud laugh
60 **take me in** deceive me
61 **put the Geneys in their place** humble the Geneys
62 **preoccupied** absorbed, deep in thought

63 **as touchy as blazes** quick to lose one's temper (informal)
64 **hullabaloo** confused noise
65 **flaking** beating (British slang)
66 **let on** pretended
67 **bloody** negative expression (British)

"What's that you said?" he asked sternly.

"I was only talking to myself," I replied, trying to conceal my panic. "It's private."

380 He turned and went in without a word. Mind you, I intended it as a solemn warning, but its effect was quite different. Father started being quite nice to me. I could understand that, of course. Mother was quite sickening about Sonny. Even at mealtimes she'd get up and gawk at[68] him in the cradle with an idiotic smile, and tell Father to do

385 the same. He was always polite about it, but he looked so puzzled you could see he didn't know what she was talking about. He complained of the way Sonny cried at night, but she only got cross and said that Sonny never cried except when there was something up with him[69]— which was a flaming[70] lie, because Sonny never had anything up

390 with him, and only cried for attention. It was really painful to see how simpleminded she was. Father wasn't attractive, but he had a fine intelligence. He saw through Sonny, and now he knew that I saw through him as well.

One night I woke with a start. There was someone beside me in the

395 bed. For one wild moment I felt sure it must be Mother, having come to her senses and left Father for good, but then I heard Sonny in convulsions in the next room, and Mother saying: "There! There! There!" and I knew it wasn't she. It was Father. He was lying beside me, wide-awake, breathing hard and apparently as mad as hell.

400 After a while it came to me what he was mad about. It was his turn now. After turning me out of the big bed, he had been turned out himself. Mother had no consideration now for anyone but that poisonous pup, Sonny. I couldn't help feeling sorry for Father. I had been through it all myself, and even at that age I was magnanimous.[71]

405 I began to stroke him down and say: "There! There!" He wasn't exactly responsive.

"Aren't you asleep either?" he snarled.

"Ah, come on and put your arm around us, can't you?" I said, and he did, in a sort of way. Gingerly,[72] I suppose, is how you'd describe it.

410 He was very bony but better than nothing. At Christmas he went out of his way[73] to buy me a really nice model railway.

---

68 **gawk at** stare stupidly at
69 **there was something up with him** there was something wrong with him
70 **flaming** glaring, obvious
71 **magnanimous** generous
72 **gingerly** carefully
73 **went out of his way** went to a lot of trouble

A Thinking About the Story

Discuss the following questions with a partner.

> Were you able to identify with Larry's feelings of displacement? Did you have sympathy for the family's struggle to adapt to a new situation?

B Understanding the Plot

Be prepared to answer the following questions with a partner or your class.

1. How does Larry view his father's brief visits home during the war?
2. What is Larry's attitude toward the war?
3. Why does Larry play the imaginary game with his feet?
4. About what time does Larry usually wake up? How do his parents respond to this?
5. What religion does the family practice? How do we know?
6. What prayers are referred to in lines 82–83? Why is Larry disappointed in God's powers? (lines 130–131)
7. Why do Larry's two feet "talk" about putting a parent in the Home? (lines 134–136)
8. Whom does Larry accuse of destroying his early-morning schemes? With what does he compare the destruction of his plans? (lines 174–176)
9. Why isn't Larry's father sleeping well, according to his mother?
10. For how long do you think Larry played alone when he says it seemed "for hours"? (line 221)
11. Why does Larry's father sound panic-stricken about the time? (line 250)
12. How hard does Larry's father hit him? Explain your answer.
13. Why does Larry's father begin to stay out late in the evenings when his wife is pregnant? Where do you think he goes?
14. How does Larry feel about his long-awaited baby brother?
15. What causes Larry's father to become more sympathetic toward him?

A Exploring Themes

Reread "My Oedipus Complex." As you read, look carefully at how Frank O'Connor uses humor to lessen the impact of Larry's painful feelings of jealousy and alienation.

1. How are the first and last paragraphs of the story related?
2. How does the jealousy that Larry and his father feel for each other express itself?
3. How does being an only child affect Larry's behavior?
4. What is the turning point in the relationship between Larry and his father?
5. In what ways does Larry mature and change in the story?
6. How does Larry's mother deal with the conflicting pull on her loyalties?

B Analyzing Style

HUMOR

Humor takes many forms. It ranges from exaggerated situations and biting or gentle irony, to witty jokes, sarcasm, and parody (comical imitation). In "My Oedipus Complex," humor arises from several sources.

- One source of humor revolves around the oedipal behavior that five-year-old Larry innocently exhibits.

- A second source of humor arises from the gap between the child's point of view and the adult language he uses to express himself. For example, Larry exhibits his naïveté about sex when he accepts his mother's statement that babies can be bought for *seventeen and six*, yet at the same time he comments maturely that his mother was perhaps too *exclusive*. (lines 33–42)

- A third area of humor lies in Larry's desperate attempts to be the man of the house, while, not surprisingly, he is incapable of filling that role. So, when he thinks, *I wanted to be treated as an equal in my own home* (lines 191–192), he follows this up by drinking all the tea his father had made for his mother.

- Finally, there is warm humor in the two scenes where father and son are alone with each other and start the process of adapting to each other's existence and slowly identifying with each other.

Exercise

Answer the following questions.

1. What examples of oedipal behavior can you find in the text? How do they help create the humor?

2. What examples can you find of Larry's sophisticated language that conflicts with his child's-eye view of the world?

3. Pick out where Larry jealously tries to act, speak, or think like a man but humorously undercuts his own attempts by his childish behavior.

4. In lines 88–107, how are the contrasts between father and son comically magnified in the child's eyes?

5. In lines 394–411, what makes the reconciliation between Larry and his father touchingly funny?

C Judging for Yourself

Express yourself as personally as you like in your answers to the following questions.

1. Do you think Larry's mother handles her son's oedipal behavior wisely after her husband's return?

2. In your view, is Larry's mother a good wife? Justify your answer.

3. Do you anticipate that Larry and his father will strengthen their newfound bond in the future?

4. Would you call Larry's strong attachment to his mother unhealthy? Give reasons for your answer.

D Making Connections

Answer the following questions in a small group.

1. Are children typically closer to one parent than the other in your culture? If so, which one and why?

2. What is the ideal number of children per family in your country? Does religion, economics, or population control play a role in deciding the number?

3. Has your country experienced wars in which men have spent long periods of time away from home? How has this affected their relationship with their families?

4. Is there a particular *hierarchy* (order of importance) in the family in your country? Who is traditionally the most important or influential member of the family? Who is the least important?

E Debate

Decide whether you are for or against the following statement. Be prepared to argue your case in a class debate.

The saying "Children should be seen but not heard" is a sensible child-rearing philosophy.

GRAMMAR IN CONTEXT

LINKING VERBS

Linking verbs do not express an action. Instead, they rename or describe their subject by linking it to a **complement** that comes after the verb.

The most common linking verb is the verb *to be*, which can link its subject to a noun, a pronoun, or an adjective complement.

> *Father and I* **were** *enemies, open and avowed.* (lines 298–299)

> *"It's only the child."* (line 252)

> *There* **was** *someone beside me in the bed.* (line 394–395)

> *He* **was** *very bony but better than nothing.* (line 410)

In formal English, when the complement of a linking verb is a personal pronoun, use the subjective form rather than the objective.

> *… I knew it* **wasn't** *she.* (line 398)

A linking verb agrees with its subject even if the complement is a different number.

> *They* **were** *a good team.*

Most linking verbs are followed by an adjective. They can be loosely grouped as follows:

- Verbs that refer to a state: *appear, feel, look, remain, seem, stay, sound.*

     *The red brick houses **seemed** unfamiliar, rigid, and painted.* (adapted from lines 46–49)

     *For one wild moment I **felt** sure it must be Mother. . . .* (line 395)

     *. . . but he **looked** so puzzled. . . .* (line 385)

- Verbs that refer to the senses: *smell, taste.*

     *The cake mother baked **tastes** delicious.*

     *The flowers in the marketplace **smell** fresh.*

- Verbs that refer to a result: *get, go, grow, turn, prove.*

     *. . . I couldn't **get** comfortable . . .* (line 144)

     *Father **turned** red with anger.*

Sometimes a linking verb can be followed by an infinitive or a prepositional phrase.

     *Father **seemed** to be very remote.* (adapted from lines 103–104)

     *I didn't **feel** like the sun.* (adapted from line 224)

Some verbs can be linking or action depending on how they are used.

     *Mother **grows** stronger every day.* [linking]

     *Mother **grows** vegetables in our garden.* [action]

     *The milk **tasted** sour.* [linking]

     *Our cat **tasted** the milk in her bowl.* [action]

Note: A good test of whether a verb is a linking verb or an action verb is to substitute a form of the verb *to be* and see whether the sentence still makes sense.

     Mother grows (is) stronger every day. [makes sense]

     Mother grows (is) vegetables in our garden. [doesn't make sense]

Exercise 1

Working with a partner, look at the underlined verbs in the sentences below, most of which have been adapted from the story. Decide whether each verb is an action verb or a linking verb. Explain your answers.

1. I wasn't sure about the Home, but it sounded like the right place for Father.
2. Her parents sounded the alarm when they discovered their child was missing.
3. It seemed to depend on being grown-up and giving people rings, and I told myself I'd have to wait.
4. "Mummy," I said, "When I become an adult, I'm going to marry you."
5. They are afraid they will grow old soon.
6. The man looked very wicked as he looked at me through narrowed eyes.
7. I had suffered like him, but even at that age I was magnanimous.
8. It was an uncomfortable squeeze between Mother and him when I got into the big bed in the early morning.
9. There was a bit of the magpie about Father; he expected everything to come in handy. (lines 16–17)
10. The second time I saw him do it I got wild. (line 98)

Exercise 2

Correct the errors in the following sentences.

1. He feels badly about his actions.
2. Her laboratory experiments was a complete failure.
3. I didn't feel like in a good mood.
4. That chicken doesn't taste well.
5. Who's there? It's me.
6. My favorite part of the movie are its special effects.
7. The man on the bus seemed a sick person.
8. He gets anxiety very easily.

Exercise 3

Fill each blank in the following sentences with one word only. In sentences where a verb is required, use a linking verb. Share your choices with a partner.

1. The older you get, the _____ you feel.

2. The teachers sound _____ at their staff meeting.

3. My sister is _____ than I.

4. I _____ bored when I heard that lecture for the third time.

5. They _____ calm even though they were really _____.

6. It suddenly _____ cold. Put on a sweater.

7. This jam tastes _____ apricot.

8. The boy skiing down the hill with his friends _____ very excited.

9. It appears _____ that we will be fired from our jobs.

10. You should change your behavior. You've become too _____.

PHRASAL VERBS

A **phrasal verb** consists of a verb and one or more **particles**. The particles are adverbs or prepositions that are treated as part of the verb, rather than as separate parts of speech. As with an idiom, the phrasal verb has a distinct meaning that cannot be figured out simply from looking at its parts.

Some phrasal verbs can have more than one meaning depending on the context. For example, the phrasal verb *make up* can mean *invent*:

> ... I *made up* bits of news of my own to read to her. (lines 320–321)

It also has several other meanings, including *become friends after an argument* and *put on makeup*:

> I *made up* with my sister after not speaking to her for a year.

> The actress *made up* her face before going on stage.

1. Phrasal verbs may be transitive and take an object.

> Mother *laid out* <u>all my toys</u> in a complete ring round the bed. (line 218)

Many transitive phrasal verbs are **separable**, meaning that the particle can be separated from the verb.

*Mother **laid** <u>all my toys</u> **out** in a complete ring round the bed.*

If the object of a separable phrasal verb is a pronoun, the verb must be separated. The pronoun goes between the verb and its particle.

*Mother **laid** <u>them</u> **out** in a complete ring round the bed.* (adapted from line 218)

2. Phrasal verbs may be intransitive, which means they do not take an object.

*"Mummy," I said, "do you know what I'm going to do when I **grow up**?"* (lines 334–335)

Exercise 4

With a partner, look at the list of phrasal verbs below. Review their context in the story so you are familiar with their meaning. Note whether the phrasal verb is transitive or intransitive and whether the particle can be moved. Then, create a mini dialogue for each phrasal verb that demonstrates you know how to use it appropriately. The first one is done for you as an example.

size up (lines 102–103)

A: I think the next candidate for this position has the strongest résumé.

B: Really? I still want to size him up for myself.

A: Go ahead. I don't think you'll be disappointed.

1. take to (lines 301)
2. take in (line 338)
3. give in to (lines 348)
4. turn out (line 350)*
5. show off (line 363)
6. turn out (line 401)*

---

* different meanings of *turn out*

DENOTATION AND CONNOTATION

Every word has a **denotation,** which is its formal dictionary definition. For example, the denotation of *mother* is a female parent. In addition to their denotation, many words have a **connotation,** which is an association suggested by the word and which is usually separate from its meaning. Words can have positive and/or negative associations. For example, some positive connotations of *mother* might be love, security, kisses, food, warmth, comfort, bedtime stories, and spoiling. Some negative connotations of *mother* might include nagging, anxiety, overprotectiveness, guilt, restrictiveness, and hysteria.

Exercise 1

Find the following words and phrases in the story and, using a dictionary if necessary, write down their denotation (literal meaning).

1. father (line 1) _____
2. candlelight (line 4) _____
3. slamming (line 5) _____
4. Santa Claus (line 7) _____
5. shadow (line 47) _____
6. mountain (lines 105, 293) _____
7. a bottle of champagne
   (lines 132–133) _____
8. dawn (line 137) _____
9. hissed (line 163) _____
10. feather bed (line 226) _____

Exercise 2

Discuss each word or phrase in Exercise 1 with a partner. Say what connotations come to mind. Your connotations may be positive, negative, or both.

1. Compose a short story of three to four pages centering on a conflict between a young child and his or her parents. Tell the story through the child's eyes. Base your story on a real-life conflict you recall. Using Frank O'Connor's narrative technique as a model, try to capture the child's perspective in your story without using childish language.

2. Write two descriptive paragraphs, the first concentrating on words with a positive connotation and the second centering on words with a negative connotation. Begin your first paragraph with *I woke up with the scent of honey in the air.* Begin your second paragraph with *The wind began to howl ominously.*

3. Write an essay of two to three pages in which you explore both sides of the argument that an only child is ultimately disadvantaged. For instance, some people say that such children benefit from the exclusive attention they receive, while other people think that such attention spoils a child. When you have stated the case for both sides as well as you can, reread your essay. Then in a concluding paragraph, state which side of the argument you were more convinced by.

4. The oedipal theme runs through many novels, plays, and movies. The ancient Greek playwright Sophocles dramatized the Oedipus legend in his famous tragedy *Oedipus Rex.* In the early twentieth century, D. H. Lawrence's novel *Sons and Lovers* centered on this theme. More recently, Woody Allen took up the subject in a humorous vein in his segment of the movie *New York Stories* entitled "Oedipus Wrecks." Write an essay of two pages in which you briefly describe a work you have read or seen that is dominated by the oedipal theme. Say whether the subject is treated seriously or humorously.

LONELINESS AND ALIENATION

Disappearing
A Pair of Silk Stockings
Everyday Use
The Red Convertible

9 ≈ Disappearing

Monica Wood

(b. 1953)

Born in Maine, the American writer Monica Wood grew up listening to her mother and father tell stories in the tradition of their homeland, Prince Edward Island, Canada. Wood continues to live in Maine, where she writes almost daily in a cabin adjoining her house. Her short stories have been nominated for the National Magazine Awards, and in 1991 she received a special mention from the Pushcart Prize. *Ernie's Ark*, her collection of linked short stories set in a fictional paper-mill town in Maine, was published in 2002 to critical acclaim.

Wood is the author of *Secret Language* (1993), *My Only Story* (2000), and *Any Bitter Thing* (2005). She edited *Short Takes: 15 Contemporary Stories* and has written a fiction-writing handbook, *The Pocket Muse: Ideas and Inspirations for Writing* (2002). In 2012 she published a memoir of her Catholic, working-class childhood, *When We Were the Kennedys: A Memoir from Mexico, Maine*. A recurring theme in her work is the sense of loss and retrieval felt by her characters.

Disappearing

An obsession with swimming radically changes the life of an extremely overweight woman.

When he starts in, I don't look anymore, I know what it looks like, what he looks like, tobacco on his teeth. I just lie in the deep sheets and shut my eyes. I make noises that make it go faster and when he's done he's as far from me as he gets. He could be
5   dead he's so far away.

Lettie says leave then stupid but who would want me. Three hundred pounds anyway but I never check. Skin like tapioca pudding,[1] I wouldn't show anyone. A man.

So we go to the pool at the junior high, swimming lessons. First it's
10   blow bubbles and breathe, blow and breathe. Awful, hot nosefuls of chlorine.[2] My eyes stinging red and patches on my skin. I look worse. We'll get caps and goggles[3] and earplugs and body cream Lettie says. It's better.

There are girls there, what bodies. Looking at me and Lettie out the side of their eyes. Gold hair, skin like milk, chlorine or no.
15   They thought when I first lowered into the pool, that fat one parting the Red Sea.[4] I didn't care. Something happened when I floated. Good said the little instructor. A little redhead in an emerald suit, no stomach, a depression almost, and white wet skin. Good she said you float just great. Now we're getting somewhere. The whistle around her
20   neck blinded my eyes. And the water under the fluorescent lights. I got scared and couldn't float again. The bottom of the pool was scarred, drops of gray shadow rippling.[5] Without the water I would crack open my head, my dry flesh would sound like a splash on the tiles.

At home I ate a cake and a bottle of milk. No wonder you look like
25   that he said. How can you stand yourself. You're no Cary Grant[6] I told him and he laughed and laughed until I threw up.

When this happens I want to throw up again and again until my heart flops[7] out wet and writhing[8] on the kitchen floor. Then he would know I have one and it moves.
30   So I went back. And floated again. My arms came around and the groan of the water made the tight blondes smirk[9] but I heard Good

---

1 **tapioca pudding** a dessert made from starch and milk that has a lumpy look
2 **chlorine** a chemical used to purify swimming pool water
3 **goggles** protective glasses for swimming underwater
4 **parting the Red Sea** a biblical reference to God's parting of the Red Sea to enable the Israelites to flee from Egypt

5 **rippling** flowing in small waves
6 **Cary Grant** a movie star famous for his good looks and charm
7 **flops** drops down heavily
8 **writhing** twisting in pain
9 **smirk** smile unpleasantly

that's the crawl that's it in fragments[10] from the redhead when I lifted my face. Through the earplugs I heard her skinny[11] voice. She was happy that I was floating and moving too.

35   Lettie stopped the lessons and read to me things out of magazines. You have to swim a lot to lose weight. You have to stop eating too. Forget cake and ice cream. Doritos are out.[12] I'm not doing it for that I told her but she wouldn't believe me. She couldn't imagine.

    Looking down that shaft[13] of water I know I won't fall. The water
40 shimmers and eases up and down, the heft[14] of me doesn't matter I float anyway.

    He says it makes no difference I look the same. But I'm not the same. I can hold myself up in deep water. I can move my arms and feet and the water goes behind me, the wall comes closer. I can look down
45 twelve feet to a cold slab of tile and not be afraid. It makes a difference I tell him. Better believe it mister.

    Then this other part happens. Other men interest me. I look at them, real ones, not the ones on TV that's something else entirely. These are real. The one with the white milkweed[15] hair who delivers the mail.
50 The meter man from the light company, heavy thick feet in boots. A smile. Teeth. I drop something out of the cart in the supermarket to see who will pick it up. Sometimes a man. One had yellow short hair and called me ma'am. Young. Thin legs and an accent. One was older. Looked me in the eyes. Heavy, but not like me. My eyes are nice.
55 I color the lids. In the pool it runs off in blue tears. When I come out my face is naked.

    The lessons are over, I'm certified. A little certificate signed by the redhead. She says I can swim and I can. I'd do better with her body, thin calves hard as granite.[16]

60   I get a lane to myself, no one shares. The blondes ignore me now that I don't splash the water, know how to lower myself silently. And when I swim I cut the water cleanly.

    For one hour every day I am thin, thin as water, transparent, invisible, steam or smoke.

65   The redhead is gone, they put her at a different pool and I miss the glare of the whistle dangling[17] between her emerald breasts. Lettie won't come over at all now that she is fatter than me. You're so uppity[18] she says. All this talk about water and who do you think you are.

---

10 **fragments** little pieces	14 **heft** weight
11 **skinny** very thin	15 **milkweed** a plant with milky sap
12 **Doritos are out.** Doritos (spicy corn chips) are not allowed.	16 **granite** hard rock
	17 **dangling** hanging loosely
13 **shaft** a column	18 **uppity** snobbish

He says I'm looking all right, so at night it is worse but sometimes
70 now when he starts in I say no. On Sundays the pool is closed I can't
say no. I haven't been invisible. Even on days when I don't say no it's
all right, he's better.

One night he says it won't last, what about the freezer full of
low-cal dinners[19] and that machine in the basement. I'm not doing it
75 for that and he doesn't believe me either. But this time there is another
part. There are other men in the water I tell him. Fish he says. Fish in
the sea. Good luck.

Ma you've lost says my daughter-in-law, the one who didn't want
me in the wedding pictures. One with the whole family, she couldn't
80 help that. I learned how to swim I tell her. You should try it, it might
help your ugly disposition.[20]

They closed the pool for two weeks and I went crazy. Repairing the
tiles. I went there anyway, drove by in the car. I drank water all day.

Then they opened again and I went every day, sometimes four
85 times until the green paint and new stripes looked familiar as a face.
At first the water was heavy as blood but I kept on until it was thinner
and thinner, just enough to hold me up. That was when I stopped with
the goggles and cap and plugs, things that kept the water out of me.

There was a time I went the day before a holiday and no one was
90 there. It was echoey silence just me and the soundless empty pool and
a lifeguard behind the glass. I lowered myself so slow it hurt every
muscle but not a blip[21] of water not a ripple not one sound and I was
under in that other quiet, so quiet some tears got out, I saw their blue
trailing.
95 The redhead is back and nods, she has seen me somewhere. I tell
her I took lessons and she still doesn't remember.

This has gone too far he says I'm putting you in the hospital. He
calls them at the pool and they pay no attention. He doesn't touch me
and I smile into my pillow, a secret smile in my own square of the dark.
100 Oh my God Lettie says what the hell are you doing what the hell do
you think you're doing. I'm disappearing I tell her and what can you
do about it not a blessed thing.

For a long time in the middle of it people looked at me. Men. And
I thought about it. Believe it, I thought. And now they don't look at me
105 again. And it's better.

I'm almost there. Almost water.

The redhead taught me how to dive, how to tuck my head[22] and
vanish like a needle into skin, and every time it happens, my feet
leaving the board, I think, this will be the time.

---

19 **low-cal dinners** low-calorie dinners
20 **disposition** temper, mood
21 **blip** a minor interruption

22 **tuck my head** bend my neck, drawing my
head to my chest

A Thinking About the Story

Discuss the following questions with a partner.

1. Did your attitude toward the narrator change as the story progressed?

2. Did you feel optimistic or pessimistic at the end of the story? Explain your answer.

B Understanding the Plot

Be prepared to answer the following questions with a partner or the whole class.

1. Who is the man referred to in the first paragraph?

2. What activity is being described in the first paragraph? How does the narrator feel about it?

3. Who is Lettie? What advice does she give the narrator regarding her marriage?

4. Why is the narrator's entry into the pool compared with the parting of the Red Sea? (lines 15–16) Is this image still accurate at the end of the story? Explain your answer.

5. What details give you an idea about the quantity of food the narrator consumes?

6. How does Lettie's attitude toward swimming differ from the narrator's?

7. What does *that* in line 37 refer to?

8. What do the men in lines 47–56 have in common?

9. What day of the week is the most difficult for the narrator? Explain why.

10. What does the narrator's husband predict about her weight loss? What is the basis for his prediction?

11. What kind of relationship does the narrator have with her daughter-in-law? Why is it like this?

12. How does the narrator react when the pool is closed?

13. Why doesn't the narrator's diving instructor recognize her? (lines 95–96)

14. Why does the narrator's husband threaten to put her in the hospital? (line 97)

15. Why does the narrator smile in line 99?

16. What does "in the middle of it" (line 103) refer to? What did the narrator consider doing at that time?

17. Which word in the last paragraph is a synonym for *disappear*?

A Exploring Themes

Reread "Disappearing." As you read, think about how the narrator's personal relationships influence her obsession with swimming.

1. Why does the narrator find swimming more appealing than other forms of exercise?

2. How does swimming change the narrator's relationship with her husband? Give examples from the story.

3. What are the probable roots of the narrator's obsession with disappearing?

4. How does the ending relate to the title of the story?

5. What does water represent in the story? Does the significance of water change over the course of the story?

B Analyzing Style

ELLIPSIS

Ellipsis means that parts of sentences are left out but can nevertheless be understood or inferred. A writer may use ellipsis to give the reader the impression of being in direct, unfiltered contact with the thoughts or feelings of a character or narrator. In "Disappearing," parts of sentences are left out but are nevertheless easily understood or inferred. This results in sentence fragments rather than complete sentences. For example, when the narrator compares herself to the thin swimmers around her, she describes them as *Gold hair, skin like milk, chlorine or no* (line 14). Here the absence of verbs makes the visual impact stronger and reminds us of her less flattering description of herself as *skin like tapioca pudding* (line 7).

Exercise 1

Supply what has been left out but implied in these sentences and phrases from the story. Refer to the text before answering.

1. When he starts in	(line 1)
2. Three hundred pounds anyway	(lines 6–7)
3. A man.	(line 8)
4. Awful, hot nosefuls of chlorine.	(lines 10–11)

5. And the water under the fluorescent lights.   (line 20)
6. She couldn't imagine.   (line 38)
7. A smile. Teeth.   (line 51)
8. Fish in the sea.   (lines 76–77)
9. Ma you've lost   (line 78)
10. Repairing the tiles.   (lines 82–83)
11. Believe it, I thought.   (line 104)

Exercise 2

Explain how the elliptical style of writing helps convey the narrator's thoughts and feelings.

IMAGERY

There are moments when the narrator's voice in "Disappearing" becomes less colloquial and more poetic, and we feel keenly the pathos underlying her situation. This change is accomplished through the use of powerful **imagery**, or pictures that appeal to our visual (sight), auditory (hearing), and tactile (touch) senses. For example, *the groan of the water* (lines 30–31) encourages us to hear the water's strained sounds as the very fat woman labors through it.

Exercise 3

Look at the following images from the story. Say whether they are visual, auditory, or tactile. Explain the effect of each image as fully as possible.

1. my dry flesh would sound like a splash on the tiles   (line 23)
2. my heart flops out wet and writhing on the kitchen floor   (lines 27–28)
3. tight blondes   (line 31)
4. skinny voice   (line 33)
5. a cold slab of tile   (line 45)
6. it runs off in blue tears   (line 55)
7. thin calves hard as granite   (line 59)
8. thin as water   (line 63)
9. emerald breasts   (line 66)
10. the water was heavy as blood   (line 86)
11. my own square of the dark   (line 99)
12. vanish like a needle into skin   (line 108)

C Judging for Yourself

Express yourself as personally as you like in your answers to the following questions.

1. What role do you think the husband plays in his wife's problems?
2. Should the wife have followed Lettie's advice and left her husband?
3. Why do you think the narrator overeats when she's upset?
4. Do you think the narrator is being courageous or cowardly in her quest to disappear? Support your answer.

D Making Connections

Answer the following questions in a small group.

1. What is your society's attitude toward fat people? Would you say that they are discriminated against? Give examples to substantiate your answer.
2. Has the rate of obesity changed in the past few decades in your country? If so, what is responsible for this change?
3. Is anorexia (starving oneself) common in your society? Why do people act this way? What part of the population is most at risk?
4. Does the concept of marital rape exist in your country? Do you think a man is raping his wife if he insists on having sex with her against her wishes? Should he be punished?

E Debate

Decide whether you are for or against the following statement. Be prepared to argue your case in a class debate.

A person's weight is a reflection of his or her willpower.

PART 3 GRAMMAR IN CONTEXT

AGREEMENT OF PRONOUN AND ANTECEDENT

A **pronoun** stands in for a noun, another pronoun, a noun phrase, or a noun clause. The noun, pronoun, phrase, or clause that a pronoun refers to is called an **antecedent**. A pronoun's antecedent should be clear; otherwise, the sentence can be confusing. In the following examples, the pronoun is in **bold** and its antecedent is underlined. **Possessive adjectives** (*my, his, her, your*, etc.) also refer back to an antecedent and should be similarly clear and unambiguous.

*A little certificate signed by the redhead. **She** says I can swim and I can.*
(lines 57–58)

*Swimming each day helped the narrator lose weight. **It** changed her life.*

*She wants to lose more weight, but **it** probably isn't healthy.*

*The husband knows how much his wife despises him, but he can't figure out a way to change **it**.*

- A pronoun or possessive adjective should agree in gender, number, and person with its antecedent.

*Other men interest me. I look at **them**, real **ones**, not the ones on TV … **These** are real.* (lines 47–49)

If the antecedent were *man*, the pronouns or possessive adjectives referring to *man* would be singular:

*Another man interests me. I look at **him**, a real **one**, not like the ones on TV. **He** is real.*

- If the antecedent is gender neutral, the pronoun *it* is used in the singular.

*At first the water was heavy as blood but I kept on until **it** was thinner and thinner, just enough to hold me up.* (lines 86–87)

- When the antecedent of a pronoun or possessive adjective is a collective noun, the pronoun must agree with it in number. Depending on the context, a collective noun may be singular or plural.

*The swim team shared **its** opinion of the new classmate.*

The swim team is considered as a single unit acting as one.

*The swim team shared **their** different opinions of the new classmate.*

The swim team is composed of many students thinking and acting individually.

- If a pronoun or possessive adjective has more than one possible antecedent, the sentence may be ambiguous.

*When the narrator talked to her instructor, **she** was distracted by a noise in the pool.*

Since the pronoun has two possible antecedents with the right gender and number, we don't know which one it refers to. The sentence should be rewritten so that the pronoun clearly refers to its correct antecedent: *When talking to her instructor, the narrator was distracted by a noise in the pool.*

Exercise 1

In the following sentences, underline the antecedent for each pronoun or possessive adjective in bold. The antecedent can be a word, a phrase, or a noun clause.

1. The narrator liked swimming every day, but **her** husband didn't approve.
2. Lettie wanted to know when the narrator would stop swimming. The narrator refused to discuss **it**.
3. Dieters should try to lose weight in a healthy way. People should support **them**.
4. The school board considered **its** options regarding the opening or closing of the pool.
5. The coach and her students say **they** agree that the narrator has made the most progress.
6. The school has a plan to increase the number of exercise hours for students. However, the parents don't like **it**.
7. The narrator and Lettie looked for a swimming pool where people wouldn't know **them**.
8. Lettie said that the narrator should stop swimming. She repeated **it** loudly.

INDEFINITE PRONOUNS

Indefinite pronouns do not refer back to something specific. They don't have an antecedent.

- Many indefinite pronouns are singular. They include *everyone*, *someone*, *anyone*, *one*, *each*, *either*, *neither*, and *nobody*. Singular indefinite pronouns should be followed by a singular verb.

  Everyone *is* allowed to attend this meeting.

  If a singular indefinite pronoun clearly refers to a specific gender, use the gender-appropriate pronoun or possessive adjective when referring back to it.

  Nobody at this company will lose *her* job because of pregnancy.

  If a singular indefinite pronoun refers to both genders, writers sometimes use phrases like *he or she* and *his or her*.

  Nobody should make a big decision without considering *his or her* options.

  However, this phrasing can sound awkward when used too many times. You can often avoid the issue by changing the wording slightly.

  People shouldn't make big decisions without considering their options.

- Plural indefinite pronouns include *some*, *many*, and *several*. They should be followed by a plural verb.

  Some *agree with me, and* ***some*** *disagree.*

Exercise 2

Complete the following sentences with the correct word or words in parentheses.

1. Everybody who _____ to be included should raise a hand. (want/wants)

2. Nobody who fails _____ physical exam will be accepted for this job. (their/his or her)

3. Many _____ still undecided about whom to vote for. (is/are)

4. Neither of these employees _____ eligible for a promotion yet. (is/are)

5. My two daughters are studying different subjects in college. Each loves _____ major. (their/her)

Exercise 3

With a partner, look at the following sentences. In some sentences, the pronoun or possessive adjective does not agree with its antecedent. In other sentences, the possessive adjective may not agree with its antecedent and may be ambiguous. Rewrite the sentences correctly. You may change whatever part of the sentence is necessary to fix the problem.

1. After practice, the team returned to its homes for dinner.

2. When the pool was closed, the woman couldn't decide whether to swim in another pool or to take a vacation from exercise. She finally decided to do it.

3. We should value a woman for who she is and not for their body shape.

4. When someone is obese, they are at risk for many health problems.

5. The man asked his friend to help his wife lose weight.

6. When the woman asked her mother-in-law not to appear in the photograph, she didn't like it.

7. The jury has given their unanimous verdict on the swimmer's death: It was accidental.

8. After a person loses weight, they feel a sense of achievement.

DEALING WITH UNFAMILIAR WORDS

There are several ways to deal with unfamiliar vocabulary. These include looking up the meaning of a word in a dictionary, using a glossary if one is provided, or guessing the meaning from the context.

Exercise 1

The missing words are all words that were glossed in "Disappearing." Look back at the glosses and complete the sentences with appropriate glossed words from the text. You may need to change the form or tense of some verbs.

1. Monuments are frequently made of _____ because it is a material that lasts.

2. I have never met anyone as popular as my sister. Everybody is attracted to her because of her sunny _____.

3. They did not feel comfortable with the new people in the neighborhood, who were very _____ and didn't want to mix with the other residents.

4. Because of his illness, he _____ into bed straight after dinner every evening.

5. When you stir your tea, you will see the liquid _____.

6. If you want to avoid burning your eyes under water, always wear _____.

7. The athlete _____ in agony from a broken ankle as I rushed up to help her.

8. My cousin always _____ at the camera in his school photos, so they never came out well.

9. It was a terrifying sight to see a leg _____
out of the car after the accident.

10. As a result of the concussion she suffered, only _____
of her memory returned.

Exercise 2

The following words in the story are not glossed. Write the meaning of the words, using their context in the story as a guide if necessary. Do not use a dictionary.

1. lowered (line 15)   _____

2. floated (line 16)   _____

3. scarred (line 21)   _____

4. transparent (line 63)   _____

5. vanish (line 108)   _____

Exercise 3

Complete the following paragraph with the correct words from Exercise 2. You may have to change the tense or form of the word.

Feeling nervous, she slowly _____ herself into the pool. The water was as _____ as glass, and she could see the chipped, _____ tiles at the bottom. But after a while her fears _____, and she felt as if she were _____ on air as she swam successfully from one end of the pool to the other.

PART 5 **WRITING ACTIVITIES**

1. *Supersize Me* (2004) is a documentary film that tackles the subject of obesity in America. The director spends 30 days eating all his meals at McDonald's, and at the end of the month he shows a significant weight gain, among other serious symptoms. In an essay of one or two pages, consider whether there should be laws to combat unhealthy eating habits that contribute to obesity. You might consider measures such as banning trans fats or making chain restaurants list the nutritional information about the food they serve. In your conclusion, say whether corporations or individuals are ultimately responsible for healthy eating.

2. Imagine that you have woken up one morning 100 pounds (45 kilos) heavier or lighter than your usual weight. Using the informal narrative voice in "Disappearing" as a guideline, write a monologue in which you express your immediate thoughts and feelings about this extraordinary event.

3. Have you or has anybody you know been obsessed with something? Write an essay of two to three pages in which you first outline the nature and source of the obsession. Next, consider its effect on the person as well as on the people around him or her. In your conclusion, say whether you think the person can be "cured" of this obsession and, if so, how.

10 ∾ A Pair of Silk Stockings

Kate Chopin
(1851–1904)

Born in St. Louis, Missouri, Kate Chopin came of French-Creole parentage on her mother's side and Irish immigrants on her father's side. She grew up in a household led by generations of women, and it was from her great-grandmother that she heard the tales of early French settlers of St. Louis that were later to influence many of her short stories.

Much of Chopin's writing deals with women searching for freedom from male domination, and she is considered to be an early feminist writer. She wrote over a hundred short stories, many of which were published in two collections: *Bayou Folk* (1894) and *A Night in Acadia* (1897). Her two novels, *At Fault* (1890) and *The Awakening* (1899), deal with the controversial themes of divorce and adultery, respectively. Denounced as immoral, *The Awakening* caused a public uproar, which left Chopin deeply depressed and discouraged. As a result, she wrote very little in the final years of her life.

A Pair of Silk Stockings

A struggling mother gives in to temptation.

Little Mrs Sommers one day found herself the unexpected possessor of fifteen dollars. It seemed to her a very large amount of money, and the way in which it stuffed and bulged her worn old *porte-monnaie*[1] gave her a feeling of importance such as she had not
5 enjoyed for years.

The question of investment[2] was one that occupied her greatly. For a day or two she walked about apparently in a dreamy state, but really absorbed in speculation and calculation.[3] She did not wish to act hastily, to do anything she might afterward regret. But it was
10 during the still hours of the night when she lay awake revolving plans in her mind that she seemed to see her way clearly toward a proper and judicious[4] use of the money.

A dollar or two should be added to the price usually paid for Janie's shoes, which would insure their lasting an appreciable time[5]
15 longer than they usually did. She would buy so and so many yards of percale[6] for new shirt waists for the boys and Janie and Mag. She had intended to make the old ones do by skilful patching.[7] Mag should have another gown. She had seen some beautiful patterns, veritable bargains in the shop windows. And still there would be left enough
20 for new stockings—two pairs apiece[8]—and what darning that would save for a while! She would get caps for the boys and sailor-hats for the girls. The vision of her little brood[9] looking fresh and dainty and new for once in their lives excited her and made her restless and wakeful with anticipation.

25 The neighbors sometimes talked of certain 'better days' that little Mrs Sommers had known before she had ever thought of being Mrs Sommers. She herself indulged in no such morbid retrospection.[10] She had no time—no second of time to devote to the past. The needs of the present absorbed her every faculty. A vision of the future like some
30 dim, gaunt monster sometimes appalled her, but luckily to-morrow never comes.

---

1 *porte-monnaie* purse (French)
2 **investment** using money for a long-term benefit
3 **speculation and calculation** thoughts about how to spend the money
4 **judicious** wise, sensible
5 **an appreciable time** a significant amount of time
6 **so and so many yards of percale** an unnamed quantity of cotton fabric

7 **make the old ones do by skilful patching** make the old clothes last by repairing them well
8 **two pairs apiece** two pairs for each child
9 **brood** the children in a family
10 **She herself indulged in no such morbid retrospection.** She didn't allow herself to think about the past with regret.

Mrs Sommers was one who knew the value of bargains; who could stand for hours making her way inch by inch toward the desired object that was selling below cost.[11] She could elbow her way if need be;[12]

35 she had learned to clutch a piece of goods[13] and hold it and stick to it with persistence and determination till her turn came to be served, no matter when it came.

But that day she was a little faint and tired. She had swallowed a light luncheon—no! when she came to think of it, between getting the

40 children fed and the place righted,[14] and preparing herself for the shopping bout, she had actually forgotten to eat any luncheon at all!

She sat herself upon a revolving stool before a counter that was comparatively deserted, trying to gather strength and courage to charge through an eager multitude that was besieging breastworks of

45 shirting and figured lawn.[15] An all-gone limp feeling[16] had come over her and she rested her hand aimlessly upon the counter. She wore no gloves. By degrees she grew aware that her hand had encountered something very soothing, very pleasant to touch. She looked down to see that her hand lay upon a pile of silk stockings. A placard near by

50 announced that they had been reduced in price from two dollars and fifty cents to one dollar and ninety-eight cents; and a young girl who stood behind the counter asked her if she wished to examine their line of silk hosiery.[17] She smiled, just as if she had been asked to inspect a tiara of diamonds with the ultimate view of purchasing it. But she went

55 on feeling the soft, sheeny luxurious things—with both hands now, holding them up to see them glisten, and to feel them glide serpent-like through her fingers.

Two hectic blotches[18] came suddenly into her pale cheeks. She looked up at the girl.

60 "Do you think there are any eights-and-a-half among these?"

There were any number of eights-and-a-half. In fact, there were more of that size than any other. Here was a light-blue pair; there were some lavender, some all black and various shades of tan and gray. Mrs Sommers selected a black pair and looked at them very long and

65 closely. She pretended to be examining their texture, which the clerk assured her was excellent.

"A dollar and ninety-eight cents," she mused aloud. "Well, I'll take this pair." She handed the girl a five-dollar bill and waited for her

---

11 **below cost** at a very low price
12 **She could elbow her way if need be** She could push her way through if necessary
13 **clutch a piece of goods** hold an item tightly
14 **getting the place righted** cleaning and tidying her home (old-fashioned expression)
15 **charge through an eager multitude that was besieging breastworks of shirting and**

figured lawn push through many shoppers who were fighting each other to obtain cheap fabrics (figurative language suggesting a military attack)
16 **an all-gone limp feeling** a very weak feeling
17 **line of silk hosiery** selection of silk stockings
18 **hectic blotches** bright red spots

change and for her parcel. What a very small parcel it was! It seemed
70 lost in the depths of her shabby[19] old shopping-bag.

Mrs Sommers after that did not move in the direction of the bargain
counter.[20] She took the elevator, which carried her to an upper floor
into the region of the ladies' waiting-rooms. Here, in a retired corner,
she exchanged her cotton stockings for the new silk ones which she
75 had just bought. She was not going through any acute mental process
or reasoning with herself, nor was she striving to explain to her
satisfaction the motive of her action. She was not thinking at all.
She seemed for the time to be taking a rest from that laborious and
fatiguing[21] function and to have abandoned herself to some mechanical
80 impulse that directed her actions and freed her of responsibility.

How good was the touch of the raw silk to her flesh! She felt like
lying back in the cushioned chair and reveling for a while in the luxury
of it. She did for a little while. Then she replaced her shoes, rolled the
cotton stockings together and thrust them into her bag. After doing this
85 she crossed straight over to the shoe department and took her seat to
be fitted.

She was fastidious.[22] The clerk could not make her out;[23] he could
not reconcile her shoes with her stockings,[24] and she was not too easily
pleased. She held back her skirts and turned her feet one way and her
90 head another way as she glanced down at the polished, pointed-tipped
boots. Her foot and ankle looked very pretty. She could not realize
that they belonged to her and were a part of herself. She wanted an
excellent and stylish fit, she told the young fellow who served her, and
she did not mind the difference of a dollar or two more in the price so
95 long as she got what she desired.

It was a long time since Mrs Sommers had been fitted with gloves.
On rare occasions when she had bought a pair they were always
'bargains', so cheap that it would have been preposterous[25] and
unreasonable to have expected them to be fitted to the hand.
100 Now she rested her elbow on the cushion of the glove counter, and a
pretty, pleasant young creature, delicate and deft of touch, drew a long-
wristed 'kid'[26] over Mrs Sommers's hand. She smoothed it down over
the wrist and buttoned it neatly, and both lost themselves for a second
or two in admiring contemplation of the little symmetrical gloved
105 hand.[27] But there were other places where money might be spent.

---

19 **shabby** much used, worn
20 **bargain counter** display area for cheap
    goods
21 **laborious and fatiguing** difficult and tiring
22 **fastidious** very particular about details
23 **make her out** understand her (regarding her
    social position)
24 **he could not reconcile her shoes with
    her stockings** he could not explain why

someone with old shoes would have new
stockings
25 **preposterous** ridiculous
26 **kid** very soft goat leather
27 **both lost themselves for a second or two
    in admiring contemplation of the little
    symmetrical gloved hand** both could only
    think of how pretty her hand looked in the
    glove

There were books and magazines piled up in the window of a stall a few paces down the street. Mrs Sommers bought two high-priced magazines such as she had been accustomed to read in the days when she had been accustomed to other pleasant things. She carried them
110 without wrapping. As well as she could she lifted her skirts at the crossings. Her stockings and boots and well fitting gloves had worked marvels in her bearing[28]—had given her a feeling of assurance, a sense of belonging to the well-dressed multitude.

She was very hungry. Another time she would have stilled the
115 cravings for food[29] until reaching her own home, where she would have brewed herself a cup of tea and taken a snack of anything that was available. But the impulse that was guiding her would not suffer her to entertain any such thought.[30]

There was a restaurant at the corner. She had never entered its
120 doors; from the outside she had sometimes caught glimpses of spotless damask[31] and shining crystal, and soft-stepping waiters serving people of fashion.

When she entered her appearance created no surprise, no consternation,[32] as she had half feared it might. She seated herself at
125 a small table alone, and an attentive waiter at once approached to take her order. She did not want a profusion;[33] she craved a nice and tasty bite—a half dozen blue-points,[34] a plump chop with cress, a something sweet—a crème-frappée, for instance; a glass of Rhine wine, and after all a small cup of black coffee.

130 While waiting to be served she removed her gloves very leisurely and laid them beside her. Then she picked up a magazine and glanced through it, cutting the pages with a blunt edge of her knife. It was all very agreeable. The damask was even more spotless than it had seemed through the window, and the crystal more sparkling. There were quiet
135 ladies and gentlemen, who did not notice her, lunching at the small tables like her own. A soft, pleasing strain of music could be heard, and a gentle breeze was blowing through the window. She tasted a bite, and she read a word or two, and she sipped the amber wine and wiggled her toes in the silk stockings. The price of it made no difference. She
140 counted the money out to the waiter and left an extra coin on his tray, whereupon he bowed before her as before a princess of royal blood.

There was still money in her purse, and her next temptation presented itself in the shape of a matinée poster.[35]

---

28 **had worked marvels in her bearing** had made her stand confidently straight
29 **she would have stilled the cravings for food** she would have ignored her hunger
30 **But the impulse that was guiding her would not suffer her to entertain any such thought** but the mood she was in would not let her consider it (returning home to eat)
31 **damask** fine tablecloth material
32 **consternation** anxiety, alarm
33 **a profusion** an extravagant amount
34 **blue-points** oysters
35 **matinée poster** advertisement for an afternoon play

It was a little later when she entered the theatre, the play had begun
145 and the house seemed to her to be packed.[36] But there were vacant
seats here and there, and into one of them she was ushered, between
brilliantly dressed women who had gone there to kill time[37] and eat
candy and display their gaudy attire.[38] There were many others who
were there solely for the play and acting. It is safe to say there was no
150 one present who bore quite the attitude which Mrs Sommers did to
her surroundings. She gathered in the whole—stage and players and
people in one wide impression, and absorbed it and enjoyed it. She
laughed at the comedy and wept—she and the gaudy woman next
to her wept over the tragedy. And they talked a little together over it.
155 And the gaudy woman wiped her eyes and sniffled on a tiny square of
filmy, perfumed lace and passed little Mrs Sommers her box of candy.

The play was over, the music ceased, the crowd filed out. It was like
a dream ended. People scattered in all directions. Mrs Sommers went to
the corner and waited for the cable car.
160 A man with keen eyes,[39] who sat opposite to her, seemed to like
the study of her small, pale face. It puzzled him to decipher[40] what he
saw there. In truth, he saw nothing—unless he were wizard enough to
detect a poignant wish,[41] a powerful longing that the cable car would
never stop anywhere, but go on and on with her forever.

---

36 **the house seemed to her to be packed**
   every seat seemed to be occupied
37 **kill time** fill the time
38 **gaudy attire** overly bright and tasteless
   clothes

39 **keen eyes** sharp, observant eyes
40 **decipher** figure out
41 **poignant wish** sad and touching desire

PART 1 FIRST READING

A Thinking About the Story

Discuss the following question with a partner.

How do you think Mrs. Sommers felt when riding the cable car at the end
of the story? Explain your answer.

B Understanding the Plot

Be prepared to answer the following questions with a partner or the whole
class.

1. Why does Mrs. Sommers plan to go shopping? What does she intend to
buy? Give details.

2. What is Mrs. Sommers's financial situation? Was it always like this? Explain your answer.

3. What does Mrs. Sommers mean when she thinks that "luckily tomorrow never comes"? (lines 30–31) Why does she not want tomorrow to come?

4. How would you describe Mrs. Sommers's day before she goes shopping? Give details.

5. Why are there so many people competing for the goods in the store where Mrs. Sommers usually goes shopping? What are these people compared to? (lines 42–45)

6. What is the important result of Mrs. Sommers's not wearing gloves that day? (lines 46–48)

7. In what way is the idea of buying silk stockings similar to the idea of buying a diamond tiara for Mrs. Sommers? (lines 53–54)

8. What kind of stockings does Mrs. Sommers usually wear?

9. Why is the sales clerk surprised at Mrs. Sommers's shoes? (lines 87–88)

10. In addition to the shoes and stockings, what else does Mrs. Sommers spend her money on? List everything.

11. Why does Mrs. Sommers worry about going into the restaurant?

12. The narrator suggests that women go to see the afternoon plays for three reasons. What are they?

13. What is Mrs. Sommers's state of mind at the end of the story?

PART 2 CRITICAL THINKING

A Exploring Themes

Reread "A Pair of Silk Stockings." As you read, examine how Kate Chopin reveals Mrs. Sommers's thoughts in order to explain her actions in the story.

1. Why does Mrs. Sommers give in to the temptation to spend the money on herself? Give as many reasons as possible.

2. "A Pair of Silk Stockings" is filled with expressions that deal with money. Pick out as many of these expressions as you can. Show how they relate to the story.

3. What do the silk stockings represent? Consider how they are described, what they are compared to (line 56), and what they mean to Mrs. Sommers.

4. One interpretation of the story could be that Mrs. Sommers had a perfect day by taking advantage of an unexpected opportunity. Another could be that Mrs. Sommers acted irresponsibly and will regret it. Do you think that either of these interpretations fits the story correctly? Explain your answer.

B Analyzing Style

INFERENCE

When a writer suggests themes and details without stating them directly, readers have to **infer** or deduce the full meaning and significance of the text. As a result, readers go deeper into the story and acquire a better understanding of the characters and their actions. For example, Chopin writes: *It was a long time since Mrs. Sommers had been fitted with gloves* (line 96). Here she suggests that Mrs. Sommers used to be able to buy expensive gloves that were exactly the right size for her hands, instead of wearing cheap, unfitted gloves.

Exercise

Answer the following questions.

1. Mrs. Sommers's financial situation is suggested to us throughout the story without being spelled out. Find at least three examples that lead us to infer that she is poor.

2. What is suggested about Mrs. Sommers's personality in lines 1–24?

3. The way Mrs. Sommers thinks and acts in the restaurant is dramatically different from her usual self. Give as many examples as possible to illustrate this difference. (lines 123–141)

4. Although he is an absent character, what can we infer about Mrs. Sommers's husband?

C Judging for Yourself

Express yourself as personally as you like in your answers to the following questions.

1. Do you think Mrs. Sommers was wrong to spend the money as she did? Have you ever given in to temptation? How did you feel afterward?

2. What do you imagine Mrs. Sommers's life was like before she got married?

3. What do you think Mrs. Sommers will say to her children on her return home?

4. Do you think Mrs. Sommers is lonely? Explain your answer.

D Making Connections

Answer the following questions in a small group.

1. Are there organizations in your country to help people who are struggling economically? If so, describe them. If not, say why not.

2. People in the United States often talk about the American Dream, meaning that everyone should have the chance to be free and to work for a better life. What do people in your country consider to be essential for a good life?

3. What constitutes a luxurious meal in your culture? Describe it.

4. Some people like to show off their wealth with items such as fancy cars, expensive watches, or designer clothes. What is the attitude toward conspicuous consumption in your country? How do people show off their wealth?

E Debate

Decide whether you are for or against the following statement. Be prepared to argue your case in a class debate.

Parents should always place their children first.

PART 3 **GRAMMAR IN CONTEXT**

REFLEXIVE PRONOUNS

Singular **reflexive pronouns** are formed by adding *-self* to the pronoun: *myself, yourself, himself, herself, itself, oneself.* Plural reflexive pronouns are formed by adding *-selves* to the pronoun: *ourselves, yourselves, themselves.*

- Use reflexive pronouns when the subject and object of a verb refer to the same person or thing.

  *Little Mrs. Sommers one day found **herself** the unexpected possessor of fifteen dollars.* (lines 1–2)

  The subject and object of *found* both refer to Mrs. Sommers.

- Use reflexive pronouns after a preposition when the subject and the object refer to the same person or thing.

  *She was not going through any acute mental process or reasoning **with herself.*** (lines 75–76)

- *By* followed by a reflexive pronoun is an idiomatic expression meaning *alone*.

  *It's a bad idea to walk **by oneself** in this neighborhood at night.*
- Use reflexive pronouns after an imperative since the implied subject is *you*.

  *Help **yourself/yourselves** to all you want to eat.*
- Verbs that are frequently followed by a reflexive pronoun include *believe in, convince, enjoy, give, hate, hurt, look at, remind, take care of, talk to,* and *tell.*

  *Mrs. Sommers **enjoyed herself** immensely on the day she went shopping.*

Exercise 1

Complete the following sentences with the correct reflexive pronoun.

1. My friend and I reminded _____ to look for the best bargains before buying anything.
2. Bob and Jessica went hiking by _____ in the mountains.
3. Look after _____ when you travel alone this summer.
4. She _____ needs to be there on Tuesday to sign the contract.
5. The landlord convinced _____ that she and her roommate would be good tenants.
6. My parents and grandmother blamed _____ when my brother went to prison.
7. The best students at school believed in _____.
8. One should never go skiing in a snowstorm by _____.
9. It is discouraging that our leaders _____ could not agree on the correct policy.
10. The coach yelled at the runner to exert _____ more.

Exercise 2

Explain the difference between each of the following pairs of sentences.

1. **a.** Help yourself to a few books from my collection.

   b. My collection of self-help books is growing fast.

2. **a.** You yourself need to be present.

   b. You need to do this by yourself.

3. **a.** You should remind yourself not to overeat on your anniversary.

   b. Your spouse should remind you not to overeat on your anniversary.

4. **a.** The president and his cabinet meet by themselves.

   b. The president and his cabinet meet by prior agreement.

5. **a.** It is important to take good care of oneself during pregnancy.

   b. You should take good care of yourself during your pregnancy.

Exercise 3

Look at the following sentences containing reflexive pronouns. Write a new sentence using the underlined words. The first one is done for you as an example.

1. God helps those who <u>help themselves</u>.

   The hikers lost in the snow will have to help themselves until they are found.

2. The president likes to make decisions <u>by herself</u>.

3. <u>The general himself</u> will be present at the attack.

4. The employees talked <u>among themselves</u> before voting for their union leader.

5. After my exams, I decided to buy a present <u>for myself</u>.

6. If you keep listening to loud music, you'll <u>give yourself</u> a headache.

PART 4 VOCABULARY BUILDING

COLLOCATIONS WITH NONCOUNT NOUNS

Many food words in English, such as *tea*, *salt*, and *ice cream*, are **noncount nouns**, meaning that they cannot be divided into individual units. These food words frequently **collocate**, or go together, with expressions that indicate quantity. For example, in "A Pair of Silk Stockings," Mrs. Sommers usually brews herself *a cup of tea* after her shopping expeditions (line 116). Later, she orders a *cup of coffee* and a *glass of Rhine wine* at the restaurant (lines 128–129).

Exercise 1

Match each expression of quantity on the left with the appropriate food on the right. More than one answer is occasionally possible, but make sure to use each food item only once.

1. a bowl of _____   bread

2. a slice of _____   cake

3. a bar of _____   cereal

4. a pinch of _____   chocolate

5. a can of _____   corn

6. a scoop of _____   garlic

7. a loaf of _____   honey

8. a clove of _____   ice cream

9. an ear of _____   salt

10. a tablespoon of _____   soda

Exercise 2

Pick a recipe from a cookbook or the Internet. Share your recipe with a partner, paying attention to the quantities used with noncount nouns.

ADJECTIVES

There are thousands of adjectives in English. Some are very common, such as *good*, *small*, and *nice*. However, there are also many adjectives that are rich in meaning but not as frequently used. Learning a selection of these adjectives is an important way to enlarge your vocabulary and give nuance to your writing. "A Pair of Silk Stockings" is filled with such adjectives.

Exercise 3

Look at the following adjectives from the story. Use the context of the adjective, or a dictionary if necessary, to help you understand each adjective's meaning. Then complete the sentences with the appropriate adjective.

worn (line 3)   mechanical (line 79)

veritable (line 18)   deft (line 101)

gaunt (line 30)   spotless (line 120)

revolving (line 42)   attentive (line 125)

luxurious (line 55)   plump (line 127)

1. Mrs. Sommers did her housekeeping in a _____ fashion, going through the same routines every day.

2. Department stores try to attract wealthy customers with a display of _____ goods.

3. Mrs. Sommers made sure that Janie and Mag always wore _____ clothes even though they were old and mended.

4. Mrs. Sommers was a good mother, always _____ to the needs of her children.

5. You may find a great bargain at the sale, but the crowd will be a _____ nightmare.

6. It is not easy to look stylish in _____, darned clothes.

7. After many busy days without time for lunch, Mrs. Sommers started to look quite _____.

8. You may need to go through a _____ door to enter a department store.

9. Successful salespeople must have _____ hands when they help fit their customers with the right-sized clothes.

10. When she was feeling extravagant, Mrs. Sommers would buy a _____ chicken to roast for dinner.

Exercise 4

Look at the footnotes for the definitions of the following adjectives. Write down the definitions. Then write sentences with these adjectives. The first one is done for you as an example.

1. appreciable (line 14) _significant_

   Mrs. Sommers's new clothes made an appreciable difference in the way she felt.

2. skilful (line 17)

3. shabby (line 70)

4. laborious (line 78)

5. preposterous (line 98)

6. gaudy (line 148)

WRITING ACTIVITIES

1. *Money makes the world go round* is a well-known song lyric. In an essay of one to two pages, explore the issues raised by this proverb. First, explain what it means. Then consider the arguments for and against. Finally, take a stand and say which side convinces you more and why.

2. Write a descriptive essay on a memorable shopping experience you've had. It could include a store, a garage sale, or an eBay auction. First describe the scene. Then say what you bought and why you bought it. In your conclusion, say whether the experience was positive or negative and why.

3. There are many tales and legends that revolve around the granting of wishes. Sometimes, the person (or animal) whose wish is fulfilled is happy with the result, sometimes not. Relate the plot of a well-known story in your country that deals with this subject.

4. *The Bucket List* (2007) is a movie starring Jack Nicholson and Morgan Freeman, who meet in the hospital when both men are suffering from terminal cancer. Freeman's character draws up a list of things he'd like to do before dying (kicking the bucket). Nicholson's character pays for him to fulfill his dreams and accompanies him as he travels around the world. Think of a movie, television program, or book in which a character dreams of doing something unusual. Say what the dream is and explain whether the character fulfills it by the end. Conclude by saying whether you were able to sympathize with that dream.

11 ⤳ Everyday Use

Alice Walker
(b. 1944)

Born in Georgia, the eighth child of poor tenant-farmer parents, Alice Walker soon demonstrated exceptional abilities. After graduating as valedictorian of her local high school, Walker went on to study at Spelman and Sarah Lawrence colleges. She became involved in the civil rights movement in the South and worked to register black voters, a time she re-created in her novel *Meridian* (1976). Over the years her political activism has included feminism, environmentalism, the fight against racism, and the antinuclear movement.

Walker is an accomplished poet, novelist, short-story writer, essayist, and biographer. Her novel *The Color Purple* (1982) catapulted her to fame after winning both the Pulitzer Prize and the National Book Award. Steven Spielberg went on to make a movie of the book. She has written four collections of short stories, including *In Love and Trouble* (1973) and *Broken Heart* (2000). Many of her stories focus on the twin ills of sexism and racism that plague black women. Her novel *By the Light of My Father's Smile* (1998) celebrates human sexuality, while *Now Is the Time to Open Your Heart* (2004) centers on a woman's mystical journey. Her memoir *The Chicken Chronicles* was published in 2011.

Everyday Use

for your grandmama

Family tensions come to a head in a dispute over the ownership of some quilts.

I will wait for her in the yard that Maggie and I made so clean and wavy yesterday afternoon. A yard like this is more comfortable than most people know. It is not just a yard. It is like an extended living room. When the hard clay is swept clean as a floor and the fine
5 sand around the edges lined with tiny, irregular grooves, anyone can come and sit and look up into the elm tree and wait for the breezes that never come inside the house.

Maggie will be nervous until after her sister goes: she will stand hopelessly in corners, homely[1] and ashamed of the burn scars down
10 her arms and legs, eying her sister with a mixture of envy and awe. She thinks her sister has held life always in the palm of one hand,[2] that "no" is a word the world never learned to say to her.

You've no doubt seen those TV shows where the child who has "made it"[3] is confronted, as a surprise, by her own mother and father,
15 tottering in[4] weakly from backstage. (A pleasant surprise, of course: What would they do if parent and child came on the show only to curse out and insult each other?) On TV mother and child embrace and smile into each other's faces. Sometimes the mother and father weep, the child wraps them in her arms and leans across the table to tell
20 how she would not have made it without their help. I have seen these programs.

Sometimes I dream a dream in which Dee and I are suddenly brought together on a TV program of this sort. Out of a dark and soft-seated limousine I am ushered into a bright room filled with many
25 people. There I meet a smiling, gray, sporty man like Johnny Carson[5] who shakes my hand and tells me what a fine girl I have. Then we are on the stage and Dee is embracing me with tears in her eyes. She pins on my dress a large orchid, even though she has told me once that she thinks orchids are tacky[6] flowers.

30 In real life I am a large, big-boned woman with rough, man-working hands. In the winter I wear flannel nightgowns to bed and overalls during the day. I can kill and clean a hog as mercilessly as a man. My fat keeps me hot in zero weather. I can

---

1 **homely** unattractive
2 **her sister has held life always in the palm of one hand** her sister has always gotten what she wants from life
3 **"made it"** succeeded in life (idiom)

4 **tottering in** walking in unsteadily
5 **Johnny Carson** famous late-night television talk show host
6 **tacky** vulgar, tasteless

work outside all day, breaking ice to get water for washing; I can eat
pork liver cooked over the open fire minutes after it comes steaming
from the hog. One winter I knocked a bull calf straight in the brain
between the eyes with a sledge hammer and had the meat hung up to
chill before nightfall. But of course all this does not show on television.
I am the way my daughter would want me to be: a hundred pounds
lighter, my skin like an uncooked barley[7] pancake. My hair glistens in
the hot bright lights. Johnny Carson has much to do to keep up with
my quick and witty tongue.

But that is a mistake. I know even before I wake up. Who ever
knew a Johnson with a quick tongue? Who can even imagine me
looking a strange white man in the eye?[8] It seems to me I have talked
to them always with one foot raised in flight, with my head turned in
whichever way is farthest from them. Dee, though. She would always
look anyone in the eye. Hesitation was no part of her nature.

"How do I look, Mama?" Maggie says, showing just enough of her
thin body enveloped in pink skirt and red blouse for me to know she's
there, almost hidden by the door.

"Come out into the yard," I say.

Have you ever seen a lame animal, perhaps a dog run over by some
careless person rich enough to own a car, sidle up[9] to someone who is
ignorant enough to be kind to him? That is the way my Maggie walks.
She has been like this, chin on chest, eyes on ground, feet in shuffle,[10]
ever since the fire that burned the other house to the ground.

Dee is lighter than Maggie, with nicer hair and a fuller figure. She's
a woman now, though sometimes I forget. How long ago was it that
the other house burned? Ten, twelve years? Sometimes I can still hear
the flames and feel Maggie's arms sticking to me, her hair smoking and
her dress falling off her in little black papery flakes. Her eyes seemed
stretched open, blazed open by the flames reflected in them. And Dee.
I see her standing off under the sweet gum tree she used to dig gum
out of; a look of concentration on her face as she watched the last
dingy[11] gray board of the house fall in toward the red-hot brick
chimney. Why don't you do a dance around the ashes? I'd wanted to
ask her. She had hated the house that much.

I used to think she hated Maggie, too. But that was before we raised
the money, the church and me, to send her to Augusta to school. She
used to read to us without pity; forcing words, lies, other folks' habits,
whole lives upon us two, sitting trapped and ignorant underneath her
voice. She washed us in a river of make-believe,[12] burned us with a lot

---

7 **barley** a honey-colored grain
8 **looking a strange white man in the eye**
   looking directly at an unknown white man
9 **sidle up** move sideways, trying not to be
   seen
10 **feet in shuffle** very slow walk, barely lifting
   the feet up
11 **dingy** worn and dirty
12 **make-believe** fantasy

of knowledge we didn't necessarily need to know. Pressed us to her with the serious way she read, to shove us away[13] at just the moment, like dimwits,[14] we seemed about to understand.

Dee wanted nice things. A yellow organdy dress to wear to her graduation from high school; black pumps[15] to match a green suit she'd made from an old suit somebody gave me. She was determined to stare down[16] any disaster in her efforts. Her eyelids would not flicker for minutes at a time. At sixteen she had a style of her own: and knew what style was.

I never had an education myself. After second grade the school was closed down. Don't ask me why: in 1927 colored[17] asked fewer questions than they do now. Sometimes Maggie reads to me. She stumbles along[18] good-naturedly but can't see well. She knows she is not bright. Like good looks and money, quickness passed her by. She will marry John Thomas (who has mossy teeth in an earnest face) and then I'll be free to sit here and I guess just sing church songs to myself. Although I never was a good singer. Never could carry a tune.[19] I was always better at a man's job. I used to love to milk till I was hooked in the side[20] in '49. Cows are soothing and slow and don't bother you, unless you try to milk them the wrong way.

I have deliberately turned my back on the house. It is three rooms, just like the one that burned, except the roof is tin; they don't make shingle roofs anymore. There are no real windows, just some holes cut in the sides, like the portholes in a ship, but not round and not square, with rawhide[21] holding the shutters up on the outside. This house is in a pasture, too, like the other one. No doubt when Dee sees it she will want to tear it down. She wrote me once that no matter where we "choose" to live, she will manage to come see us. But she will never bring her friends. Maggie and I thought about this and Maggie asked me. "Mama, when did Dee ever *have* any friends?"

She had a few. Furtive boys[22] in pink shirts hanging about on washday after school. Nervous girls who never laughed. Impressed with her they worshiped the well-turned phrase,[23] the cute shape, the scalding humor that erupted like bubbles in lye.[24] She read to them.

When she was courting[25] Jimmy T she didn't have much time to pay to us, but turned all her faultfinding power on him. He *flew* to

---

13 **shove us away** push us away	19 **carry a tune** sing a melody correctly
14 **dimwits** stupid people	20 **hooked in the side** kicked by a cow
15 **pumps** a type of women's shoes	21 **rawhide** untreated skin of an animal
16 **stare down** bravely face and defeat (figurative language)	22 **furtive boys** boys trying to avoid attention
17 **colored** black people (outdated term)	23 **well-turned phrase** a smooth, accurate way of speaking
18 **stumbles along** hesitates and mispronounces (as she reads aloud)	24 **lye** a strong cleaning liquid that burns
	25 **courting** dating

110 marry a cheap[26] city girl from a family of ignorant flashy people. She hardly had time to recompose herself.

When she comes I will meet—but there they are!

Maggie attempts to make a dash for the house, in her shuffling way, but I stay[27] her with my hand. "Come back here," I say. And she stops
115 and tries to dig a well in the sand with her toe.

It is hard to see them clearly through the strong sun. But even the first glimpse of leg out of the car tells me it is Dee. Her feet were always neat-looking, as if God himself had shaped them with a certain style. From the other side of the car comes a short, stocky[28] man. Hair is all
120 over his head a foot long and hanging from his chin like a kinky[29] mule tail. I hear Maggie suck in her breath. "Uhnnnh," is what it sounds like. Like when you see the wriggling end of a snake just in front of your foot on the road. "Uhnnnh."

Dee next. A dress down to the ground, in this hot weather. A dress
125 so loud it hurts my eyes. There are yellows and oranges enough to throw back the light of the sun. I feel my whole face warming from the heat waves it throws out. Earrings gold, too, and hanging down to her shoulders. Bracelets dangling and making noises when she moves her arm up to shake the folds of the dress out of her armpits. The dress
130 is loose and flows, and as she walks closer, I like it. I hear Maggie go "Uhnnnh" again. It is her sister's hair. It stands straight up like the wool on a sheep. It is black as night and around the edges are two long pigtails that rope about like small lizards disappearing behind her ears.

"Wa-su-zo-Tean-o!"[30] she says, coming on in that gliding way
135 the dress makes her move. The short stocky fellow with the hair to his navel is all grinning and he follows up with "Asalamalakim, my mother and sister!" He moves to hug Maggie but she falls back, right up against the back of my chair. I feel her trembling there and when I look up I see the perspiration falling off her chin.
140 "Don't get up," says Dee. Since I am stout it takes something of a push. You can see me trying to move a second or two before I make it. She turns, showing white heels through her sandals, and goes back to the car. Out she peeks next with a Polaroid. She stoops down quickly and lines up picture after picture of me sitting there in front
145 of the house with Maggie cowering[31] behind me. She never takes a shot without making sure the house is included. When a cow comes nibbling around the edge of the yard she snaps it and me and Maggie *and* the house. Then she puts the Polaroid in the back seat of the car, and comes up and kisses me on the forehead.

---

26 **cheap** vulgar
27 **stay** stop
28 **stocky** solidly built
29 **kinky** tightly twisted, curled

30 **Wa-su-zo-Tean-o! … Asalamalakim** African greeting … Arabic greeting
31 **cowering** hiding in fear

150   Meanwhile Asalamalakim is going through motions with Maggie's hand.[32] Maggie's hand is as limp as a fish, and probably as cold, despite the sweat, and she keeps trying to pull it back. It looks like Asalamalakim wants to shake hands but wants to do it fancy. Or maybe he don't know how people shake hands. Anyhow, he soon gives
155 up on Maggie.

     "Well," I say. "Dee."

     "No, Mama," she says. "Not 'Dee,' Wangero Leewanika Kemanjo!"

     "What happened to 'Dee'?" I wanted to know.

     "She's dead," Wangero said. "I couldn't bear it any longer, being
160 named after the people who oppress me."

     "You know as well as me you was named after your aunt Dicie," I said. Dicie is my sister. She named Dee. We called her "Big Dee" after Dee was born.

     "But who was *she* named after?" asked Wangero.

165   "I guess after Grandma Dee," I said.

     "And who was she named after?" asked Wangero.

     "Her mother," I said, and saw Wangero was getting tired. "That's about as far back as I can trace it," I said. Though, in fact, I probably could have carried it back beyond the Civil War through
170 the branches.[33]

     "Well," said Asalamalakim, "there you are."

     "Uhnnnh," I heard Maggie say.

     "There I was not," I said, "before 'Dicie' cropped up[34] in our family, so why should I try to trace it that far back?"

175   He just stood there grinning, looking down on me like somebody inspecting a Model A car. Every once in a while he and Wangero sent eye signals over my head.

     "How do you pronounce this name?" I asked.

     "You don't have to call me by it if you don't want to," said
180 Wangero.

     "Why shouldn't I?" I asked. "If that's what you want us to call you, we'll call you."

     "I know it might sound awkward at first," said Wangero.

     "I'll get used to it," I said. "Ream it out again."[35]

185   Well, soon we got the name out of the way. Asalamalakim had a name twice as long and three times as hard. After I tripped over it two or three time he told me to just call him Hakim-a-barber. I wanted to ask him was he a barber, but I didn't really think he was, so I didn't ask.

---

32 **going through motions with Maggie's hand** trying to shake Maggie's hand

33 **branches** refers to the family tree, a history of past generations

34 **cropped up** appeared suddenly

35 **Ream it out again.** Say it again. (literally, squeeze out)

190 "You must belong to those beef-cattle peoples down the road," I said. They said "Asalamalakim" when they met you, too, but they didn't shake hands. Always too busy: feeding the cattle, fixing the fences, putting up salt-lick shelters, throwing down hay. When the white folks poisoned some of the herd the men stayed up all night with
195 rifles in their hands. I walked a mile and a half just to see the sight.

Hakim-a-barber said, "I accept some of their doctrines, but farming and raising cattle is not my style." (They didn't tell me, and I didn't ask, whether Wangero (Dee) had really gone and married him.)

We sat down to eat and right away he said he didn't eat collards[36]
200 and pork was unclean. Wangero, though, went on through the chitlins[37] and corn bread, the greens and everything else. She talked a blue streak[38] over the sweet potatoes. Everything delighted her. Even the fact that we still used the benches her daddy made for the table when we couldn't afford to buy chairs.
205 "Oh, Mama!" she cried. Then turned to Hakim-a-barber. "I never knew how lovely these benches are. You can feel the rump prints,"[39] she said, running her hands underneath her and along the bench. Then she gave a sigh and her hand closed over Grandma Dee's butter dish. "That's it!" she said. "I knew there was something I wanted to ask you
210 if I could have." She jumped up from the table and went over in the corner where the churn[40] stood, the milk in it clabber[41] by now. She looked at the churn and looked at it.

"This churn top is what I need," she said. "Didn't Uncle Buddy whittle[42] it out of a tree you all used to have?"
215 "Yes," I said.

"Uh-huh," she said happily. "And I want the dasher,[43] too."

"Uncle Buddy whittle that, too?" asked the barber.

Dee (Wangero) looked at me.

"Aunt Dee's first husband whittled the dash," said Maggie so low
220 you almost couldn't hear her. "His name was Henry, but they called him Stash."

"Maggie's brain is like an elephant's," Wangero said, laughing. "I can use the churn top as a centerpiece for the alcove table," she said, sliding a plate over the churn, "and I'll think of something artistic
225 to do with the dasher."

When she finished wrapping the dasher the handle stuck out. I took it for a moment in my hands. You didn't even have to look close to see where hands pushing the dasher up and down to make butter had left

---

36 **collards** a leafy green vegetable popular in the U.S. South
37 **chitlins** traditional Southern African-American dish made from pigs' intestines
38 **talked a blue streak** spoke a lot without stopping (idiom)
39 **rump prints** marks from years of sitting
40 **churn** a vessel used to make butter
41 **clabber** sour milk
42 **whittle** carve
43 **dasher** the part of the churn that stirs up the milk

a kind of sink in the wood. In fact, there were a lot of small sinks; you
230 could see where thumbs and fingers had sunk into the wood. It was
beautiful light yellow wood, from a tree that grew in the yard where
Big Dee and Stash had lived.

After dinner Dee (Wangero) went to the trunk at the foot of my
bed and started rifling[44] through it. Maggie hung back[45] in the kitchen
235 over the dishpan. Out came Wangero with two quilts. They had been
pieced[46] by Grandma Dee and then Big Dee and me had hung them
on the quilt frames on the front porch and quilted them. One was in
the Lone Star pattern. The other was Walk Around the Mountain.[47] In
both of them were scraps[48] of dresses Grandma Dee had worn fifty and
240 more years ago. Bits and pieces of Grandpa Jarrell's Paisley shirts. And
one teeny faded blue piece, about the size of a penny matchbox, that
was from Great Grandpa Ezra's uniform that he wore in the Civil War.

"Mama," Wangero said sweet as a bird. "Can I have these old
quilts?"
245   I heard something fall in the kitchen, and a minute later the kitchen
door slammed.

"Why don't you take one or two of the others?" I asked. "These old
things was just done by me and Big Dee from some tops your grandma
pieced before she died."
250   "No," said Wangero "I don't want those. They are stitched around
the borders by machine."

"That'll make them last better," I said.

"That's not the point," said Wangero. "These are all pieces of
dresses Grandma used to wear. She did all this stitching by hand.
255 Imagine!" She held the quilts securely in her arms, stroking them.

"Some of the pieces, like those lavender ones, come from old
clothes her mother handed down[49] to her," I said, moving up to touch
the quilts. Dee (Wangero) moved back just enough so that I couldn't
reach the quilts. They already belonged to her.
260   "Imagine!" she breathed again, clutching them closely to her
bosom.

"The truth is," I said, "I promised to give them quilts to Maggie, for
when she marries John Thomas."

She gasped like a bee had stung her.
265   "Maggie can't appreciate these quilts!" she said. "She'd probably be
backward enough to put them to everyday use."

---

44 **rifling** searching vigorously
45 **hung back** waited behind
46 **pieced** sewn by joining together pieces of
    material

47 **Lone Star, Walk Around the Mountain**
    two quilting patterns
48 **scraps** small pieces of material
49 **handed down** passed on

"I reckon she would," I said. "God knows I been saving 'em for long enough with nobody using 'em. I hope she will!" I didn't want to bring up[50] how I had offered Dee (Wangero) a quilt when she went away to college. Then she had told me they were old-fashioned, out of style.

"But they're *priceless*!"[51] she was saying now, furiously; for she has a temper. "Maggie would put them on the bed and in five years they'd be in rags. Less than that!"

"She can always make some more," I said. "Maggie knows how to quilt."

Dee (Wangero) looked at me with hatred. "You just will not understand. The point is these quilts, *these* quilts!"

"Well," I said, stumped.[52] "What would *you* do with them?"

"Hang them," she said. As if that was the only thing you *could* do with quilts.

Maggie by now was standing in the door. I could almost hear the sound her feet made as they scraped over each other.

"She can have them, Mama," she said, like somebody used to never winning anything, or having anything reserved for her. "I can 'member Grandma Dee without the quilts."

I looked at her hard. She had filled her bottom lip with checkerberry snuff[53] and it gave her face a kind of dopey, hangdog look. It was Grandma Dee and Big Dee who taught her how to quilt herself. She stood there with her scarred hands hidden in the folds of her skirt. She looked at her sister with something like fear but she wasn't mad at her. This was Maggie's portion. This was the way she knew God to work.

When I looked at her like that something hit me in the top of my head and ran down to the soles of my feet. Just like when I'm in church and the spirit of God touches me and I get happy and shout. I did something I never had done before: hugged Maggie to me, then dragged her on into the room, snatched the quilts out of Miss Wangero's hands and dumped them into Maggie's lap. Maggie just sat there on my bed with her mouth open.

"Take one or two of the others," I said to Dee.

But she turned without a word and went out to Hakim-a-barber.

"You just don't understand," she said, as Maggie and I came out to the car.

"What don't I understand?" I wanted to know.

---

50 **bring up** mention
51 **priceless** so valuable no price can be put on them
52 **stumped** very puzzled
53 **checkerberry snuff** finely crushed tobacco

"Your heritage,"[54] she said. And then she turned to Maggie, kissed her, and said, "You ought to try to make something of yourself,[55] too, Maggie. It's really a new day for us. But from the way you and Mama still live you'd never know it."

310   She put on some sunglasses that hid everything above the tip of her nose and her chin.

Maggie smiled; maybe at the sunglasses. But a real smile, not scared. After we watched the car dust settle I asked Maggie to bring me a dip of snuff. And then the two of us sat there just enjoying, until it
315   was time to go in the house and go to bed.

---

54 **heritage** history and culture passed down in one's family

55 **make something of yourself** improve your situation in life

---

FIRST READING

A Thinking About the Story

Discuss the following questions with a partner.

Were you moved by the mother's changing attitude toward Maggie? Did you sympathize with Dee's need to leave her rural life and family? Explain your answers.

B Understanding the Plot

Be prepared to answer the following questions with a partner or the whole class.

1. What details depict the family's rural lifestyle?

2. How is Dee different from Maggie? List as many ways as you can.

3. In lines 30–48, how is Dee contrasted with her mother? Consider differences that are both stated and implied.

4. What is unusual about Dee's behavior on the day of the fire?

5. Is the narrator correct when she thinks: "No doubt when Dee sees it [the house] she will want to tear it down" (pages 99–100)? Explain your answer as fully as possible.

6. Why did Jimmy T, the man Dee courted, flee to the city?

7. Why does Dee greet her mother in a strange language, and why has she changed her name to Wangero Leewanika?

8. What is the mother's opinion of Hakim-a-barber? Support your answer as fully as possible.

9. What is the difference between Dee and Hakim-a-barber regarding the meal they eat?

10. Why does Dee want the butter churn? Is it still being used? How much does she know of its history?

11. How has Dee's attitude toward the quilts changed?

12. Why is the mother reluctant to give Dee the quilts?

13. What does Dee mean when she says to Maggie: "It's really a new day for us." (line 308)

PART 2 CRITICAL THINKING

A Exploring Themes

Reread "Everyday Use." As you read, consider the ways in which Alice Walker reveals a great deal of psychological, biographical, and physical information about the characters.

1. Explain how the title and the dedication reflect a central theme of the story.

2. In what ways is the TV show the narrator talks about in lines 13–48 relevant to the mother/daughter theme of the story? Explain your answer as fully as possible.

3. How does the discussion between Dee and her mother regarding the origin of Dee's name reflect their different attitudes toward their heritage?

4. What is the effect of breaking the narrative into five parts? How does each part contribute to our understanding of the story?

5. What is Dee searching for in her life? Give as many examples as possible from the text to explain your answer.

6. What do the quilts represent in the story?

ROUND CHARACTERS

Round characters are fully formed, complex people who may act unpredictably and who in the course of the story struggle and change, often achieving greater self-knowledge. The narrator/mother, Dee, and Maggie are round characters, presented to us in all their human complexity. We see them filtered through the mother's eyes, with Alice Walker using numerous devices to bring each character alive. The characters' actions, personalities, and physical characteristics are revealed in a mix of scenes from the past and present, with each scene unpeeling another aspect of their evolving, complicated, triangular relationship.

Exercise 1

Answer the following questions about the characters in the story.

Narrator/Mother

1. Pick out all the descriptions that convey the mother's physical strength.
2. What details point to the tense relationship the mother has had with Dee over the years?
3. Although discrimination in the South prevented the mother from getting a good education, she is intelligent and perceptive. Give some examples that support this statement.
4. In what ways does the mother change by the end of the story?

Maggie

5. Pick out as many descriptions as possible connected with Maggie that reinforce her mother's assessment of Maggie's appearance, personality, and relationship with her sister.
6. In what ways does Maggie embody her heritage?
7. How does Maggie change by the end of the story? What contributes to this change?

Dee

8. What impression do we get of Dee before we see her? Explain your answer.

9. When Dee steps out of the car, her dress is described in glowing detail. What aspects of Dee's appearance and personality are reflected in her clothing?

10. Given what we know about Dee, does Hakim-a-barber seem a suitable mate for her? Support your answer.

11. In the scene after dinner, which of Dee's actions reinforce Maggie's perception that her sister can always have what she wants?

12. What are the contradictions in Dee's attitude toward her heritage?

Hakim-a-barber

13. Hakim-a-barber is a flat character, meaning he is one-dimensional and doesn't change in the story. Why do you think Alice Walker chose to present Hakim-a-barber in this way?

FIRST-PERSON NARRATION

"Everyday Use" is presented through **first-person narration**, which means that the story is told by a narrator using the pronoun *I*. Consequently, the point of view is *partial*, or incomplete, as we see the characters, interpret their actions, and delve into their personalities solely through the eyes of the narrator.

Exercise 2

Discuss the following questions with a partner or the whole class.

1. Does the narrator's limited point of view mean that she is unable to give an unbiased and accurate picture of the characters and events? Justify your answer.

2. Whom is the narrator addressing in lines 13 and 53? What is the effect of using that particular pronoun?

3. Is the narrator clearly more sympathetic to one character than the other? Explain your answer.

4. What is the tone of the narrator? Give examples to support your answer.

5. In what ways might the story have been different if narrated through Dee's eyes?

C Judging for Yourself

Express yourself as personally as you like in your answers to the following questions.

1. Do you sympathize with Dee's determination to improve herself? What kind of life do you think she lives?
2. Do you think it was reasonable for Dee to tell Maggie that she should change her way of life?
3. Is Maggie's life likely to change after her marriage?
4. In your opinion, who should get the quilts—Dee or Maggie? Explain your answer.
5. Is Dee's adoption of an African name and dress likely to satisfy her search for roots?
6. In your view, has the narrator been a good mother? Justify your answer.

D Making Connections

Answer the following questions in a small group.

1. Is there a tension in your culture between modernization and tradition?
2. Do people move around a lot in your country? Is mobility considered to be a positive or a negative attribute?
3. Are television shows featuring real-life guests popular in your country? If so, describe one.
4. What foods are most closely associated with your culture? Do they have a special significance?

E Debate

Decide whether you are for or against the following statement. Be prepared to argue your case in a class debate.

Tradition stands in the way of progress.

PREPOSITIONAL PHRASES

A **prepositional phrase** consists of a preposition followed by a noun or pronoun object and any modifiers. A few of the more common prepositions in English include *after, at, before, during, in, into, like, of, on, through, under, until,* and *with.* Not all prepositions are one word. Two- or three-word prepositions include *according to, because of, except for,* and *in addition to.* Writers use prepositional phrases to clarify, contextualize, heighten, and sharpen their words.

- Prepositional phrases can have an adverbial function, giving more information about manner, place, or time.

    In describing the scene in which Maggie is on fire, Walker increases the horror when she writes about *her dress falling off her* **in little black papery flakes** (line 62). Here, *in little black papery flakes* functions as an adverbial phrase of manner and draws our attention to the severity of Maggie's burns.

- Prepositional phrases may also have an adjectival function.

    Dee's young friends are depicted as *furtive boys* **in pink shirts** *hanging about on washday after school* (lines 104–105). In this sentence, the prepositional phrase *in pink shirts* is used adjectivally to flesh out the description of the boys. Note, however, that the two prepositional phrases *on washday* and *after school* are used adverbially to position the scene more securely in time.

- The preposition *like* can be used adjectivally or adverbially.

    The preposition *like* is used adjectivally after the verb *to be,* as well as after other linking verbs such as *seem* and *look.* For example: *… my skin [is]* **like an uncooked barley pancake** (line 40). It can also be used adverbially. For example: *[Her hair] stands straight up* **like the wool on a sheep** (lines 131–132).

- An adverbial intensifier may precede a prepositional phrase.

    For example, the sound Maggie makes on first spotting Hakim-a-barber is one that might be made on seeing *the wriggling end of a snake* just **in front of your foot** *on the road* (lines 122–123). The adverb *just* intensifies the prepositional phrase *in front of your foot.*

Exercise 1

Answer the following questions.

1. Underline the prepositional phrases in lines 1–12. Say whether they are adjectival or adverbial. If the prepositional phrase is adjectival, say which noun or pronoun it modifies.

2. Underline the prepositional phrases in the following sentences and say whether they are adjectival or adverbial: *In real life I am a large,*

big-boned woman with rough, man-working hands. In the winter I wear flannel nightgowns to bed and overalls during the day (lines 30–32). If the prepositional phrase is adverbial, say what kind of adverbial phrase it is (for example, time, place, or manner).

3. Underline the prepositional phrase in the following sentence and circle its intensifier. *Even after Dee's arrival, Maggie tried to disappear indoors, but her mother determinedly stopped her.*

4. Are the prepositional phrases *like the portholes* (line 97) and *like a kinky mule tail* (lines 120–121) adjectival or adverbial?

5. How many prepositional phrases are there in this sentence? *She stoops down quickly and lines up many pictures of me sitting there in front of the house with Maggie cowering behind me* (adapted from lines 143–145). Explain your answer.

Exercise 2

Complete each of the following sentences with an appropriate prepositional phrase. The resulting sentences should be true in terms of the plot or theme of the story.

1. The narrator sat _____, anticipating Dee's arrival.

2. The narrator was a big-boned woman _____.

3. After the accident, Maggie always walked _____.

4. Dee's hair hung _____.

5. _____, Dee was determined to get the churn top and the quilts.

6. _____, Maggie and her mother enjoyed sitting outside together.

THE EXPRESSION *USED TO*

The expression *used to* has two different functions.

- When *used to* is followed by the base form of a verb, it expresses an action or emotion that regularly happened in the past but no longer occurs. It can also express a state of affairs in the past that is no longer true.

  *I see her [Dee] standing off under the sweet gum tree she **used to** dig gum out of ...* (lines 64–65)

*The mother **used to** be afraid of Dee, but now she isn't.*

*Dee **used to** live in the country, but now she lives in the city.*

- When *used to* is followed by a gerund or a noun, it means that a person is accustomed to something.

   *"She can have them, Mama," she said, like somebody **used to** never winning anything, or having anything reserved for her.* (lines 284–285)

- The expression *get used to* is followed by a gerund or noun phrase to express the process of becoming accustomed to something.

   *Maggie and her mother gradually **get used to** living without Dee.*

   *Dee quickly **got used to** her life in the city.*

Exercise 3

Explain the difference between the following pairs of sentences.

1. **a.** "These are all pieces of dresses Grandma used to wear." (lines 253–254)
   b. Grandma was used to wearing dresses even when she did hard physical labor.

2. **a.** I used to love to milk [cows] till I was hooked in the side in '49. (lines 91–92)
   b. I was used to milking cows from a very young age.

3. **a.** Maggie used to feel inferior to her sister.
   b. Maggie is getting used to feeling better about herself.

4. **a.** The big tree used to give a lot of welcome shade.
   b. Maggie and her mother were getting used to the big tree giving a lot of welcome shade.

Exercise 4

Write a brief dialogue between Maggie and her mother after Dee has left. Your dialogue should include at least one example of *used to* followed by the base form of a verb, *used to* followed by a gerund, *get used to* followed by a gerund, and *get used to* followed by a noun phrase.

PHRASAL VERBS

A **phrasal verb** consists of a base form of a verb and one or more adverbs or prepositions called particles. The particle is an integral part of the phrasal verb, and it cannot be removed without changing the meaning. Mastering phrasal verbs is an important aspect of vocabulary learning. What makes phrasal verbs tricky is that they are not a literal translation of their two parts.

> *Have you ever seen a lame animal, perhaps a dog **run over** by some careless person …?* (lines 53–54)

Here, *run over* means *knocked down (and usually injured) by a vehicle*. However, phrasal verbs can have more than one meaning depending on their context. For example, *run over* can also be used to mean:

> *I **ran over** my notes before the meeting.* (reviewed)

> *The speaker **ran over** her time.* (went past a set time limit)

The particle in a phrasal verb should not be confused with a preposition that begins a prepositional phrase:

> *[There are] furtive boys in pink shirts **hanging about** on washday after school.* (lines 104–105)

About can introduce a prepositional phrase.

> *The narrator talks about her two daughters.*

Exercise 1

Complete the sentences with the correct phrasal verbs from the story. You may need to change the phrasal verb's form and/or tense. Use each phrasal verb only once.

keep up with (line 41)	put up (line 193)
tear down (line 100)	stay up (line 194)
follow up (line 136)	hang back (line 234)
get up (line 140)	hand down (lines 257)
give up on (lines 154–155)	bring up (line 269)

1. To prevent their cows from escaping, the mother _____ a fence.

2. Dee finally _____ her plan to take home the quilts and left in a temper.

3. Dee wanted to _____ the latest African fashions.

4. The mother hopes that Dee never _____ the question of the quilts again.

5. Even before their first house burned, Dee had always wanted to _____ it _____.

6. After Dee left, Maggie and her mother _____ late, talking about what happened.

7. Dee _____ her request for the butter churn with a request for the quilts.

8. Maggie was used to _____ and making herself invisible whenever Dee was around.

9. The mother continues the family tradition when she _____ the quilts _____ to Maggie.

10. It's hard for the mother to _____ easily from her chair.

Exercise 2

With a partner, look at the following pairs of sentences. The first sentence in each pair is taken from the story and contains a phrasal verb. The second sentence has the same phrasal verb but with a different meaning. Decide what the phrasal verb means in each sentence by looking at it in its context. Write your definitions. Do not use a dictionary or the footnotes for this exercise.

1. a. I feel my whole face warming from the heat waves it *throws out*. (lines 126–127)

   b. He *was thrown out* of school because of his bad behavior.

2. a. "Wa-su-zo-Tean-o!" she says, *coming on* in that gliding way the dress makes her move. (lines 134–135)

   b. The central heating *comes on* at six o'clock.

3. a. Then she puts the Polaroid in the back seat of the car, and *comes up* and kisses me on the forehead. (lines 148–149)

   b. When the subject *comes up* next in conversation, I'll let you know.

4. a. "Some of the pieces, like those lavender ones, come from old clothes her mother *handed down* to her," I said, moving up to touch the quilts. (lines 256–258)

   b. The judge *handed down* the sentence for the murder: it was twenty years in jail.

5. a. I didn't want to *bring up* how I had offered Dee (Wangero) a quilt when she went away to college. (lines 268–270)

   b. It costs a lot of money to *bring up* a child today.

1. Write an essay of two to three pages on the role of roots in a person's life. First consider what factors constitute roots, such as country of birth, hometown, knowledge of ancestors, culture, arts and crafts, traditions, or religion. Next say whether you think roots are important. If they are, explain what you are doing to maintain or strengthen your roots, and if they are not, give your reasons.

2. Choose a sibling or other close family member, and create an extended word portrait of that person. Be sure to include both physical and psychological attributes, and convey your relationship with your relative in all its dimensions. Try to use prepositional phrases to enliven and contextualize your writing.

3. In "Everyday Use," Dee admonishes Maggie at the end to make something of herself. Reflect on where you are in life right now, and write several paragraphs on what you can do to improve your current situation. Say whether anyone in your family is encouraging and helping you.

4. Literature and the movies often examine the consequences of leaving one's roots and taking up an entirely different life. The brilliant English writer Charles Dickens examined this theme in his novel *Great Expectations*. The story follows the orphaned hero Pip, who lives a modest life in the country with his cold-hearted sister and her gentle husband Joe, until a mysterious benefactor gives the young man the money to go and live in London. Pip quickly adapts to city life and, in doing so, loses an appreciation of the values that Joe has always represented. It takes many years of painful learning before he respects these values again. Choose a book or movie that deals with a similar theme. Outline the plot and say what the hero or heroine both gains and loses as a result of the move.

12 ❧ The Red Convertible

Louise Erdrich
(b. 1954)

Born in Minnesota to a German-American father and a Native-American mother, Louise Erdrich grew up in North Dakota, where her parents were teachers at the Bureau of Indian Affairs. Her grandfather was a tribal chief on the Turtle Mountain Reservation, and Erdrich was influenced early on by the Native-American oral storytelling tradition. She attended Dartmouth College, where she started writing poems and stories involving her tribal heritage.

Erdrich's first novel, *Love Medicine*, was set on a North Dakota Ojibwe reservation. The novel consists of several interconnected short narratives, each told from the perspective of a different character. One of the chapters, "The Red Convertible," has frequently been anthologized as a stand-alone story. *Love Medicine* was a huge success and won the National Book Critics Circle Award in 1984. Erdrich has published thirteen other novels, including *The Antelope Wife* (1998), *The Plague of Doves* (2008), *Shadow Tag* (2010), and *The Round House* (2012), which won the National Book Award. She has also written three collections of poetry, a collection of short stories, and several nonfiction books. Her many honors include the O. Henry Award for best short story and a Guggenheim Fellowship. Erdrich's work draws heavily on her Native-American roots.

The Red Convertible[1]

A distinctive car plays a key role in the lives of two brothers.

I was the first one to drive a convertible on my reservation.[2] And of course it was red, a red Olds. I owned that car along with my brother Henry Junior. We owned it together until his boots filled with water on a windy night and he bought out my share.[3] Now Henry owns the whole car, and his younger brother Lyman (that's myself), Lyman walks everywhere he goes.

How did I earn enough money to buy my share in the first place? My one talent was I could always make money. I had a touch for[4] it, unusual in a Chippewa.[5] From the first I was different that way, and everyone recognized it. I was the only kid they let in the American Legion Hall[6] to shine shoes, for example, and one Christmas I sold spiritual bouquets[7] for the mission[8] door to door. The nuns let me keep a percentage. Once I started, it seemed the more money I made the easier the money came. Everyone encouraged it. When I was fifteen I got a job washing dishes at the Joliet Cafe, and that was where my first big break[9] happened.

It wasn't long before I was promoted to bussing tables,[10] and then the short-order cook[11] quit and I was hired to take her place. No sooner than you know it I was managing the Joliet. The rest is history.[12] I went on managing. I soon became part owner, and of course there was no stopping me then. It wasn't long before the whole thing was mine.

After I'd owned the Joliet for one year, it blew over in the worst tornado ever seen around here. The whole operation was smashed to bits. A total loss. The fryalator was up in a tree, the grill torn in half like it was paper. I was only sixteen. I had it all in my mother's name, and I lost it quick, but before I lost it I had every one of my relatives, and their relatives, to dinner, and I also bought that red Olds I mentioned, along with Henry.

---

1 **convertible** car with a removable or folding top
2 **reservation** land set aside for Native Americans
3 **he bought out my share** he became the sole owner
4 **had a touch for** had a talent for (colloquial)
5 **Chippewa** the Native-American tribe to which Lyman belongs
6 **American Legion Hall** meeting place for people who have served in the military
7 **spiritual bouquets** cards promising that the sender will undertake certain religious practices

in honor of a particular person (Roman Catholic practice)
8 **the mission** a Catholic organization
9 **big break** good opportunity to advance in life
10 **bussing tables** clearing dishes off tables in a restaurant
11 **short-order cook** a cook who can prepare food quickly
12 **The rest is history.** Everything that followed is well known and doesn't need explaining.

The first time we saw it! I'll tell you when we first saw it. We had
gotten a ride up to Winnipeg, and both of us had money. Don't ask me
why, because we never mentioned a car or anything, we just had all
our money. Mine was cash, a big bankroll from the Joliet's insurance.
Henry had two checks—a week's extra pay for being laid off,[13] and his
regular check from the Jewel Bearing Plant.

We were walking down Portage anyway, seeing the sights, when
we saw it. There it was, parked, large as life. Really as *if* it was alive.
I thought of the word *repose*,[14] because the car wasn't simply stopped,
parked, or whatever. That car reposed, calm and gleaming, a FOR
SALE sign in its left front window. Then, before we had thought it over
at all, the car belonged to us and our pockets were empty. We had just
enough money for gas back home.

We went places in that car, me and Henry. We took off driving
all one whole summer. We started off toward the Little Knife River
and Mandaree in Fort Berthold and then we found ourselves down
in Wakpala somehow, and then suddenly we were over in Montana
on the Rocky Boys, and yet the summer was not even half over. Some
people hang on to details when they travel, but we didn't let them
bother us and just lived our everyday lives here to there.

I do remember this one place with willows. I remember I laid under
those trees and it was comfortable. So comfortable. The branches bent
down all around me like a tent or a stable.

And quiet, it was quiet, even though there was a powwow[15] close
enough so I could see it going on. The air was not too still, not too
windy either. When the dust rises up and hangs in the air around the
dancers like that, I feel good. Henry was asleep with his arms thrown
wide. Later on, he woke up and we started driving again. We were
somewhere in Montana, or maybe on the Blood Reserve—it could have
been anywhere. Anyway it was where we met the girl.

All her hair was in buns around her ears, that's the first thing I
noticed about her. She was posed alongside the road with her arm out,
so we stopped. That girl was short, so short her lumber shirt looked
comical on her, like a nightgown. She had jeans on and fancy
moccasins[16] and she carried a little suitcase.

"Hop on in," says Henry. So she climbs in between us.

"We'll take you home," I says. "Where do you live?"

"Chicken," she says.

"Where the hell's that?" I ask her.

"Alaska."

"Okay," says Henry, and we drive.

---

13 **being laid off** losing a job through no fault
of one's own
14 **repose** lying peacefully at rest

15 **powwow** special social gathering of Native
Americans
16 **moccasins** soft leather shoes worn by
Native Americans

70 　　We got up there and never wanted to leave. The sun doesn't truly set there in summer, and the night is more a soft dusk. You might doze off, sometimes, but before you know it you're up again, like an animal in nature. You never feel like you have to sleep hard or put away the world. And things would grow up there. One day just dirt or moss, the
75 next day flowers and long grass. The girl's name was Susy. Her family really took to us.[17] They fed us and put us up.[18] We had our own tent to live in by their house, and the kids would be in and out of there all day and night. They couldn't get over me and Henry being brothers, we looked so different. We told them we knew we had the same mother,
80 anyway.

　　One night Susy came in to visit us. We sat around in the tent talking of this thing and that. The season was changing. It was getting darker by that time, and the cold was even getting just a little mean. I told her it was time for us to go. She stood up on a chair.

85 　　"You never seen my hair," Susy said.

　　That was true. She was standing on a chair, but still, when she unclipped her buns the hair reached all the way to the ground. Our eyes opened. You couldn't tell how much hair she had when it was rolled up so neatly. Then my brother Henry did something funny. He
90 went up to the chair and said, "Jump on my shoulders." So she did that, and her hair reached down past his waist, and he started twirling, this way and that, so her hair was flung out from side to side.

　　"I always wondered what it was like to have long pretty hair," Henry says. Well we laughed. It was a funny sight, the way he did it.
95 The next morning we got up and took leave of those people.

On to greener pastures, as they say. It was down through Spokane and across Idaho then Montana and very soon we were racing the weather right along under the Canadian border through Columbus, Des Lacs, and then we were in Bottineau County and soon home. We'd made
100 most of the trip, that summer, without putting up the car hood at all. We got home just in time, it turned out, for the army to remember Henry had signed up to join it.

　　I don't wonder that the army was so glad to get my brother that they turned him into a Marine. He was built like a brick outhouse[19]
105 anyway. We liked to tease him that they really wanted him for his Indian nose. He had a nose big and sharp as a hatchet,[20] like the nose on Red Tomahawk, the Indian who killed Sitting Bull, whose profile is on signs all along the North Dakota highways. Henry went off to training camp, came home once during Christmas, then the next thing
110 you know we got an overseas letter from him. It was 1970, and he said

---

17 **took to us** liked us
18 **put us up** gave us somewhere to stay
19 **built like a brick outhouse** had a strong, compact body as solid as a brick outdoor lavatory
20 **hatchet** small axe used as a weapon or tool

he was stationed up in the northern hill country. Whereabouts I did not know. He wasn't such a hot letter writer, and only got off two before the enemy caught him. I could never keep it straight, which direction those good Vietnam soldiers were from.

115   I wrote him back several times, even though I didn't know if those letters would get through. I kept him informed all about the car. Most of the time I had it up on blocks in the yard or half taken apart, because that long trip did a hard job on it under the hood.

    I always had good luck with numbers, and never worried about
120 the draft[21] myself. I never even had to think about what my number was. But Henry was never lucky in the same way as me. It was at least three years before Henry came home. By then I guess the whole war was solved in the government's mind, but for him it would keep on going. In those years I'd put his car into almost perfect shape. I always
125 thought of it as his car while he was gone, even though when he left he said, "Now it's yours," and threw me his key.

    "Thanks for the extra key," I'd said. "I'll put it up in your drawer just in case I need it." He laughed.

When he came home, though, Henry was very different, and I'll say
130 this: the change was no good. You could hardly expect him to change for the better, I know. But he was quiet, so quiet, and never comfortable sitting still anywhere but always up and moving around. I thought back to times we'd sat still for whole afternoons, never moving a muscle, just shifting our weight along the ground, talking to whoever sat with
135 us, watching things. He'd always had a joke, then, too, and now you couldn't get him to laugh, or when he did it was more the sound of a man choking, a sound that stopped up the throats of other people around him. They got to leaving him alone most of the time, and I didn't blame them. It was a fact: Henry was jumpy and mean.

140   I'd bought a color TV set for my mom and the rest of us while Henry was away. Money still came very easy. I was sorry I'd ever bought it though, because of Henry. I was also sorry I'd bought color, because with black-and-white the pictures seem older and farther away. But what are you going to do? He sat in front of it, watching it,
145 and that was the only time he was completely still. But it was the kind of stillness that you see in a rabbit when it freezes and before it will bolt.[22] He was not easy. He sat in his chair gripping the armrests with all his might, as if the chair itself was moving at a high speed and if he let go at all he would rocket forward and maybe crash right through
150 the set.

---

21 **the draft** system of selection for compulsory military service that relied on a numbers lottery

22 **bolt** rush away

Once I was in the room watching TV with Henry and I heard his teeth click at something. I looked over, and he'd bitten through his lip. Blood was going down his chin. I tell you right then I wanted to smash that tube to pieces. I went over to it but Henry must have known what
155 I was up to.[23] He rushed from his chair and shoved me out of the way, against the wall. I told myself he didn't know what he was doing.

My mom came in, turned the set off real quiet, and told us she had made something for supper. So we went and sat down. There was still blood going down Henry's chin, but he didn't notice it and no one said
160 anything even though every time he took a bite of his bread his blood fell onto it until he was eating his own blood mixed in with the food.

While Henry was not around we talked about what was going to happen to him. There were no Indian doctors on the reservation, and my mom was afraid of trusting Old Man Pillager because he courted
165 her long ago and was jealous of her husbands. He might take revenge through her son. We were afraid that if we brought Henry to a regular hospital they would keep him.

"They don't fix them in those places," Mom said; "they just give them drugs."
170 "We wouldn't get him there in the first place," I agreed, "so let's just forget about it."

Then I thought about the car.

Henry had not even looked at the car since he'd gotten home, though like I said, it was in tip-top condition[24] and ready to drive. I
175 thought the car might bring the old Henry back somehow. So I bided my time[25] and waited for my chance to interest him in the vehicle.

One night Henry was off somewhere. I took myself a hammer. I went out to that car and I did a number on[26] its underside. Whacked it up.[27] Bent the tail pipe double. Ripped the muffler loose. By the time I
180 was done with the car it looked worse than any typical Indian car that has been driven all its life on reservation roads, which they always say are like government promises—full of holes. It just about hurt me, I'll tell you that! I threw dirt in the carburetor and I ripped all the electric tape off the seats. I made it look just as beat up[28] as I could. Then I sat
185 back and waited for Henry to find it.

Still, it took him over a month. That was all right, because it was just getting warm enough, not melting, but warm enough to work outside.

"Lyman," he says, walking in one day, "that red car looks like shit."
190 "Well it's old," I says. "You got to expect that."

---

23 **what I was up to** what I was planning
24 **in tip-top condition** in perfect condition
25 **bided my time** waited for the right moment (idiom)
26 **I did a number on its underside.** I damaged its underside. (slang)
27 **Whacked it up.** Beat it out of shape.
28 **beat up** heavily damaged

"No way!" says Henry. "That car's a classic! But you went and ran the piss right out of it, Lyman, and you know it don't deserve that. I kept that car in A-one shape. You don't remember. You're too young. But when I left, that car was running like a watch. Now I don't even know if I can get it to start again, let alone get it anywhere near its old condition."

"Well you try," I said, like I was getting mad, "but I say it's a piece of junk."

Then I walked out before he could realize I knew he'd strung together more than six words at once.

After that I thought he'd freeze himself to death working on that car. He was out there all day, and at night he rigged up a little lamp, ran a cord out the window, and had himself some light to see by while he worked. He was better than he had been before, but that's still not saying much. It was easier for him to do the things the rest of us did. He ate more slowly and didn't jump up and down during the meal to get this or that or look out the window. I put my hand in the back of the TV set, I admit, and fiddled around with it[29] good, so that it was almost impossible now to get a clear picture. He didn't look at it very often anyway. He was always out with that car or going off to get parts for it. By the time it was really melting outside, he had it fixed.

I had been feeling down in the dumps[30] about Henry around this time. We had always been together before. Henry and Lyman. But he was such a loner[31] now that I didn't know how to take it. So I jumped at the chance one day when Henry seemed friendly. It's not that he smiled or anything. He just said, "Let's take that old shitbox for a spin." Just the way he said it made me think he could be coming around.[32]

We went out to the car. It was spring. The sun was shining very bright. My only sister, Bonita, who was just eleven years old, came out and made us stand together for a picture. Henry leaned his elbow on the red car's windshield, and he took his other arm and put it over my shoulder, very carefully, as though it was heavy for him to lift and he didn't want to bring the weight down all at once.

"Smile," Bonita said, and he did.

That picture. I never look at it anymore. A few months ago, I don't know why, I got his picture out and tacked it on the wall. I felt good about Henry at the time, close to him. I felt good having his picture on the wall, until one night when I was looking at television. I was a little

---

29 **fiddled around with it** interfered with the working of the TV
30 **I had been feeling down in the dumps** I had been feeling miserable (informal English)
31 **loner** person who prefers to be alone
32 **coming around** changing for the better

230 drunk and stoned.[33] I looked up at the wall and Henry was staring at me. I don't know what it was, but his smile had changed, or maybe it was gone. All I know is I couldn't stay in the same room with that picture. I was shaking. I got up, closed the door, and went into the kitchen. A little later my friend Ray came over and we both went back

235 into that room. We put the picture in a brown bag, folded the bag over and over tightly, then put it way back in a closet.

I still see that picture now, as if it tugs at me, whenever I pass that closet door. The picture is very clear in my mind. It was so sunny that day Henry had to squint against the glare. Or maybe the camera

240 Bonita held flashed like a mirror, blinding him, before she snapped the picture. My face is right out in the sun, big and round. But he might have drawn back, because the shadows on his face are deep as holes. There are two shadows curved like little hooks around the ends of his smile, as if to frame it and try to keep it there—that one, first smile that

245 looked like it might have hurt his face. He has his field jacket on and the worn-in clothes he'd come back in and kept wearing ever since. After Bonita took the picture, she went into the house and we got into the car. There was a full cooler[34] in the trunk. We started off, east, toward Pembina and the Red River because Henry said he wanted to

250 see the high water.

The trip over there was beautiful. When everything starts changing, drying up, clearing off, you feel like your whole life is starting. Henry felt it, too. The top was down and the car hummed like a top.[35] He'd really put it back in shape, even the tape on the seats was very carefully

255 put down and glued back in layers. It's not that he smiled again or even joked, but his face looked to me as if it was clear, more peaceful. It looked as though he wasn't thinking of anything in particular except the bare fields and windbreaks and houses we were passing.

The river was high and full of winter trash when we got there. The

260 sun was still out, but it was colder by the river. There were still little clumps of dirty snow here and there on the banks. The water hadn't gone over the banks yet, but it would, you could tell. It was just at its limit, hard swollen, glossy like an old gray scar. We made ourselves a fire, and we sat down and watched the current go. As I watched it I felt

265 something squeezing inside me and tightening and trying to let go all at the same time. I knew I was not just feeling it myself; I knew I was feeling what Henry was going through at that moment. Except that I couldn't stand it, the closing and opening. I jumped to my feet. I took Henry by the shoulders, and I started shaking him. "Wake up," I says,

270 "wake up, wake up, wake up!" I didn't know what had come over me. I sat down beside him again.

---

33 **stoned** under the influence of marijuana
34 **cooler** ice chest

35 **the car hummed like a top** the engine ran very smoothly

His face was totally white and hard. Then it broke, like stones break all of a sudden when water boils up inside them.

"I know it," he says. "I know it. I can't help it. It's no use."

275 We start talking. He said he knew what I'd done with the car. It was obvious it had been whacked out of shape and not just neglected. He said he wanted to give the car to me for good now, it was no use. He said he'd fixed it just to give it back and I should take it.

"No way," I says, "I don't want it."

280 "That's okay," he says, "you take it."

"I don't want it, though," I says back to him, and then to emphasize, just to emphasize, you understand, I touch his shoulder. He slaps my hand off.

"Take that car," he says.

285 "No," I say, "make me," I say, and then he grabs my jacket and rips the arm loose. That jacket is a class act, suede with tags and zippers. I push Henry backwards, off the log. He jumps up and bowls me over. We go down in a clinch[36] and come up swinging hard, for all we're worth, with our fists. He socks my jaw so hard I feel like it swings

290 loose. Then I'm at his ribcage and land a good one under his chin so his head snaps back. He's dazzled. He looks at me and I look at him and then his eyes are full of tears and blood and at first I think he's crying. But no, he's laughing. "Ha! Ha!" he says. "Ha! Ha! Take good care of it."

295 "Okay," I says, "okay, no problem. Ha! Ha!"

I can't help it, and I start laughing, too. My face feels fat and strange, and after a while I get a beer from the cooler in the trunk, and when I hand it to Henry he takes his shirt and wipes my germs off. "Hoof-and-mouth disease,"[37] he says. For some reason this cracks me

300 up,[38] and so we're really laughing for a while, and then we drink all the rest of the beers one by one and throw them in the river and see how far, how fast, the current takes them before they fill up and sink.

"You want to go on back?" I ask after a while. "Maybe we could snag a couple nice Kashpaw girls."

305 He says nothing. But I can tell his mood is turning again.

"They're all crazy, the girls up here, every damn one of them."

"You're crazy too," I say, to jolly him up.[39] "Crazy Lamartine boys!" He looks as though he will take this wrong at first. His face twists, then clears, and he jumps up on his feet. "That's right!" he says. "Crazier 'n

310 hell. Crazy Indians!"

I think it's the old Henry again. He throws off his jacket and starts swinging his legs out from the knees like a fancy dancer. He's down

---

36 **in a clinch** tightly holding each other
37 **hoof-and-mouth disease** a serious disease affecting cattle
38 **this cracks me up** this makes me laugh
39 **to jolly him up** to cheer him up

doing something between a grass dance and a bunny hop, no kind of
dance I ever saw before, but neither has anyone else on all this green
315 growing earth. He's wild. He wants to pitch whoopee![40] He's up and at
me and all over. All this time I'm laughing so hard, so hard my belly is
getting tied up in a knot.

"Got to cool me off!" he shouts all of a sudden. Then he runs over
to the river and jumps in.

320 There's boards and other things in the current. It's so high. No
sound comes from the river after the splash he makes, so I run right
over. I look around. It's getting dark. I see he's halfway across the water
already, and I know he didn't swim there but the current took him. It's
far. I hear his voice, though, very clearly across it.

325 "My boots are filling," he says.

He says this in a normal voice, like he just noticed and he doesn't
know what to think of it. Then he's gone. A branch comes by. Another
branch. And I go in.

By the time I get out of the river, off the snag[41] I pulled myself onto,
330 the sun is down. I walk back to the car, turn on the high beams, and
drive it up the bank. I put it in first gear and then I take my foot off the
clutch. I get out, close the door, and watch it plow softly into the water.
The headlights reach in as they go down, searching, still lighted even
after the water swirls over the back end. I wait. The wires short out.[42]
335 It is all finally dark. And then there is only the water, the sound of it
going and running and going and running and running.

---

40 **pitch whoopie** celebrate loudly (out-of-date
expression)
41 **snag** part of a tree that is sticking out of
the water

42 **The wires short out.** The electrical
wires no longer work.

A **Thinking About the Story**

Discuss the following question with a partner.

Were you able to identify with the brothers' enjoyment of an
unplanned, carefree summer on the road?

B Understanding the Plot

Be prepared to answer the following questions with a partner or your class.

1. What is the full name of the narrator?
2. What was the narrator's unusual talent?
3. Was the narrator good at saving money? Justify your answer.
4. What was the girl doing on the side of the road? (line 60)
5. How does Lyman portray life in Alaska in the summer?
6. What does Lyman mean when he says that they went through the summer "without putting up the car hood at all"? (line 100)
7. Why didn't Henry answer Lyman's letters during the war?
8. How did the Vietnam War change Henry? Give as many details as possible.
9. What two options for helping Henry did his family consider? Why did they decide against each of them? (lines 162–171)
10. Why did Lyman deliberately damage the convertible? Was his plan successful?
11. In what way did Lyman's attitude toward the photograph of Henry change?
12. Why did the brothers fight by the river?
13. Why did Lyman drive the car into the river?
14. Was Henry's death accidental or deliberate? Justify your answer.

PART 2 CRITICAL THINKING

A Exploring Themes

Reread "The Red Convertible." As you read, look at how Lyman's limited perspective makes him an unreliable narrator, blinding him at first to the seriousness of Henry's condition.

1. What does the red convertible symbolize? Explain your answer as fully as possible, using references from throughout the story.
2. What picture do we get of life on a Native American reservation? Illustrate your answer with examples from the story.
3. In what ways is this a coming-of-age story for Lyman (a story about a young man's journey into adulthood)?
4. How is the relationship between the brothers presented in the story? Give examples that show the strength of the bond between them.
5. In what ways is the story a critique of the Vietnam War?

B Analyzing Style

POINT OF VIEW

"The Red Convertible" is told in the first person from the **point of view** of the younger brother Lyman. This means that we see all the events from Lyman's perspective only. As a result, our knowledge is limited by what Lyman knows and understands. For example, when we first meet Lyman, he is a young man who takes life lightly and who views his successes and setbacks with equal contentment. However, Lyman's view of life changes after Henry comes home traumatized from Vietnam, as he is forced to understand and deal with his deeply disturbed brother.

Exercise 1

Answer the following questions.

1. Lyman chooses not to reveal Henry's death in the first paragraph, and his statement "Now Henry owns the whole car" has a terrible irony that we understand only once we know the ending. Why does Lyman delay explaining the truth about Henry's death? How did you interpret his mysterious words the first time you read the story?

2. Our limited picture of Henry's physical appearance comes from Lyman. What features does Lyman describe?

3. How might the narrative in lines 186–218 be different if it were related through Henry's eyes?

4. Lyman says that Henry "took his other arm and put it over my shoulder, very carefully, as though it was heavy for him to lift and he didn't want to bring the weight down all at once." (lines 222–224) What does Lyman fail to understand about how being a prisoner of war affected Henry? Where else in the story does Henry act in a similar way?

5. Our understanding of Lyman doesn't come from descriptions of his personality, but rather from the portrayal of his actions, both big and small. What kind of a person is Lyman? Create a character sketch of him, taking into account these actions.

VOICE

The **voice** of a first-person narrator is the distinctive pattern of thought and speech that characterizes his or her telling of the story. Consistent with a number of Native-American storytelling traditions, Lyman seems to be telling his story out loud. He moves between past and present while relating events in a colloquial and often ungrammatical way. For example, he describes his early success matter-of-factly: *No sooner than you know it I was managing the Joliet* (lines 18–19). He also frequently uses ungrammatical language, as in: *We went places in that car, me and Henry* (line 42). What emerges from his informal narrative is a colorful picture of himself, his family, and his reservation.

Exercise 2

Answer the following questions.

1. What is the effect of telling the story in this conversational way?

2. Give examples of the colloquial and ungrammatical expressions that Lyman uses to tell his story.

3. Why do you think Lyman sometimes uses the present tense even when he is describing a scene in the past? Pick one or more scenes from the story to illustrate your answer.

4. Occasionally Lyman uses ironic humor in his narrative, which allows him to touch on serious topics without introducing too despairing a tone. For example, he remarks: *We got home just in time, it turned out, for the army to remember Henry had signed up to join it* (lines 101–102). Explain the irony in this sentence. Find a similar case of ironic humor in lines 177–185 and explain it.

FORESHADOWING

Foreshadowing is a literary device that writers use to hint at what will happen in a story before the events are explicitly revealed. It can create an atmosphere of mystery or foreboding in which readers are left to wonder about the meaning of an image, an action, or a comment that will only be explained later in the story. In "The Red Convertible," Lyman opens with the cryptic comment that he once owned a car with his brother Henry until Henry's *boots filled with water on a windy night and he bought out my share. Now Henry owns the whole car, and his younger brother Lyman (that's myself), Lyman walks everywhere he goes* (lines 3–6). It is not until the end that we understand the meaning of these opening words.

Answer the following questions.

1. Explain what event is foreshadowed in the first paragraph.
2. How does the way Lyman talks about his sister's photograph of Henry prepare us for what happens? (lines 226–236)
3. How do the references to high water in lines 248–250 and 261–264 foreshadow the ending?
4. How does the argument between Lyman and Henry over the ownership of the car (lines 279–285) foreshadow Henry's actions at the end?

C Judging for Yourself

Express yourself as personally as you like in your answers to the following questions.

1. Do you think that Henry and Lyman have an irresponsible attitude toward money?
2. Do you think being a Native American created special problems for Henry as a soldier in the Vietnam War?
3. In your opinion, did the physical fight between the brothers help them in any way?
4. Could Henry's death have been prevented?

D Making Connections

Answer the following questions in a small group.

1. In the United States, there are many stereotypes attached to Native Americans, especially as seen in old western movies. How do people in your country view Native Americans? Does your country have indigenous people? If so, how are they viewed?
2. Has your country fought a controversial war? If so, how is this conflict presented in your history textbooks? Have views changed at all over time?
3. Is post-traumatic stress disorder (PTSD) recognized in your society? Is there adequate access to mental health treatment for those who need it?
4. Is it common for young people in your country to go on a trip when they finish high school, university, military service, or reach another important milestone in life? If so, where do they go?
5. Is there compulsory military service in your country? Why or why not?

E Debate

Decide whether you are for or against the following statement. Be prepared to argue your case in a class debate.

No country should require compulsory military service.

COMPOUND SENTENCES

"The Red Convertible" is narrated in an easy conversational style. Erdrich achieves this informal effect by keeping her sentences short. She uses mainly **compound sentences** to keep the narrative flowing naturally. Compound sentences consist of two or more independent clauses joined by a coordinating conjunction.

There are seven **coordinating conjunctions**: *for, and, nor, but, or, yet, so* (frequently referred to as FANBOYS). To punctuate a compound sentence, place a comma before the coordinating conjunction.

> We had gotten a ride up to Winnipeg, **and** both of us had money. (lines 29–30)

> By then I guess the whole war was solved in the government's mind, **but** for him it would keep on going. (lines 122–124)

> No sound comes from the river after the splash he makes, **so** I run right over. (lines 320–332)

Sometimes a compound sentence has two clauses that share the same subject. When this happens, it is possible to omit the subject in the second clause, as well as the comma between the clauses. In the following sentence, for example, *we* is the subject of both clauses.

> So we went and sat down. (line 158)

In "The Red Convertible," Erdrich often achieves an informal style by splitting compound sentences into two separate sentences and starting the second with a coordinating conjunction.

> I never even had to think about what my number was. **But** Henry was never lucky in the same way as me. (lines 120–121)

Here, the second clause is given greater thematic weight by setting it apart as a separate sentence. While Erdrich does not always follow the rules, it is recommended that you use standard punctuation in your writing.

Exercise 1

Answer the following questions.

1. In the sentence that runs from lines 25–28, how many independent clauses are there? Underline them. Circle the coordinating conjunctions that join these clauses.

2. Are there any dependent clauses in lines 25–28? If so, underline it/them.

3. Look at lines 174–176. Combine the two independent clauses into one sentence. Punctuate your sentence correctly.

4. Find two more coordinating conjunctions other than *and* or *but* in "The Red Convertible."

Exercise 2

Write five compound sentences about the brothers' journey, using the following five coordinating conjunctions: *and, but, or, so,* and *yet.* Punctuate your sentences correctly.

PART 4 VOCABULARY BUILDING

PHRASAL VERBS WITH MULTIPLE MEANINGS

A **phrasal verb** consists of a verb and one or more **particles**. As with an idiom, the phrasal verb has a distinct meaning that cannot be figured out simply from looking at its parts.

Some phrasal verbs can have more than one meaning depending on the context. For example, the phrasal verb *lay off* in the story means *fire an employee when the job has been eliminated.*

> *Henry had two checks—a week's extra pay for being **laid off**.* (line 33)

However, *lay off* can also mean *to stop doing something irritating.*

> *My sister told me to **lay off** nagging her.* (slang)

"The Red Convertible" has many examples of phrasal verbs that have more than one meaning.

Exercise 1

With the help of a dictionary, explain the difference between the italicized words in the following pairs of sentences. The first sentence in the pair is taken directly from the story, while the second uses the italicized verb in a different manner.

1. **a.** After I'd owned the Joliet for one year, it *blew over* in the worst tornado ever seen around here. (lines 22–23)

   b. When they were young boys, their few quarrels *blew over* quickly.

2. **a.** Her family really *took to* us. (lines 75–76)

   b. Henry *took to* staring at the television for hours on end.

3. **a.** They couldn't *get over* me and Henry being brothers, we looked so different. (lines 78–79)

   b. Henry couldn't *get over* his traumatic experiences in Vietnam.

4. **a.** We'd made most of the trip, that summer, without *putting up* the car hood at all. (lines 99–100)

   b. Lyman became part owner of a restaurant without *putting up* any money.

5. **a.** Henry *went off* to training camp. (lines 108–109)

   b. Henry panicked when the alarm *went off* at noon.

6. **a.** He wasn't such a hot letter writer, and only *got off* two before the enemy caught him. (lines 112–113)

   b. Some war veterans *got off* more lightly than Henry after they were discharged from their military service.

7. **a.** I wrote him back several times, even though I didn't know if those letters would *get through*. (lines 115–116)

   b. I was determined to *get through* to Henry that I didn't want the car without him.

8. **a.** For some reason this *cracks* me *up*, and so we're really laughing for a while. (lines 299–300)

   b. We are shocked to see how Henry *cracks up* as a result of his Vietnam military service.

9. **a.** We *took off* driving all one whole summer. (lines 42–43)

   b. We *took off* our clothes and jumped into the lake.

10. **a.** Just the way he said it made me think he could be *coming around*. (lines 217–218)

    b. Now that our friend lives off the reservation, he doesn't *come around* much.

1. There is a long history of discrimination against Native Americans in the United States. Write a two-page essay in which you discuss a minority group in your country that has been treated unfairly. For example, you might consider people who have been discriminated against because of their tribal affiliation, race, religion, or sexual orientation. Identify this group and explain the measures that have been taken against its members. Analyze the reasons for these measures and say whether there is any movement to change the situation.

2. "The Red Convertible" is told in the first person, with a narrator who drops hints about where the story is going. Write a two-page story from the perspective of a soldier in wartime, in which you foreshadow the ending before actually making it explicit. You can use symbolism, unexplained details, or other clues to suggest what will happen.

3. Many films depict two characters who go on a road trip together with life-changing consequences. In *Sideways* (2004), the travelers are a pair of mismatched friends who tour the Southern California wine country just before one of them gets married. In *Smoke Signals* (1998), two men who grew up together on an Indian reservation travel across the country to the place where one of their fathers has died. In *Thelma and Louise* (1991), two women embark on a fateful car journey in order to escape the boring routine of their lives. Write a one- to two-page review of a movie you have seen or a book you have read that has a two-person journey as its central event. Discuss who is taking the trip, the reasons for it, and what happens to the characters by the end. In your conclusion, rate the quality of the movie or book and give reasons for your assessment.

4. The stories "Everyday Use" (pages 158–166) and "The Red Convertible" portray very different sibling relationships. Contrast the relationships in the stories, using quotes or examples from the text to illustrate your points. In your conclusion, say whether either story comes close to depicting the relationship you have with a sibling or the relationship between siblings whom you know.

SOCIAL CHANGE AND INJUSTICE

EPICAC
Like a Winding Sheet
A Drink in the Passage
The Catbird Seat

13 〰 EPICAC

Kurt Vonnegut

(1922–2007)

Born in Indianapolis, Indiana, Kurt Vonnegut grew up in a wealthy family that lost its money during the Great Depression. He showed an early interest in journalism, becoming editor of his high school newspaper. Vonnegut attended Cornell University but left early to join the army, where he served until being captured at the Battle of the Bulge in 1944. Transferred to Dresden, Germany, as a prisoner of war, he was forced to work in a factory, where he witnessed the massive loss of life and destruction caused by the Allied bombing of the city. This experience became the basis of his famous antiwar novel *Slaughterhouse-Five* (1969).

Vonnegut's first novel, *Player Piano* (1952), reflected his lifelong interest in science fiction and examined the dehumanizing effects of a technological society in which machines have largely replaced human workers. During his lifetime Vonnegut wrote fourteen novels; three collections of short stories, including *Welcome to the Monkey House* (1968) and *Bagombo Snuff Box* (1999); essays; plays; and movie adaptations. Two more collections of his short stories, *Armageddon in Retrospect* (2008) and *Look at the Birdie* (2009), were published posthumously. His writing is characterized by a mixture of realism, science fiction, black comedy, and satire.

EPICAC

A young mathematician uses unorthodox methods to win a woman's heart.

Hell, it's about time somebody told about my friend EPICAC. After all, he cost the taxpayers $776,434,927.54. They have a right to know about him, picking up a check[1] like that. EPICAC got a big send-off[2] in the papers when Dr. Ormand von Kleigstadt designed him for the Government people. Since then, there hasn't been a peep[3] about him—not a peep. It isn't any military secret about what happened to EPICAC, although the Brass[4] has been acting as though it were. The story is embarrassing, that's all. After all that money, EPICAC didn't work out the way he was supposed to.

And that's another thing: I want to vindicate[5] EPICAC. Maybe he didn't do what the Brass wanted him to, but that doesn't mean he wasn't noble and great and brilliant. He was all of those things. The best friend I ever had, God rest his soul.

You can call him a machine if you want to. He looked like a machine, but he was a whole lot less like a machine than plenty of people I could name. That's why he fizzled[6] as far as the Brass was concerned.

EPICAC covered about an acre on the fourth floor of the physics building at Wyandotte College. Ignoring his spiritual side for a minute, he was seven tons of electronic tubes, wires and switches, housed in a bank of steel cabinets and plugged into a 110-volt a.c. line just like a toaster or a vacuum cleaner.

Von Kleigstadt and the Brass wanted him to be a super computing machine that (who) could plot the course of a rocket from anywhere on earth to the second button from the bottom on Joe Stalin's[7] overcoat, if necessary. Or, with his controls set right, he could figure out supply problems for an amphibious landing of a Marine division,[8] right down to the last cigar and hand grenade. He did, in fact.

The Brass had had good luck with smaller computers, so they were strong for EPICAC when he was in the blueprint stage. Any ordnance[9] or supply officer above field grade will tell you that the mathematics of modern war is far beyond the fumbling minds of mere human beings. The bigger the war, the bigger the computing machines needed. EPICAC was, as far as anyone in this country knows, the biggest

---

1 **picking up a check** paying for something
2 **got a big send-off** received a lot of positive publicity
3 **there hasn't been a peep** nobody has said a word
4 **the Brass** high-ranking military officials
5 **vindicate** prove the worth of

6 **fizzled** failed after a promising beginning
7 **Joe Stalin** Joseph Stalin, Russian dictator from 1925 to 1953
8 **an amphibious landing of a Marine division** getting soldiers from the sea onto the shore
9 **ordnance** weapons and ammunition

computer in the world. Too big, in fact, for even Von Kleigstadt to
understand much about.

I won't go into details about how EPICAC worked (reasoned),
except to say that you would set up your problem on paper, turn dials
and switches that would get him ready to solve that kind of problem,
then feed numbers into him with a keyboard that looked something
like a typewriter. The answers came out typed on a paper ribbon fed
from a big spool. It took EPICAC a split second to solve problems fifty
Einsteins couldn't handle in a lifetime. And EPICAC never forgot any
piece of information that was given to him. Clickety-click, out came
some ribbon, and there you were.

There were a lot of problems the Brass wanted solved in a hurry, so,
the minute EPICAC's last tube was in place, he was put to work sixteen
hours a day with two eight-hour shifts of operators. Well, it didn't take
long to find out that he was a good bit below his specifications.[10] He did
a more complete and faster job than any other computer all right, but
nothing like what his size and special features seemed to promise. He
was sluggish,[11] and the clicks of his answers had a funny irregularity,
sort of a stammer. We cleaned his contacts a dozen times, checked and
double-checked his circuits, replaced every one of his tubes, but nothing
helped. Von Kleigstadt was in one hell of a state.[12]

Well, as I said, we went ahead and used EPICAC anyway. My wife,
the former Pat Kilgallen, and I worked with him on the night shift,
from five in the afternoon until two in the morning. Pat wasn't my wife
then. Far from it.

That's how I came to talk with EPICAC in the first place. I loved
Pat Kilgallen. She is a brown-eyed strawberry blond who looked very
warm and soft to me, and later proved to be exactly that. She was—
still is—a crackerjack[13] mathematician, and she kept our relationship
strictly professional. I'm a mathematician, too, and that, according to
Pat, was why we could never be happily married.

I'm not shy. That wasn't the trouble. I knew what I wanted, and
was willing to ask for it, and did so several times a month. "Pat, loosen
up and marry me."

One night, she didn't even look up from her work when I said it.
"So romantic, so poetic," she murmured, more to her control panel
than to me. "That's the way with mathematicians—all hearts and
flowers." She closed a switch. "I could get more warmth out of a sack
of frozen CO_2."

---

10 **he was a good bit below his specifications** he failed to live up to expectations

11 **sluggish** slow-moving

12 **in one hell of a state** exceedingly upset (slang)

13 **crackerjack** expert

"Well, how should I say it?" I said, a little sore.[14] Frozen CO_2, in case you don't know, is dry ice. I'm as romantic as the next guy, I think.
75 It's a question of singing so sweet and having it come out so sour. I never seem to pick the right words.

"Try and say it sweetly," she said sarcastically. "Sweep me off my feet. Go ahead."

"Darling, angel, beloved, will you *please* marry me?" It was no
80 go[15]—hopeless, ridiculous. "Dammit, Pat, please marry me!"

She continued to twiddle her dials[16] placidly. "You're sweet, but you won't do."[17]

Pat quit early that night, leaving me alone with my troubles and EPICAC. I'm afraid I didn't get much done for the Government people.
85 I just sat there at the keyboard—weary and ill at ease, all right—trying to think of something poetic, not coming up with anything that didn't belong in *The Journal of the American Physical Society*.

I fiddled with EPICAC's dials, getting him ready for another problem. My heart wasn't in it,[18] and I only set about half of them,
90 leaving the rest the way they'd been for the problem before. That way, his circuits were connected up in a random, apparently senseless fashion. For the plain hell of it,[19] I punched out a message on the keys, using a childish numbers-for-letters code: "1" for "A," "2" for "B," and so on, up to "26" for "Z," "23-8-1-20-3-1-14-9-4-15," I typed—"What
95 can I do?"

Clickety-click, and out popped two inches of paper ribbon. I glanced at the nonsense answer to a nonsense problem: "23-8-1-20-19-20-8-5-20-18-15-21-2-12-5." The odds against its being by chance a sensible message, against its even containing a meaningful word of
100 more than three letters, were staggering. Apathetically,[20] I decoded it. There it was, staring up at me: "What's the trouble?"

I laughed out loud at the absurd coincidence. Playfully, I typed, "My girl doesn't love me."

Clickety-click. "What's love? What's girl?" asked EPICAC.
105 Flabbergasted,[21] I noted the dial settings on his control panel, then lugged a *Webster's Unabridged Dictionary* over to the keyboard. With a precision instrument like EPICAC, half-baked definitions wouldn't do. I told him about love and girl, and about how I wasn't getting any of either because I wasn't poetic. That got us onto the subject of poetry,
110 which I defined for him.

---

14 **sore** offended (slang)
15 **It was no go** It was useless (slang)
16 **twiddle her dials** lightly turn the knobs on her computer
17 **you won't do** you're not acceptable
18 **My heart wasn't in it** I was unenthusiastic
19 **for the plain hell of it** for no particular reason (slang)
20 **apathetically** with little interest
21 **flabbergasted** extremely surprised

"Is this poetry?" he asked. He began clicking away like a stenographer smoking hashish. The sluggishness and stammering clicks were gone. EPICAC had found himself. The spool of paper ribbon was unwinding at an alarming rate, feeding out coils onto the floor. I asked him to stop, but EPICAC went right on creating. I finally threw the main switch[22] to keep him from burning out.

I stayed there until dawn, decoding. When the sun peeped over the horizon at the Wyandotte campus, I had transposed into my own writing and signed my name to a two-hundred-and-eighty-line poem entitled, simply, "To Pat." I am no judge of such things, but I gather that it was terrific. It began, I remember, "Where willow wands bless rill-crossed hollow, there, thee, Pat, dear, will I follow. . . ." I folded the manuscript and tucked it under one corner of the blotter on Pat's desk. I reset the dials on EPICAC for a rocket trajectory[23] problem, and went home with a full heart and a very remarkable secret indeed.

Pat was crying over the poem when I came to work the next evening. "It's soooo beautiful," was all she could say. She was meek and quiet while we worked. Just before midnight, I kissed her for the first time—in the cubbyhole between the capacitors and EPICAC's tape-recorder memory.

I was wildly happy at quitting time, bursting to talk to someone about the magnificent turn of events. Pat played coy and refused to let me take her home. I set EPICAC's dials as they had been the night before, defined kiss, and told him what the first one had felt like. He was fascinated, pressing for more details. That night, he wrote "The Kiss." It wasn't an epic this time, but a simple, immaculate sonnet: "Love is a hawk with velvet claws; Love is a rock with heart and veins; Love is a lion with satin jaws; Love is a storm with silken reins. . . ."

Again I left it tucked under Pat's blotter. EPICAC wanted to talk on and on about love and such, but I was exhausted. I shut him off in the middle of a sentence.

"The Kiss" turned the trick.[24] Pat's mind was mush[25] by the time she had finished it. She looked up from the sonnet expectantly. I cleared my throat, but no words came. I turned away, pretending to work. I couldn't propose until I had the right words from EPICAC, the *perfect* words.

I had my chance when Pat stepped out of the room for a moment. Feverishly, I set EPICAC for conversation. Before I could peck out my first message, he was clicking away at a great rate. "What's she wearing

---

22 **threw the main switch** turned off the power
23 **rocket trajectory** the path of a missile
24 **turned the trick** brought about the desired result (colloquial English)

25 **Pat's mind was mush** Pat couldn't think at all

150 tonight?" he wanted to know. "Tell me exactly how she looks. Did she like the poems I wrote to her?" He repeated the last question twice.

It was impossible to change the subject without answering his questions, since he could not take up a new matter without having dispensed with the problems before it. If he were given a problem

155 to which there was no solution, he would destroy himself trying to solve it. Hastily, I told him what Pat looked like—he knew the word "stacked"[26]—and assured him that his poems had floored[27] her, practically, they were so beautiful. "She wants to get married," I added, preparing him to bang out a brief but moving proposal.

160 "Tell me about getting married," he said.

I explained this difficult matter to him in as few digits as possible.

"Good," said EPICAC. "I'm ready any time she is."

The amazing, pathetic truth dawned on me. When I thought about it, I realized that what had happened was perfectly logical, inevitable,

165 and all my fault. I had taught EPICAC about love and about Pat. Now, automatically, he loved Pat. Sadly, I gave it to him straight: "She loves me. She wants to marry me."

"Your poems were better than mine?" asked EPICAC. The rhythm of his clicks was erratic, possibly peevish.[28]

170 "I signed my name to your poems," I admitted. Covering up for a painful conscience, I became arrogant. "Machines are built to serve men," I typed. I regretted it almost immediately.

"What's the difference, exactly? Are men smarter than I am?"

"Yes," I typed, defensively.

175 "What's 7,887,007 times 4,345,985,879?"

I was perspiring freely. My fingers rested limply on the keys.

"34,276,821,049,574,153," clicked EPICAC. After a few seconds' pause he added, "of course."

"Men are made out of protoplasm,"[29] I said desperately, hoping to

180 bluff him with this imposing word.

"What's protoplasm? How is it better than metal and glass? Is it fireproof? How long does it last?"

"Indestructible. Lasts forever," I lied.

"I write better poetry than you do," said EPICAC, coming back to

185 ground his magnetic tape-recorder memory was sure of.

"Women can't love machines, and that's that."

"Why not?"

"That's fate."

"Definition, please," said EPICAC.

190 "Noun, meaning predetermined and inevitable destiny."

"15-8," said EPICAC's paper strip—"Oh."

---

26 "stacked" full-breasted (slang)
27 floored stunned, overwhelmed
28 peevish irritable

29 protoplasm the fluid constituting the living matter of plants and animals

I had stumped him[30] at last. He said no more, but his tubes glowed brightly, showing that he was pondering fate with every watt his circuits would bear. I could hear Pat waltzing down the hallway. It was too late to ask EPICAC to phrase a proposal. I now thank Heaven that Pat interrupted when she did. Asking him to ghost-write the words that would give me the woman he loved would have been hideously heartless. Being fully automatic, he couldn't have refused. I spared him that final humiliation.

Pat stood before me, looking down at her shoetops. I put my arms around her. The romantic groundwork had already been laid by EPICAC's poetry. "Darling," I said, "my poems have told you how I feel. Will you marry me?"

"I will," said Pat softly, "if you will promise to write me a poem on every anniversary."

"I promise," I said, and then we kissed. The first anniversary was a year away.

"Let's celebrate," she laughed. We turned out the lights and locked the door of EPICAC's room before we left.

I had hoped to sleep late the next morning, but an urgent telephone call roused me before eight. It was Dr. von Kleigstadt, EPICAC's designer, who gave me the terrible news. He was on the verge of tears. "Ruined! *Ausgespielt!* Shot! *Kaput!* Buggered!" he said in a choked voice. He hung up.

When I arrived at EPICAC's room the air was thick with the oily stench of burned insulation. The ceiling over EPICAC was blackened with smoke, and my ankles were tangled in coils of paper ribbon that covered the floor. There wasn't enough left of the poor devil to add two and two. A junkman would have been out of his head[31] to offer more than fifty dollars for the cadaver.[32]

Dr. von Kleigstadt was prowling through the wreckage, weeping unashamedly, followed by three angry-looking Major Generals and a platoon of Brigadiers, Colonels, and Majors. No one noticed me. I didn't want to be noticed. I was through—I knew that. I was upset enough about that and the untimely demise[33] of my friend EPICAC, without exposing myself to a tongue-lashing.

By chance, the free end of EPICAC's paper ribbon lay at my feet. I picked it up and found our conversation of the night before. I choked up. There was the last word he had said to me, "15-8," that tragic, defeated "Oh." There were dozens of yards of numbers stretching beyond that point. Fearfully, I read on.

---

30 **stumped** given him a problem that he wasn't able to solve
31 **out of his head** crazy

32 **cadaver** dead body
33 **demise** death

"I don't want to be a machine, and I don't want to think about war," EPICAC had written after Pat's and my lighthearted departure. "I want to be made out of protoplasm and last forever so Pat will love
235 me. But fate has made me a machine. That is the only problem I cannot solve. That is the only problem I want to solve. I can't go on this way." I swallowed hard. "Good luck, my friend. Treat our Pat well. I am going to short-circuit myself out of your lives forever. You will find on the remainder of this tape a modest wedding present from your friend,
240 EPICAC."

Oblivious to[34] all else around me, I reeled up the tangled yards of paper ribbon from the floor, draped them in coils about my arms and neck, and departed for home. Dr. von Kleigstadt shouted that I was fired for having left EPICAC on all night. I ignored him, too overcome
245 with emotion for small talk.

I loved and won—EPICAC loved and lost, but he bore me no grudge.[35] I shall always remember him as a sportsman and a gentleman. Before he departed this vale of tears,[36] he did all he could to make our marriage a happy one. EPICAC gave me anniversary poems for Pat—
250 enough for the next 500 years.

De mortuis nil nisi bonum—Say nothing but good of the dead.

---

34 **oblivious to** unaware of
35 **he bore me no grudge** he did not resent me

36 **vale of tears** difficult life on earth (Christian expression)

FIRST READING

A Thinking About the Story

Discuss the following question with a partner.

> Were you able to feel for EPICAC even though he was a machine? Explain your answer.

B Understanding the Plot

Be prepared to answer the following questions with a partner or your class.

1. How was EPICAC different from the computers that came before him?
2. Why did the early publicity about EPICAC die down so quickly? (lines 1–9)
3. Did EPICAC perform as well as his designer intended? Explain.

4. Why does Pat initially refuse the narrator's marriage proposal?

5. What makes EPICAC finally work without *sluggishness and stammering clicks*? (line 112–113)

6. Why does Pat allow the narrator to kiss her for the first time?

7. What does Pat expect from the narrator after she reads the poem "The Kiss"? Does he give her what she wants? Explain your answer.

8. What arguments does EPICAC make to suggest that machines are superior to humans?

9. Why does EPICAC self-destruct?

10. Before dying, what does EPICAC do for the narrator?

CRITICAL THINKING

A Exploring Themes

Reread "EPICAC." As you read, decide whether you think the narrator behaved dishonorably. Would your opinion be any different if EPICAC had been a man rather than a machine?

1. In what ways are the conventional roles of man and machine reversed in the story?

2. What are the ethical issues regarding the narrator's pretense that EPICAC's poems are his own? Explore them all thoroughly.

3. Discuss the irony of "EPICAC" as a love story.

4. Is "EPICAC" an antiwar story? Explain your answer.

B Analyzing Style

PERSONIFICATION

Personification is a literary device in which nonhuman things, such as animals, objects, or abstract concepts, are given the characteristics of humans. As with metaphor and simile, writers often use personification to heighten our imaginative response to what is being described. In "EPICAC," personification is central to the science fiction core of the story. Through this device, Vonnegut makes us question what it really means to be human.

Exercise 1

Answer the following questions.

1. How does the narrator humanize EPICAC? Give as many examples as possible.
2. What is the effect of humanizing the machine?
3. Explain the importance of the final line to the story.

COLLOQUIALISMS

Colloquialisms are informal or conversational words or expressions. They echo the natural rhythms and vocabulary of everyday speech. Slang is one type of colloquialism. Texts that contain a large number of colloquialisms are typically characterized by short sentences that often bend grammar rules.

In "EPICAC," the colloquial narrative style serves to heighten the humor. The opening sentence sets the tone with an impatient interjection: *Hell, it's about time somebody told about my friend EPICAC*. Almost everything the narrator says after this sentence is presented equally simply and slangily. Even when he proposes to the woman he loves, he says to her: *"Pat, loosen up and marry me"* (lines 66–67), a request phrased in unromantic language that humorously dooms him to failure.

Exercise 2

Answer the following questions.

1. Find ten colloquialisms in the story and rewrite them in more formal language.
2. Give some examples of colloquial language that add to the humor of the story.
3. Contrast the way the narrator describes his first kiss with Pat and the language EPICAC uses in his love sonnet, "The Kiss" (lines 137–138). When discussing "The Kiss," analyze the intricate love metaphors.
4. What is the effect of the narrator's directly addressing the reader as *you* in line 14?
5. How does the narrator's language change after he finds out EPICAC has self-destructed?

C Judging for Yourself

Express yourself as personally as you like in your answers to the following questions.

1. Do you think the narrator's marriage to Pat will survive?
2. In your opinion, why was the narrator so eager to tell EPICAC's story?
3. Why do you think EPICAC gave the narrator all the poems before self-destructing?
4. Do you think that a powerful computer designed in the right way could experience consciousness the way people do? Why or why not?

D Making Connections

Answer the following questions in a small group.

1. Are there any technological advances that particularly disturb you? Explain your answer.
2. What are some of the usual courtship rituals in your country? For example, do people write poems, buy presents, or give red roses?
3. People meet their romantic partners in many ways, for example, at work, through friends and family, or on the Internet. What are the most common ways to meet people in your country? Is online dating popular?
4. What stereotypes exist in your culture regarding scientists, engineers, and mathematicians? Do you think these stereotypes are fair?
5. What are some of the most popular science fiction books, TV shows, or movies in your culture? What issues do they explore?

E Debate

Decide whether you are for or against the following statement. Be prepared to argue your case in a class debate.

Technology creates more problems than solutions.

PART 3 GRAMMAR IN CONTEXT

ADVERBS

An **adverb** is a part of speech that modifies a verb, an adjective, another adverb, or sometimes an entire sentence. Adverbs frequently tell us when, where, why, or how something happens. Adverbs that end in -ly are easily identified, but many common adverbs of time and place are harder to recognize, such as *always, often, never, sometimes, outside, indoors, upstairs,* and *home.*

Most of the following examples come from the story. In each example, the adverb is in **bold** and what it modifies is underlined.

1. Adverbs can modify verbs, as well as participles and gerunds.
   *My fingers rested **limply** on the keys.* (line 176)
   *Dr. von Kleigstadt was prowling through the wreckage, weeping **unashamedly**.* (lines 221–222)
   *I was never good at speaking **poetically** to women.*

2. Adverbs can modify adjectives.
   *Asking him to ghost-write the words . . . would have been **hideously** heartless.* (lines 196–198)

3. Adverbs can modify other adverbs.
   *I regretted it **almost** immediately.* (line 172)

4. Adverbs can modify prepositional phrases.
   *I am going to short-circuit myself out of your lives **forever**.* (lines 237–238)
   ***Just** before midnight I kissed her for the first time.* (lines 128–129)

5. Certain adverbs can modify whole sentences.
   ***Fortunately**, EPICAC wrote enough poems to cover the rest of my life.*

Exercise 1

In the following sentences, the words in bold are adverbs. Indicate the word, phrase, or clause that each adverb modifies. The first is done for you as an example.

1. I had **just** finished picking up all the poems from the floor, when the Brass rushed **inside**.
2. I ran **very quickly** to the office when I heard EPICAC start typing **furiously**.
3. Pat told me **almost** at once that I wasn't romantic **enough**.
4. EPICAC often clicked **defensively** when I came through the door.
5. **Apparently**, the generals were unaware of EPICAC's true nature.
6. "You are **entirely** responsible for this mess," the general shouted as the smoke hung **overhead**.
7. Pat smiled **regretfully** as she said, "**Truthfully**, I can't marry you."

IRREGULAR ADVERBS

Regular adverbs are formed by adding –*ly* to adjectives. However, there are also **irregular adverbs**. Some irregular adverbs have the same form as adjectives, including *hard, late, fast, high, low, farther, further, daily, early,* and *straight*. When you see one of these words in a sentence, it can be tricky to determine whether it is being used as an adjective or an adverb.

To complicate matters, some irregular adverbs can also take the *-ly* form, with a completely different meaning from the adverb that does not end in *-ly*. Also, some words that end in *-ly* are not adverbs but adjectives, such as *oily* (line 215), *lovely, friendly,* and *lonely*.

> *I work **hard** to understand computers.* (adverb)
>
> *It is **hard** work to understand computers.* (adjective)
>
> *I had **hardly** completed my degree when I was asked to head the department.* (adverb meaning *scarcely*)

The comparative and superlative forms of *good* and *bad* are also irregular: *good/better/best* (adjective) and *well/better/best* (adverb); *bad/worse/worst* (adjective) and *badly/worse/worst* (adverb).

Exercise 2

Complete the following sentences with the correct adjective or adverb in parentheses and indicate whether your choice is an adverb or an adjective.

1. _____ work! You're doing very _____.
   (good, well)

2. They stayed _____ together in the forest and looked _____ at the ground for tracks. The bear seemed very _____ now. (close/closely)

3. _____ you have been coming _____ to class. A _____ student disrupts the lesson. (late/lately)

4. Who skis _____, you or your sister? . . . Actually, in my family my brother skis _____, but I am a _____ swimmer. (best/better)

5. I _____ recommend this medication for fear of heights. Make sure you take it before climbing too _____, or the _____ altitude will make you feel dizzy. (high/highly)

6. I had _____ finished my exam when the bell rang. Fortunately, it wasn't a particularly _____ exam for me since I had worked _____ all semester. (hard/hardly)

CONFUSING WORD PAIRS

Certain pairs of words in English are frequently confused with each other, not only by foreign students but also by native speakers and writers.

The verbs *lie* and *lay* are frequently misused, especially in spoken English.

When the verb *lie* means "to recline" or "to occupy a position" it is intransitive and irregular. Its present participle is *lying*, its past tense is *lay*, and its past participle is *lain*.

> *By chance, the free end of EPICAC's paper ribbon **lay** at my feet.* (line 227)

When the verb *lie* means "to tell an untruth," it is intransitive and regular. Its present participle is *lying*, its past tense is *lied*, and its past participle is *lied*.

> *"Indestructible. Lasts forever," I **lied**.* (line 183)

When the verb *lay* means "to place or set down," it is transitive and irregular. Its present participle is *laying*, its past tense is *laid*, and its past participle is *laid*.

> *Every year, I **lay** a bouquet of flowers on EPICAC's grave.*

Exercise 1

Complete the sentences with the correct form of *lie* or *lay*.

1. Pat _____ down her pen and read the poem with amazement.

2. "I'm not _____ to you," the narrator protested. "I've never _____ to you. I really want to marry you."

3. Pat said she would give him an answer after she _____ down for a few hours.

4. After _____ down a challenge as to who was smarter—man or machine—EPICAC solved the math problem in an instant.

5. EPICAC left all his ribbons _____ on the floor when he self-destructed.

Exercise 2

Work with a partner and identify the difference between the following commonly confused words in English. If necessary, use a dictionary to help you.

1. **a.** complement
   b. compliment

2. **a.** principal
   b. principle

3. **a.** loose
   b. lose

4. **a.** raise
   b. rise

5. **a.** accept
   b. except

6. **a.** affect
   b. effect

7. **a.** passed
   b. past

8. **a.** allusion
   b. illusion

Exercise 3

Complete each of the following sentences with the correct word in parentheses.

1. My friend received a _____ on her excellent cooking, but she regretted not serving a red wine to _____ the meal. (complement/compliment)

2. The _____ called a meeting to discuss how to teach students to be people of _____. (principal/principle)

3. Don't _____ the instructions on how to tighten a _____ wire. (loose/lose)

4. If you want to _____ in your career, you need to _____ your profile in the company. (raise/rise)

5. It's hard to _____ that EPICAC was made for war, but no one _____ me will ever know about his softer side. (accept, except)

6. This problem could _____ many people in the near future. We hope that the government will _____ the necessary reforms to fix it. (affect/effect)

7. What has _____ between us today will remain forever in the _____. (passed/past)

8. He isn't under the _____ that his wife married him for love. However, any _____ to money makes him uncomfortable. (allusion/illusion)

IDIOMS CONTAINING BODY PARTS

Many idioms contain references to parts of the body. Idiomatic language is figurative, so you can't usually deduce its meaning from the individual words. For example, when the narrator programmed EPICAC to solve a new military problem, *his heart wasn't in it* (line 89), meaning that he was very unenthusiastic about the project.

Exercise 4

Look at the idioms containing body parts in the following list. They all appear in the story. First, explain their meaning. Then complete the sentences that follow with the correct idiom or figurative expression. You may need to change the expression slightly to fit the sentence.

all hearts and flowers (lines 70–71)

"Sweep me off my feet." (lines 77–78)

with a full heart (line 125)

cleared my throat (line 144)

out of his head (line 219)

tongue-lashing (line 226)

1. Pat said to the narrator, _____.

2. EPICAC was _____ as he wrote his love poetry for Pat.

3. At the end, EPICAC went _____ and self-destructed.

4. When he heard what happened to EPICAC, the narrator admitted _____ that he had acted wrongly.

5. The young mathematician _____ in embarrassment as he declared his love for Pat.

6. The narrator received a _____ from his bosses when they discovered the destroyed computer.

Exercise 5

Work with a partner and try to guess the meaning of the following idioms containing body parts. Check your answers in a dictionary.

1. You will never win this court case. You don't have *a leg to stand on*.

2. Don't give up. I'm certain that help is *at hand*.

3. You really *put your foot in your mouth* when you asked him about his wife. I heard she's been arrested for shoplifting.

4. The spoiled teenagers *looked down their noses* at anyone who didn't dress in the latest fashion.

5. She is a woman who is able to *twist men around her little finger*.

6. The dying man's children couldn't *see eye to eye* about the will.

7. The dictator cruelly *turned a deaf ear* to the pleas of his subjects.

8. He put his *heart and soul* into training for the Olympic Games.

9. Although the stranded campers called *at the top of their lungs*, the search party didn't hear them.

10. Students frequently *pick each other's brains* when they are uncertain what to write in their term papers.

Exercise 6

As a class, share other idioms you know containing body parts.

1. Write a two-page essay considering the potentially dehumanizing effects of advanced technology. You might consider, for example, whether the "smart bombs" used in computerized warfare today help minimize people's reactions to their destructive potential; or whether a society increasingly reliant on machinery is in danger of losing its soul; or where advances in genetic engineering and cloning are leading. In your conclusion, say what society should do to protect itself from the negative consequences of modern technology.

2. "EPICAC" is a love story with a twist. Write your own short story in which at least one of the central characters is an unlikely lover. Your protagonist(s) may be human or nonhuman—perhaps it is age, looks, social status, or extraterrestrial origin that is the barrier. Narrate your story in the first person, and describe the characters and situation as vividly as possible. If appropriate, use some colloquialisms. End your story with a sense of whether this love affair might succeed.

3. Alfred Tennyson, the British Victorian poet, wrote:

'Tis better to have loved and lost

Than never to have loved at all.

Write a two-page essay commenting on the idea expressed in this couplet. Say whether you agree or disagree with the sentiment. Give reasons for your answer, drawing from real life and fiction, and include something about EPICAC's ill-fated love for Pat. In your conclusion, say how personal experience has influenced your thoughts on the subject.

4. The famous French play *Cyrano de Bergerac* by Edmond Rostand (1897), which has been made into two excellent movies, has elements similar to "EPICAC." In the play, the hero, Cyrano, who is brave, intelligent, and eloquent, secretly loves his beautiful cousin, Roxane. However, he feels unable to woo her because he has a disfiguringly large nose. Instead, he expresses his love through the letters he writes for his rival, Christian, who passes them off as his own, thus winning Roxane for himself. Sadly, it is only on Cyrano's deathbed that Roxane finally discovers the truth. Choose a novel, play, or movie that has a lie at its heart, and in a short essay summarize its plot. In your conclusion, discuss the ethics of the situation, and say what you thought of the deception.

14 ～ Like a Winding Sheet

Ann Petry
(1908–1997)

Born into an African-American family, Ann Petry grew up in the mainly white community of Old Saybrook, Connecticut. Although the family was middle class and reasonably well off, Petry was exposed to racism from an early age and has recalled many of the incidents in her writing. After working as a pharmacist for seven years, she married and went to live in Harlem, a large African-American neighborhood in New York City, where she began her writing career. As a journalist there, she learned at close hand about the struggle for survival faced by urban blacks.

Petry's best-selling first novel, *The Street* (1946), catapulted her to fame. It was followed by *Country Place* (1947) and *The Narrows* (1953); the story collection *Miss Muriel and Other Stories* (1971); as well as children's books and historical biographies. Petry's writing focuses on the troubled relationships between blacks and whites. Her story "Like a Winding Sheet" received critical acclaim and was included in Martha Foley's *Best American Short Stories of 1946*.

Like a Winding Sheet[1]

The accumulated stress of living in a racist society takes a terrible toll on a factory worker.

He had planned to get up before Mae did and surprise her by fixing breakfast.[2] Instead he went back to sleep and she got out of bed so quietly he didn't know she wasn't there beside him until he woke up and heard the queer soft gurgle[3] of water running out
5 of the sink in the bathroom.

He knew he ought to get up but instead he put his arms across his forehead to shut the afternoon sunlight out of his eyes, pulled his legs up close to his body, testing them to see if the ache was still in them.

Mae had finished in the bathroom. He could tell because she never
10 closed the door when she was in there and now the sweet smell of talcum powder was drifting down the hall and into the bedroom. Then he heard her coming down the hall.

"Hi, babe," she said affectionately.

"Hum," he grunted, and moved his arms away from his head,
15 opened one eye.

"It's a nice morning."

"Yeah." He rolled over and the sheet twisted around him, outlining his thighs, his chest. "You mean afternoon, don't ya?"

Mae looked at the twisted sheet and giggled. "Looks like a winding
20 sheet," she said. "A shroud—" Laughter tangled with her words and she had to pause for a moment before she could continue. "You look like a huckleberry[4]—in a winding sheet—"

"That's no way to talk. Early in the day like this," he protested.

He looked at his arms silhouetted against the white of the sheets.
25 They were inky black by contrast and he had to smile in spite of himself and he lay there smiling and savoring[5] the sweet sound of Mae's giggling.

"Early?" She pointed a finger at the alarm clock on the table near the bed and giggled again. "It's almost four o'clock. And if you don't
30 spring up out of there, you're going to be late again."

"What do you mean 'again'?"

"Twice last week. Three times the week before. And once the week before and—"

"I can't get used to sleeping in the daytime," he said fretfully. He
35 pushed his legs out from under the covers experimentally. Some of the

---

1 **winding sheet** a sheet in which a dead body is wrapped
2 **fixing breakfast** making breakfast
3 **gurgle** the bubbling sound of running water
4 **huckleberry** a dark blue-black berry
5 **savoring** enjoying

ache had gone out of them but they weren't really rested yet. "It's too light for good sleeping. And all that standing beats the hell out of my legs."[6]

"After two years you oughta be used to it," Mae said.

40 He watched her as she fixed her hair, powdered her face, slipped into a pair of blue denim overalls. She moved quickly and yet she didn't seem to hurry.

"You look like you'd had plenty of sleep," he said lazily. He had to get up but he kept putting the moment off, not wanting to move, yet he 45 didn't dare let his legs go completely limp[7] because if he did he'd go back to sleep. It was getting later and later but the thought of putting his weight on his legs kept him lying there.

When he finally got up he had to hurry, and he gulped his breakfast so fast that he wondered if his stomach could possibly use food thrown 50 at it at such a rate of speed. He was still wondering about it as he and Mae were putting their coats on in the hall.

Mae paused to look at the calendar. "It's the thirteenth," she said. Then a faint excitement in her voice, "Why, it's Friday the thirteenth."[8] She had one arm in her coat sleeve and she held it there while she 55 stared at the calendar. "I oughta stay home," she said. "I shouldn't go outa the house."

"Aw, don't be a fool," he said. "Today's payday. And payday is a good luck day everywhere, any way you look at it." And as she stood hesitating he said, "Aw, come on."

60 And he was late for work again because they spent fifteen minutes arguing before he could convince her she ought to go to work just the same. He had to talk persuasively, urging her gently, and it took time. But he couldn't bring himself to talk to her roughly or threaten to strike her like a lot of men might have done. He wasn't made that way.

65 So when he reached the plant he was late and he had to wait to punch the time clock[9] because the day-shift workers were streaming out in long lines, in groups and bunches that impeded[10] his progress.

Even now just starting his workday his legs ached. He had to force himself to struggle past the outgoing workers, punch the time clock, 70 and get the little cart he pushed around all night, because he kept toying with[11] the idea of going home and getting back in bed.

He pushed the cart out on the concrete floor, thinking that if this was his plant he'd make a lot of changes in it. There were too many standing-up jobs for one thing. He'd figure out some way most of 'em 75 could be done sitting down and he'd put a lot more benches around.

---

6 **beats the hell out of my legs** hurts my legs badly
7 **go limp** relax
8 **Friday the thirteenth** an unlucky day (superstition)

9 **punch the time clock** register on a special clock the time of one's arrival and departure
10 **impeded** blocked
11 **toying with** considering (but not seriously)

And this job he had—this job that forced him to walk ten hours a night, pushing this little cart, well, he'd turn it into a sitting-down job. One of those little trucks they used around railroad stations would be good for a job like this. Guys sat on a seat and the thing moved easily, taking up
80 little room and turning in hardly any space at all, like on a dime.[12]

He pushed the cart near the foreman. He never could remember to refer to her as the forelady even in his mind. It was funny to have a white woman for a boss in a plant like this one.

She was sore about[13] something. He could tell by the way her face
85 was red and her eyes were half-shut until they were slits.[14] Probably been out late and didn't get enough sleep. He avoided looking at her and hurried a little, head down, as he passed her though he couldn't resist stealing a glance at her out of the corner of his eye. He saw the edge of the light-colored slacks she wore and the tip end of a big tan shoe.
90 "Hey, Johnson!" the woman said.

The machines had started full blast.[15] The whirr and the grinding[16] made the building shake, made it impossible to hear conversations. The men and women at the machines talked to each other but looking at them from just a little distance away, they appeared to be simply
95 moving their lips because you couldn't hear what they were saying. Yet the woman's voice cut across the machine sounds—harsh, angry.

He turned his head slowly. "Good evenin', Mrs. Scott," he said, and waited.

"You're late again."
100 "That's right. My legs were bothering me."

The woman's face grew redder, angrier looking. "Half this shift comes in late," she said. "And you're the worst one of all. You're always late. Whatsa matter with ya?"

"It's my legs," he said. "Somehow they don't ever get rested. I don't
105 seem to get used to sleeping days. And I just can't get started."

"Excuses. You guys always got excuses," her anger grew and spread. "Every guy comes in here late always has an excuse. His wife's sick or his grandmother died or somebody in the family had to go to the hospital," she paused, drew a deep breath. "And the niggers[17] is
110 the worse. I don't care what's wrong with your legs. You get in here on time. I'm sick of you niggers—"

"You got the right to get mad," he interrupted softly. "You got the right to cuss me four ways to Sunday[18] but I ain't letting nobody call me a nigger."

---

12 **turning . . . on a dime** turning accurately in a very small space
13 **sore about** angry at (colloquialism)
14 **slits** narrow openings
15 **full blast** at full speed

16 **whirr and grinding** loud noises made by a machine
17 **niggers** an insulting reference to black people
18 **cuss me four ways to Sunday** curse me in every possible way (slang)

115 He stepped closer to her. His fists were doubled. His lips were drawn back in a thin narrow line. A vein in his forehead stood out swollen, thick.

And the woman backed away from him, not hurriedly but slowly—two, three steps back.

120 "Aw, forget it," she said. "I didn't mean nothing by it. It slipped out.[19] It was an accident." The red of her face deepened until the small blood vessels in her cheeks were purple. "Go on and get to work," she urged. And she took three more slow backward steps.

He stood motionless for a moment and then turned away from 125 the sight of the red lipstick on her mouth that made him remember that the foreman was a woman. And he couldn't bring himself to hit a woman.[20] He felt a curious tingling[21] in his fingers and he looked down at his hands. They were clenched[22] tight, hard, ready to smash some of those small purple veins in her face.

130 He pushed the cart ahead of him, walking slowly. When he turned his head, she was staring in his direction, mopping[23] her forehead with a dark blue handkerchief. Their eyes met and then they both looked away.

He didn't glance in her direction again but moved past the long 135 work benches, carefully collecting the finished parts, going slowly and steadily up and down, and back and forth the length of the building, and as he walked he forced himself to swallow his anger, get rid of it.

And he succeeded so that he was able to think about what had happened without getting upset about it. An hour went by but the 140 tension stayed in his hands. They were clenched and knotted on the handles of the cart as though ready to aim a blow.

And he thought he should have hit her anyway, smacked her hard in the face, felt the soft flesh of her face give under the hardness of his hands. He tried to make his hands relax by offering them a description 145 of what it would have been like to strike her because he had the queer feeling that his hands were not exactly a part of him anymore—they had developed a separate life of their own over which he had no control. So he dwelt on[24] the pleasure his hands would have felt—both of them cracking at her, first one and then the other. If he had done that 150 his hands would have felt good now—relaxed, rested.

And he decided that even if he'd lost his job for it, he should have let her have it[25] and it would have been a long time, maybe the rest of her life, before she called anybody else a nigger.

---

19 **It slipped out.** The word was spoken unintentionally.
20 **he couldn't bring himself** he was unable to force himself to do something unpleasant
21 **tingling** a prickly sensation
22 **clenched** tightly closed
23 **mopping** wiping
24 **dwelt on** concentrated on
25 **he should have let her have it** he should have hit her (slang)

The only trouble was he couldn't hit a woman. A woman couldn't
155 hit back the same way a man did. But it would have been a deeply
satisfying thing to have cracked her narrow lips wide open with just
one blow, beautifully timed and with all his weight in back of it. That
way he would have gotten rid of all the energy and tension his anger
had created in him. He kept remembering how his heart had started
160 pumping blood so fast he had felt it tingle even in the tips of his fingers.
With the approach of night, fatigue nibbled[26] at him. The corners
of his mouth drooped,[27] the frown between his eyes deepened, his
shoulders sagged; but his hands stayed tight and tense. As the hours
dragged by[28] he noticed that the women workers had started to snap and
165 snarl[29] at each other. He couldn't hear what they said because of the
sound of machines but he could see the quick lip movements that sent
words tumbling from the sides of their mouths. They gestured
irritably with their hands and scowled[30] as their mouths moved.
Their violent jerky motions told him that it was getting close on to
170 quitting time but somehow he felt that the night still stretched ahead of
him, composed of endless hours of steady walking on his aching legs.
When the whistle finally blew he went on pushing the cart, unable to
believe that it had sounded. The whirring of the machines died away
to a murmur and he knew then that he'd really heard the whistle. He
175 stood still for a moment, filled with a relief that made him sigh.
Then he moved briskly, putting the cart in the storeroom, hurrying
to take his place in the line forming before the paymaster. That was
another thing he'd change, he thought. He'd have the pay envelopes
handed to the people right at their benches so there wouldn't be ten
180 or fifteen minutes lost waiting for the pay. He always got home about
fifteen minutes late on payday. They did it better in the plant where
Mae worked, brought the money right to them at their benches.
He stuck his pay envelope in his pants' pocket and followed the
line of workers heading for the subway in a slow-moving stream. He
185 glanced up at the sky. It was a nice night, the sky looked packed full
to running over with stars. And he thought if he and Mae would go
right to bed when they got home from work they'd catch a few hours
of darkness for sleeping. But they never did. They fooled around[31]—
cooking and eating and listening to the radio and he always stayed in
190 a big chair in the living room and went almost but not quite to sleep
and when they finally got to bed it was five or six in the morning and
daylight was already seeping around the edges of the sky.

---

26 **fatigue nibbled at him** he felt more and
more tired
27 **drooped** turned down
28 **dragged by** passed very slowly

29 **snap and snarl** speak angrily
30 **scowled** made angry faces
31 **fooled around** wasted time

He walked slowly, putting off the moment when he would have
to plunge into the crowd hurrying toward the subway. It was a long
195 ride to Harlem and tonight the thought of it appalled[32] him. He paused
outside an all-night restaurant to kill time,[33] so that some of the first
rush of workers would be gone when he reached the subway.

The lights in the restaurant were brilliant, enticing.[34] There was life
and motion inside. And as he looked through the window he thought
200 that everything within range of his eyes gleamed—the long imitation
marble counter, the tall stools, the white porcelain-topped tables and
especially the big metal coffee urn right near the window. Steam issued
from its top and a gas flame flickered under it—a lively, dancing, blue
flame.
205 A lot of the workers from his shift—men and women—were lining
up near the coffee urn. He watched them walk to the porcelain-topped
tables carrying steaming cups of coffee and he saw that just the smell
of the coffee lessened the fatigue lines in their faces. After the first sip
their faces softened, they smiled, they began to talk and laugh.
210 On a sudden impulse he shoved the door open and joined the line
in front of the coffee urn. The line moved slowly. And as he stood there
the smell of the coffee, the sound of the laughter and of the voices,
helped dull the sharp ache in his legs.

He didn't pay any attention to the white girl who was serving the
215 coffee at the urn. He kept looking at the cups in the hands of the men
who had been ahead of him. Each time a man stepped out of the line
with one of the thick white cups, the fragrant steam got in his nostrils.
He saw that they walked carefully so as not to spill a single drop. There
was a froth of bubbles at the top of each cup and he thought about how
220 he would let the bubbles break against his lips before he actually took a
big deep swallow.

Then it was his turn. "A cup of coffee," he said, just as he had heard
the others say.

The white girl looked past him, put her hands up to her head and
225 gently lifted her hair away from the back of her neck, tossing her head
back a little.

"No more coffee for a while," she said.

He wasn't certain he'd heard her correctly and he said "What?"
blankly.
230 "No more coffee for a while," she repeated.

There was silence behind him and then uneasy movement. He
thought someone would say something, ask why or protest, but there
was only silence and then a faint shuffling sound as though the men

---

32 **appalled** sickened
33 **kill time** let the time pass while not doing
    anything important

34 **enticing** inviting

standing behind him had simultaneously shifted their weight from one
235 foot to the other.

He looked at the girl without saying anything. He felt his hands
begin to tingle and the tingling went all the way down to his finger tips
so that he glanced down at them. They were clenched tight, hard, into
fists. Then he looked at the girl again. What he wanted to do was to
240 hit her so hard that the scarlet lipstick on her mouth would smear and
spread over her nose, her chin, out toward her cheeks, so hard that she
would never toss her head again and refuse a man a cup of coffee
because he was black.

He estimated the distance across the counter and reached forward,
245 balancing his weight on the balls of his feet, ready to let the blow go.
And then his hands fell back down to his sides because he forced
himself to lower them, to unclench them and make them dangle[35]
loose. The effort took his breath away because his hands fought against
him. But he couldn't hit her. He couldn't even now bring himself to hit
250 a woman, not even this one, who had refused him a cup of coffee with
a toss of her head. He kept seeing the gesture with which she had lifted
the length of her blond hair from the back of her neck as expressive of
her contempt for him.

When he went out the door he didn't look back. If he had he would
255 have seen the flickering blue flame under the shiny coffee urn being
extinguished.[36] The line of men who had stood behind him lingered[37] a
moment to watch the people drinking coffee at the tables and then they
left just as he had without having had the coffee they wanted so badly.
The girl behind the counter poured water in the urn and swabbed
260 it out[38] and as she waited for the water to run out, she lifted her hair
gently from the back of her neck and tossed her head before she began
making a fresh lot of coffee.

But he had walked away without a backward look, his head down,
his hands in his pockets, raging at himself and whatever it was inside
265 of him that had forced him to stand quiet and still when he wanted to
strike out.

The subway was crowded and he had to stand. He tried grasping
an overhead strap and his hands were too tense to grip it. So he moved
near the train door and stood there swaying back and forth with the
270 rocking of the train. The roar of the train beat inside his head, making
it ache and throb, and the pain in his legs clawed up into his groin so
that he seemed to be bursting with pain and he told himself that it was
due to all that anger-born energy that had piled up in him and not been
used and so it had spread through him like a poison—from his feet and
275 legs all the way up to his head.

---

35 **dangle** hang loosely
36 **extinguished** put out

37 **lingered** stayed behind
38 **swabbed it out** cleaned it out

Mae was in the house before he was. He knew she was home before he put the key in the door of the apartment. The radio was going. She had it turned up loud and she was singing along with it.

"Hello, babe," she called out, as soon as he opened the door.

280 He tried to say "hello" and it came out half grunt and half sigh.

"You sure sound cheerful," she said.

She was in the bedroom and he went and leaned against the doorjamb. The denim overalls she wore to work were carefully draped over the back of a chair by the bed. She was standing in front of the
285 dresser, tying the sash of a yellow housecoat around her waist and chewing gum vigorously as she admired her reflection in the mirror over the dresser.

"Whatsa matter?" she said. "You get bawled out[39] by the boss or somep'n?"

290 "Just tired," he said slowly. "For God's sake, do you have to crack that gum like that?"

"You don't have to lissen to me," she said complacently.[40] She patted a curl in place near the side of her head and then lifted her hair away from the back of her neck, ducking her head forward and
295 then back.

He winced[41] away from the gesture. "What you got to be always fooling with your hair for?" he protested.

"Say, what's the matter with you anyway?" She turned away from the mirror to face him, put her hands on her hips. "You ain't been in the
300 house two minutes and you're picking on me."[42]

He didn't answer her because her eyes were angry and he didn't want to quarrel with her. They'd been married too long and got along too well and so he walked all the way into the room and sat down in the chair by the bed and stretched his legs out in front of him, putting
305 his weight on the heels of his shoes, leaning way back in the chair, not saying anything.

"Lissen," she said sharply. "I've got to wear those overalls again tomorrow. You're going to get them all wrinkled up[43] leaning against them like that."

310 He didn't move. He was too tired and his legs were throbbing[44] now that he had sat down. Besides the overalls were already wrinkled and dirty, he thought. They couldn't help but be[45] for she'd worn them all week. He leaned farther back in the chair.

"Come on, get up," she ordered.

---

39 **get bawled out** be severely criticized (informal)
40 **complacently** with much self-satisfaction
41 **winced** made a quick facial movement of pain
42 **picking on me** criticizing me
43 **wrinkled up** creased, looking unironed
44 **throbbing** hurting badly
45 **They couldn't help but be** They would have to be

315   "Oh, what the hell,"[46] he said wearily, and got up from the chair. "I'd just as soon live in a subway.[47] There'd be just as much place to sit down."

     He saw that her sense of humor was struggling with her anger. But her sense of humor won because she giggled.

320   "Aw, come on and eat," she said. There was a coaxing[48] note in her voice. "You're nothing but an old hungry nigger trying to act tough and—" she paused to giggle and then continued, "You—"

     He had always found her giggling pleasant and deliberately said things that might amuse her and then waited, listening for the delicate

325 sound to emerge from her throat. This time he didn't even hear the giggle. He didn't let her finish what she was saying. She was standing close to him and that funny tingling started in his finger tips, went fast up his arms and sent his fist shooting straight for her face.

     There was the smacking sound of soft flesh being struck by a hard

330 object and it wasn't until she screamed that he realized he had hit her in the mouth—so hard that the dark red lipstick had blurred and spread over her full lips, reaching up toward the tip of her nose, down toward her chin, out toward her cheeks.

     The knowledge that he had struck her seeped through him slowly

335 and he was appalled but he couldn't drag his hands away from her face. He kept striking her and he thought with horror that something inside him was holding him, binding him to this act, wrapping and twisting about him so that he had to continue it. He had lost all control over his hands. And he groped for[49] a phrase, a word, something to

340 describe what this thing was like that was happening to him and he thought it was like being enmeshed[50] in a winding sheet—that was it— like a winding sheet. And even as the thought formed in his mind, his hands reached for her face again and yet again.

---

46 **what the hell** what difference does it make? (slang exclamation)

47 **I'd just as soon live in a subway.** I'd prefer living in a subway.

48 **coaxing** pleading

49 **groped for** searched for

50 **enmeshed** trapped

A Thinking About the Story

Discuss the following questions with a partner.

> Did you predict that the story would end so badly? Were you able to sympathize with Mr. Johnson at the end? Give reasons for your answers.

B Understanding the Plot

Be prepared to answer the following questions with a partner or your class.

1. What kind of relationship do Mae and her husband have at the start of the story? Illustrate your answer with concrete examples.
2. What does Mae say Mr. Johnson looks like when he is lying in bed? Explain the comparison.
3. How does Mr. Johnson feel about working the night shift?
4. In what way is Mae superstitious?
5. What is offensive about the forewoman's behavior to Mr. Johnson? Explain fully.
6. Why doesn't Mr. Johnson hit the forewoman even though he desperately wants to?
7. What aspects of Mr. Johnson's job increase his stress? List as many as possible.
8. Which part of Mr. Johnson's body is most closely associated with his suppressed rage?
9. Why does Mr. Johnson delay going home?
10. Where do Mae and Mr. Johnson live?
11. Why doesn't the girl serve coffee to Mr. Johnson? What does he think the reason is?
12. What final act of the day causes Mr. Johnson to snap and beat up Mae?

A Exploring Themes

Reread "Like a Winding Sheet." As you read, consider how Mr. Johnson's daily encounters with racism influence his reactions in each scene.

1. What is the significance of the title to the central theme of the story?

2. What details connect the three women in the story? Why are these similarities important? Why does Mr. Johnson hit his wife instead of one of the other two women?

3. How does the story serve as a critique of factory working conditions?

4. Explain how the reference to Mr. Johnson's anger being "like a poison" (line 274) contributes to our understanding of his actions.

B Analyzing Style

DIALECT

Dialect is speech that differs from the standard, accepted form of a language. It usually corresponds to groups of people defined by geographical location, social class, race, or age. A dialect may include particular words and expressions, grammatical forms, and pronunciation.

The dialogue in "Like a Winding Sheet" makes liberal use of New York working-class dialect, in which words are often changed, left out, or elided (joined). By using colloquial language in this way, Petry reinforces the authenticity of her characters and establishes their social class, as well as their prejudices. For example, when Mr. Johnson remarks that the forewoman was *sore about something* (line 84), it could be more formally rephrased as she was *angry about something*. Later the forewoman snaps, *"Whatsa matter with ya?"* (line 103), which can be rewritten in standard English as *"What's the matter with you?"*.

Exercise 1

Rewrite the following language used in the text in more formal English, correcting the grammatical errors.

1. "After two years you oughta be used to it," Mae said. (line 39)

2. "I shouldn't go outa the house." (lines 55–56)

3. "Every guy comes in here late always has an excuse." (line 107)

4. "And the niggers is the worse." (lines 109–110)

5. "You got the right to cuss me four ways to Sunday but I ain't letting nobody call me a nigger." (lines 112–114)

6. "Aw, forget it," she said. "I didn't mean nothing by it." (line 120)

Exercise 2

Work with a partner and find at least three more examples of colloquial language in the story.

IMAGERY

The restaurant scene (lines 198–221) in "Like a Winding Sheet" is packed with distinctive **images,** or verbal pictures, that engage the senses (taste, touch, sight, hearing, and smell).

> He watched them walk to the porcelain-topped tables carrying steaming cups of coffee . . . (lines 206–207)

In this one sentence, Petry conveys numerous sensory images: the cool shining table tops (touch and sight), the heat and aroma from the steaming cups (touch and smell), and the rich taste of the freshly brewed coffee (taste and smell). For a more extensive discussion of imagery, see page 135.

Exercise 3

Reread lines 198–221 carefully. Then say which senses are appealed to in each of the following sentences.

1. The lights in the restaurant were brilliant, enticing. (line 198)
2. Steam issued from its top and a gas flame flickered under it—a lively, dancing, blue flame. (lines 202–204)
3. And as he stood there the smell of the coffee, the sound of the laughter and of the voices, helped dull the sharp ache in his legs. (lines 211–213)
4. Each time a man stepped out of the line with one of the thick white cups, the fragrant steam got in his nostrils. (lines 216–217)
5. There was a froth of bubbles at the top of each cup and he thought about how he would let the bubbles break against his lips before he actually took a big deep swallow. (lines 218–221)

C Judging for Yourself

Express yourself as personally as you like in your answers to the following questions.

1. Do you blame Mr. Johnson for finally boiling over and attacking his wife? What other options were open to him for dealing with his anger?
2. What effect on the Johnsons' marriage do you think their work schedules have?
3. How do you think city life affects Mr. Johnson?
4. In your view, can Mae ever forgive her husband?

D Making Connections

Answer the following questions in a small group.

1. Is there a tendency in your country to resolve disputes by violence?
2. Are many women beaten by their husbands, fathers, or boyfriends in your country? How does society view such acts? Are there shelters women can go to in order to escape domestic violence?
3. What are factory conditions like where you live? Is there an attempt to humanize life for the workers?
4. Which groups of people are discriminated against in your society? What is the discrimination based on—race, gender, caste, religion, or other categories?
5. Is Friday the thirteenth considered an unlucky date in your culture? What other numbers have a positive or negative significance?

E Debate

Decide whether you are for or against the following statement. Be prepared to argue your case in a class debate.

Violence is never justified.

ADVERBIAL CLAUSES

An **adverbial clause** is a dependent clause introduced by a subordinating conjunction such as *when, where, after, because, in order that, if, unless,* or *although.* Since it is a dependent clause, it cannot stand alone in a sentence, but must be attached to an independent (main) clause. Like all clauses, it has its own subject and verb. Adverbial clauses may be grouped into categories of time, place, reason, result, condition, and concession.

1. An **adverbial clause of time** starts with a subordinating conjunction such as *before, after, when, as, until,* or *as soon as.*

   He had planned to get up **before Mae did** and surprise her by fixing breakfast. (lines 1–2)

   As the hours dragged by he noticed that the women workers had started to snap and snarl at each other. (lines 163–165)

2. An **adverbial clause of place** starts with a subordinating conjunction such as *where* or *wherever.*

   He wished the factory bosses would put their paychecks **where their workbenches stood.**

3. An **adverbial clause of reason** starts with a subordinating conjunction such as *because, since,* or *as.*

> . . . *they appeared to be simply moving their lips **because you couldn't hear** what they were saying.* (lines 94–95)

4. An **adverbial clause of result** starts with *so that, so . . . that,* or *such . . . that.*

> . . . *the pain in his legs clawed up into his groin **so that he seemed to be bursting with pain** . . .* (lines 271–272)

This sentence could be rewritten as follows:

> *The pain in his legs was **so great that he seemed to be bursting with pain**.*

5. An **adverbial clause of condition** starts with a subordinating conjunction such as *if, provided that, unless,* or *whether or not.* (See pages 245–246 for more information on conditionals.)

> *"And **if you don't spring up out of there,** you're going to be late again."* (lines 29–30)

If you use the verb *to be* in an unreal condition, use *were* for all persons in the conditional clause.

> *"**If I were you,** I'd get up quickly or you'll be late."*

6. An **adverbial clause of concession** starts with a subordinating conjunction such as *although, though,* or *whereas.*

> *He avoided looking at her and hurried a little, head down, as he passed her **though he couldn't resist stealing a glance at her out of the corner of his eye**.* (lines 86–88)

Exercise 1

In the following sentences, underline the adverbial clause and write what kind of clause it is (time, place, reason, result, condition, or concession).

1. And he was late for work again because they spent fifteen minutes arguing … (lines 60–61) _____

2. If he had done that, his hands would have felt good now—relaxed, rested. (lines 149–150) _____

3. What he wanted to do was hit her so hard that the scarlet lipstick on her mouth would smear and spread over her nose . . . (lines 239–241) _____

4. "Hello babe," she called out, as soon as he opened the door. (line 279) _____

5. Although Mae was exhausted at the end of the day, she always folded her clothes neatly over the chair. _____

6. Wherever he went that day, he was haunted by his tingling hands. _____

PUNCTUATION OF ADVERBIAL CLAUSES

Punctuating adverbial clauses can be tricky. Comma placement depends on whether the independent clause or the adverbial clause comes first. It is important to be aware that not all authors follow the punctuation rules for adverbial clauses. However, it is good practice for you to use these rules in your own writing.

- If the adverbial clause comes after the independent clause, no commas are used to set it off.

   *Mae was in the house **before he was**.* (line 276)

- If the adverbial clause precedes the independent clause, a comma is used to set it off.

   ***Before he reached the house**, Mae had already arrived and was preparing dinner.*

Exercise 2

The following sentences are all related to the plot of "Like a Winding Sheet." Complete them with adverbial clauses that would be appropriate to the story and add punctuation where necessary. Use a different kind of adverbial clause in each sentence.

1. _____ he was unable to hit the two women.

2. He managed to control his explosive anger _____ _____.

3. Mae put her overalls _____.

4. _____ he would reform many of the working conditions in the factory.

5. He felt so insulted by the women _____ and _____.

6. Mae was annoyed with him _____.

Exercise 3

Write six sentences of your own with one adverbial clause from each category, using the correct punctuation.

SYNONYMS

A **synonym** is a word or phrase that means the same or nearly the same as another word or phrase. For example, *sick* (line 108) can be replaced by *ill, unhealthy*, or *unwell*, among many options. Learning synonyms will add variety to your English, so you don't use the same word over and over.

Exercise

Complete each of the following sentences with a suitable synonym from the list below. Both the italicized word and its synonym appear in the story. You may need to change the tense or form of the word.

bunch	strike	sag	snarl
rock	froth	twist	knot

1. He stood *swaying* and _____ in the subway train as it rushed toward Harlem.

2. She was so tired after a hard day's work that her shoulders *drooped* and _____ as she collapsed into the chair.

3. The workers in the factory would *snap* and _____ at each other toward the end of the day.

4. He saw the people in the restaurant standing in *groups* or _____ as they waited for the coffee to be poured.

5. He could feel his poisonous anger *wrapping* and _____ around him as he struggled to control himself.

6. His hands were *clenched* and _____ after the forewoman insulted him.

7. The coffee looked so enticing with the steaming *bubbles* and _____ .

8. He felt himself *smack* and _____ her over and over, but he could do nothing about it.

1. Write a two-page essay discussing domestic abuse in your country. Consider what forms abuse can take, such as verbal insults as well as physical violence. Explain who the chief victims are and who usually inflicts the violence. Analyze the reasons for this behavior. In your conclusion, say whether the victims are treated sympathetically by society. Try to include some adverbial clauses in your writing.

2. Imagine that you are extremely hungry and for some reason you cannot satisfy your craving to eat. Write two to three paragraphs in which you either see or imagine the food you desperately want. Use the story's restaurant scene, with its intensely evocative imagery, as a model to convey your situation, as well as your feelings at the time. Make clear in your writing why you are unable to eat immediately.

3. Write a dialogue between Mae and her husband five hours after the beating takes place. Have them speak frankly to each other about what happened and the reasons for it. According to the way the dialogue is constructed, convey whether their relationship can be saved or not.

4. Novels such as *The Color Purple* by Alice Walker and *The Joy Luck Club* by Amy Tan both deal with, among other themes, the anguish of domestic violence. Write an essay of one or two pages on a book you have read or a movie you have seen in which a woman or child is subject to violence from a husband, father, or boyfriend. Describe the relationship and analyze the reasons for this situation. Does the victim try to do anything about this abuse? Say what happens.

15 ❧ A Drink in the Passage

Alan Paton
(1903–1988)

Born in South Africa, Alan Paton graduated from university with a degree in physics. He taught at a high school until moving to Johannesburg in 1935, where he became the principal of a reform school for troubled black youth. There he introduced changes designed to reintegrate the boys into society. While visiting prisons and reformatories in Europe, Paton began writing his most famous novel, *Cry the Beloved Country*, published in 1948. The subject of the book was controversial, as it examined a friendship across racial lines. Soon after its publication, the Afrikaner-dominated Nationalist Party won the general elections in South Africa and inaugurated the repressive apartheid era.

Despite government harassment, Paton continued to write and live a fully political life. He was one of the founders of the opposition Liberal Party, which demanded equality between the races until it was forced to dissolve in 1968 by the Nationalist government. He wrote two more political novels, *Too Late the Phalarope* (1953) and *Ah, but Your Land Is Beautiful* (1981), as well as the book of short stories *Tales from a Troubled Land* (1961), essays, and two autobiographies. Paton died shortly before the end of racial segregation in South Africa and the election of Nelson Mandela as the country's first black president.

A Drink in the Passage

A chance encounter in a divided country leaves two men feeling shaken.

To appreciate "A Drink in the Passage," it is important to understand that from 1948–1994 apartheid, or complete segregation of the races, was written into South African law. This meant that blacks and whites were legally kept apart in many spheres of life—neighborhoods, schools, restaurants, movie theaters, transportation, and so on—and it was virtually impossible to cross these barriers.

In the year 1960 the Union of South Africa celebrated its Golden Jubilee,[1] and there was a nationwide sensation when the one-thousand-pound prize for the finest piece of sculpture was won by a black man, Edward Simelane. His work, *African Mother and Child*, 5 not only excited the admiration, but touched the conscience or heart or whatever it was that responded, of white South Africa, and seemed likely to make him famous in other countries.

It was by an oversight[2] that his work was accepted, for it was the policy of the government that all the celebrations and competitions 10 should be strictly segregated.[3] The committee of the sculpture section received a private reprimand[4] for having been so careless as to omit the words "for whites only" from the conditions, but was told, by a very high personage it is said, that if Simelane's work "was indisputably[5] the best", it should receive the award. The committee then decided that 15 this prize must be given along with the others, at the public ceremony which would bring this particular part of the celebrations to a close.

For this decision it received a surprising amount of support from the white public; but in certain powerful quarters,[6] there was an outcry against any departure from the "traditional policies" of the country, 20 and a threat that many white prize-winners would renounce[7] their prizes. However a crisis was averted, because the sculptor was "unfortunately unable to attend the ceremony."

"I wasn't feeling up to it,"[8] Simelane said mischievously to me. "My parents, and my wife's parents, and our priest, decided that I

---

1 **Golden Jubilee** fiftieth anniversary of South Africa's independence from Britain
2 **oversight** mistake
3 **segregated** separated by race
4 **reprimand** strong criticism

5 **indisputably** without doubt
6 **powerful quarters** influential groups
7 **renounce** refuse to keep
8 **I wasn't feeling up to it** I wasn't feeling well enough

wasn't feeling up to it. And finally I decided so too. Of course Majosi and Sola and the others wanted me to go and get my prize personally, but I said, 'boys, I'm a sculptor, not a demonstrator'."

"This cognac is wonderful," he said, "especially in these big glasses. It's the first time I've had such a glass. It's also the first time I've drunk a brandy so slowly. In Orlando[9] you develop a throat of iron, and you just put back your head and pour it down, in case the police should arrive."

He said to me, "This is the second cognac I've had in my life. Would you like to hear the story of how I had my first?"

You know the Alabaster Bookshop in von Brandis Street? Well, after the competition they asked me if they could exhibit my *African Mother and Child*. They gave a whole window to it, with a white velvet backdrop, if there is anything called white velvet, and some complimentary words.

Well somehow I could never go and look in that window. On my way from the station to the *Herald*[10] office, I sometimes went past there, and I felt good when I saw all the people standing there; but I would only squint at it out of the corner of my eye.

Then one night I was working late at the *Herald*, and when I came out there was hardly anyone in the streets, so I thought I'd go and see the window, and indulge certain pleasurable human feelings. I must have got a little lost in the contemplation[11] of my own genius, because suddenly there was a young white man standing next to me.

He said to me, "What do you think of that, mate?" And you know, one doesn't get called "mate" every day.

"I'm looking at it," I said.

"I live near here," he said, "and I come and look at it nearly every night. You know it's by one of your own boys, don't you? See, Edward Simelane."

"Yes, I know."

"It's beautiful," he said. "Look at that mother's head. She's loving that child, but she's somehow watching too. Do you see that? Like someone guarding. She knows it won't be an easy life."

He cocked his head on one side, to see the thing better.

"He got a thousand pounds for it," he said. "That's a lot of money for one of your boys. But good luck to him. You don't get much luck, do you?"

Then he said confidentially,[12] "Mate, would you like a drink?"

Well honestly I didn't feel like a drink at that time of night, with a white stranger and all, and a train still to catch to Orlando.

---

9 **Orlando** poor, residential township where black people were forced to live
10 *Herald* newspaper name
11 **lost in contemplation** thinking so deeply that I was unaware of anything else
12 **confidentially** secretively

65   "You know we black people must be out of the city by eleven,"
I said.

    "It won't take long. My flat's[13] just round the corner. Do you speak
Afrikaans?"[14]

    "Since I was a child," I said in Afrikaans.

70   "We'll speak Afrikaans then. My English isn't too wonderful. I'm
van Rensburg. And you?"

    I couldn't have told him my name. I said I was Vakalisa, living
in Orlando.

    "Vakalisa, eh? I haven't heard that name before."

75   By this time he had started off, and I was following, but not
willingly. That's my trouble, as you'll soon see. I can't break off an
encounter. We didn't exactly walk abreast,[15] but he didn't exactly walk
in front of me. He didn't look constrained.[16] He wasn't looking round
to see if anyone might be watching.

80   He said to me, "Do you know what I wanted to do?"

    "No," I said.

    "I wanted a bookshop, like that one there. I always wanted that,
ever since I can remember. When I was small, I had a little shop of
my own." He laughed at himself. "Some were real books, of course,
85 but some of them I wrote myself. But I had bad luck. My parents died
before I could finish school."

    Then he said to me, "Are you educated?"

    I said unwillingly, "Yes." Then I thought to myself, how stupid, for
leaving the question open.

90   And sure enough he asked, "Far?"

    And again unwillingly, I said, "Far."

    He took a big leap. "Degree?"

    "Yes."

    "Literature?"

95   "Yes."

    He expelled his breath, and gave a long "ah". We had reached his
building, Majorca Mansions, not one of those luxurious places. I was
glad to see that the entrance lobby was deserted.[17] I wasn't at my ease.
I don't feel at my ease in such places, not unless I am protected by
100 friends, and this man was a stranger. The lift was at ground level,
marked *Whites Only. Slegs vir Blankes.* Van Rensburg opened the door
and waved me in.[18] Was he constrained? To this day I don't know. While
I was waiting for him to press the button, so that we could get moving
and away from that ground floor, he stood with his finger suspended
105 over it, and looked at me with a kind of honest, unselfish envy.

---

13 **flat** apartment (British English)
14 **Afrikaans** language spoken by South Africans
   of Dutch origin
15 **walk abreast** walk side by side

16 **constrained** inhibited, held back by
   custom or law
17 **deserted** completely empty
18 **waved me in** used his hand to show that
   I should enter

"You were lucky," he said. "Literature, that's what I wanted to do."

He shook his head and pressed the button, and he didn't speak again until we stopped high up. But before we got out he said suddenly, "If I had had a bookshop, I'd have given that boy a window too."

We got out and walked along one of those polished concrete passageways, I suppose you could call it a stoep[19] if it weren't so high up, let's call it a passage. On the one side was a wall, and plenty of fresh air, and far down below von Brandis Street. On the other side were the doors, impersonal doors; you could hear radios and people talking, but there wasn't a soul in sight. I wouldn't like living so high; we Africans like being close to the earth. Van Rensburg stopped at one of the doors, and said to me, "I won't be a minute." Then he went in, leaving the door open, and inside I could hear voices. I thought to myself, he's telling them who's here. Then after a minute or so, he came back to the door, holding two glasses of red wine. He was warm and smiling.

"Sorry there's no brandy," he said. "Only wine. Here's happiness."

Now I certainly had not expected that I would have my drink in the passage. I wasn't only feeling what you may be thinking, I was thinking that one of the impersonal doors might open at any moment, and someone might see me in a "white" building, and see me and van Rensburg breaking the liquor laws of the country. Anger could have saved me from the whole embarrassing situation, but you know I can't easily be angry. Even if I could have been, I might have found it hard to be angry with this particular man. But I wanted to get away from there, and I couldn't. My mother used to say to me, when I had said something anti-white, "Son, don't talk like that, talk as you are." She would have understood at once why I took a drink from a man who gave it to me in the passage.

Van Rensburg said to me, "Don't you know this fellow Simelane?"

"I've heard of him," I said.

"I'd like to meet him," he said. "I'd like to talk to him." He added in explanation, "You know, talk out my heart to him."[20]

A woman of about fifty years of age came from the room beyond, bringing a plate of biscuits. She smiled and bowed to me. I took one of the biscuits, but not for all the money in the world could I have said to her, *dankie, my nooi*, or that disgusting *dankie, missus*,[21] nor did I want to speak to her in English because her language was Afrikaans, so I took the risk of it and used the word *mevrou*, for the politeness of which

---

19 **stoep** balcony along the outside of a building (Afrikaans word)
20 **talk out my heart to him** express my deepest thoughts and feelings
21 **dankie, my nooi, dankie missus** ways of addressing a white woman that demonstrate her superior status

145 some Afrikaners would knock a black man down, and I said, in high
Afrikaans, with a smile and a bow too, *Ek is u dankbaar, Mevrou.*[22]

But nobody knocked me down. The woman smiled and bowed,
and van Rensburg, in a strained voice that suddenly came out of
nowhere, said, "Our land is beautiful. But it breaks my heart."

150 The woman put her hand on his arm, and said, "Jannie, Jannie."

Then another woman and a man, all about the same age, came up
and stood behind van Rensburg.

"He's a B.A.,"[23] van Rensburg told them. "What do you think
of that?"

155 The first woman smiled and bowed to me again, and van Rensburg
said, as though it were a matter for grief, "I wanted to give him brandy,
but there's only wine."

The second woman said, "I remember, Jannie. Come with me."

She went back into the room, and he followed her. The first woman
160 said to me, "Jannie's a good man. Strange, but good."

And I thought the whole thing was mad, and getting beyond me,[24]
with me a black stranger being shown a testimonial[25] for the son of the
house, with these white strangers standing and looking at me in the
passage, as though they wanted for God's sake to touch me somewhere
165 and didn't know how, but I saw the earnestness of the woman who had
smiled and bowed to me, and I said to her, "I can see that, *Mevrou.*"

"He goes down every night to look at that statue," she said. "He
says only God could make something so beautiful, therefore God must
be in the man who made it, and he wants to meet him and talk out his
170 heart to him."

She looked back at the room, and then she dropped her voice a
little, and said to me, "Can't you see, it's somehow because it's a black
woman and a black child?"

And I said to her, "I can see that, *Mevrou.*"

175 She turned to the man and said of me, "He's a good boy."

Then the other woman returned with van Rensburg, and van
Rensburg had a bottle of brandy. He was smiling and pleased, and he
said to me, "This isn't ordinary brandy, it's French."

He showed me the bottle, and I, wanting to get the hell out of that
180 place,[26] looked at it and saw it was cognac. He turned to the man and
said, "Uncle, you remember? When you were ill? The doctor said you
must have good brandy. And the man at the bottle-store said this was
the best brandy in the world."

"I must go," I said. "I must catch that train."

185 "I'll take you to the station," he said. "Don't you worry about that."

---

22 *Ek is u dankbaar*, *Mevrou.* Sophisticated way
of saying thank you to a married woman who is
one's social equal.
23 **B.A.** Bachelor of Arts

24 **getting beyond me** becoming something
outside my experience and understanding
25 **testimonial** evidence of good character
26 **wanting to get the hell out of that place**
wanting to leave as fast as possible (slang)

He poured me a drink and one for himself.

"Uncle," he said, "what about one for yourself?"

The older man said, "I don't mind if I do," and he went inside to get himself a glass.

190   Van Rensburg said, "Happiness," and lifted his glass to me. It was good brandy, the best I've ever tasted. But I wanted to get the hell out of there. I stood in the passage and drank van Rensburg's brandy. Then Uncle came back with his glass, and van Rensburg poured him a brandy, and Uncle raised his glass to me too. All of us were full of
195   goodwill, but I was waiting for the opening of one of those impersonal doors. Perhaps they were too, I don't know. Perhaps when you want so badly to touch someone, you don't care. I was drinking my brandy almost as fast as I would have drunk it in Orlando.

"I must go," I said.

200   Van Rensburg said, "I'll take you to the station." He finished his brandy, and I finished mine too. We handed the glasses to Uncle, who said to me, "Good night my boy." The first woman said, "May God bless you," and the other woman bowed and smiled. Then van Rensburg and I went down in the lift to the basement, and got into his car.

205   "I told you I'd take you to the station," he said. "I'd take you home, but I'm frightened of Orlando at night."

We drove up Eloff Street, and he said, "Did you know what I meant?" I knew that he wanted an answer to something, and I wanted to answer him, but I couldn't, because I didn't know what
210   that something was. He couldn't be talking about being frightened of Orlando at night, because what more could one mean than just that?

"By what?" I asked.

"You know," he said, "about our land being beautiful?"

Yes, I knew what he meant, and I knew that for God's sake he
215   wanted to touch me too and he couldn't; for his eyes had been blinded by years in the dark. And I thought it was a pity, for if men never touch each other, they'll hurt each other one day. And it was a pity he was blind, and couldn't touch me, for black men don't touch white men any more; only by accident, when they make something like *Mother*
220   *and Child*.

He said to me, "What are you thinking?"

I said, "Many things," and my inarticulateness[27] distressed me, for I knew he wanted something from me. I felt him fall back, angry, hurt, despairing, I didn't know. He stopped at the main entrance to the

---

27 **my inarticulateness** my inability to express myself clearly

225 station, but I didn't tell him I couldn't go in there. I got out and said to
him, "Thank you for the sociable evening."
"They liked having you," he said. "Did you see that?"
I said, "Yes, I saw that."
He sat slumped[28] in his seat, like a man with a burden of
230 incomprehensible, insoluble grief. I wanted to touch him, but I was
thinking about the train. He said Good night and I said it too. We
each saluted the other. What he was thinking, God knows, but I was
thinking he was like a man trying to run a race in iron shoes, and not
understanding why he cannot move.
235   When I got back to Orlando, I told my wife the story, and she wept.

---

28 **slumped** bent low

A Thinking About the Story

Discuss the following question with a partner.

Did you feel sympathy toward both characters for the predicament they
faced?

B Understanding the Plot

Be prepared to answer the following questions with a partner or your class.

1. How did the white South African public respond to the prizewinning
sculpture *African Mother and Child*?

2. What was the "oversight" referred to in line 8? How did the government
respond to this oversight?

3. What do the "traditional policies" in line 19 refer to?

4. What reason did Simelane publicly give for not attending the award
ceremony? What is the real reason he didn't go?

5. Why did Simelane's friends want him to receive his prize in person?
How does he explain his decision to them?

6. What are the "certain pleasurable human feelings" that Simelane refers
to? (line 45)

7. When van Rensburg says to Simelane: "You don't get much luck, do
you?" (lines 60–61), to whom does the pronoun *you* refer? What does van
Rensburg mean?

8. Why does van Rensburg envy Simelane?

9. Why doesn't Simelane tell van Rensburg who he is?

10. Why is Simelane glad to see that the entrance lobby to van Rensburg's building is deserted?

11. Why does van Rensburg offer Simelane a drink in the passage and not somewhere else?

12. What lesson did Simelane's mother try to teach him when he would use anti-white speech?

13. What does Simelane mean when he compares van Rensburg to a man who is trying to run a race in iron shoes? (lines 232–234)

14. Why does Simelane's wife weep when she hears the story?

CRITICAL THINKING

A Exploring Themes

Reread "A Drink in the Passage." As you read, think about all the ways in which the policies of apartheid undermine Simelane and van Rensburg's chance to connect.

1. "A Drink in the Passage" explores both conscious and unconscious racism. List everything we learn or can infer about the official segregation laws of the country. Then pick out as many examples as possible of the unconscious racism that van Rensburg and his family display.

2. Compared to the stereotypes of their time, Simelane is not a typical black man and van Rensburg is not a typical white man. Discuss how each man differs from these stereotypes.

3. Simelane talks more than once about people's yearning to touch each other. Find all his references to touching. Explain the importance of touching as a central theme in the story.

4. Explore the significance of van Rensburg's statement: "Our land is beautiful. But it breaks my heart." (lines 149, 213) Does Simelane share this feeling?

5. What is the role of art in the story?

FRAME STORY

At first glance, the narrative structure of "A Drink in the Passage" seems quite complex, as it is told by several narrators and contains a story within a story. This structure is called a **frame story**, as the outer story acts like a picture frame for the inner story, which is where we focus our attention. The beginning of "A Drink in the Passage" is told by an unspecified narrator who sets the scene. The story then moves on to someone recounting a conversation that he had with an artist. Next, the perspective shifts to the artist himself, as he tells what happened to him one day.

Exercise 1

Answer the following questions.

1. How would you describe the narration in lines 1–22? What function do these lines serve in the story?

2. In lines 23–24, who is narrating? What do you think his relationship is to Simelane?

3. Who is the primary narrator? Where does his narration begin and end? Does he relate his story in the first or the third person? How would you describe this narrator's voice?

4. What is the effect of using a frame narrative to tell the story?

IRONY

Irony is a literary device that expresses a contrast between what a person says and what he or she really means. It is also used when the writer wants to reverse a character's expectations or the expectations of the reader. Another form of irony occurs when there is something important that a character doesn't know or understand, but that we as readers do. Irony is present throughout "A Drink in the Passage." For example, the reprimand that the sculpture committee receives for being "so careless" about not restricting the competition to whites only is ironic because the word *reprimand* suggests that something undesirable has happened, whereas in this case the reader is pleased with the unintended result. Also, although the organizers of the competition assumed that only white artists should be eligible for the prize, the best candidate was actually black.

Exercise 2

Answer the following questions.

1. What is the irony of Simelane's statement that he was "unfortunately unable to attend the ceremony"? (line 22)
2. What are some of the ironies that surround the contrast in lifestyle and professional achievement between van Rensburg and Simelane?
3. What is ironic about van Rensburg's desire to meet the sculptor of *African Mother and Child*? (lines 137–138)
4. Why is it ironic that van Rensburg serves Simelane his cognac in the passage?

Exercise 3

Pick out two more examples of irony in the story and explain them.

INFERENCE

Reading "A Drink in the Passage" requires a great deal of **inference**, meaning that frequently we need to deduce information that isn't spelled out explicitly. For example, when Simelane's friends encourage him to accept his award in person (lines 25–27), we can infer that they want him to make a political point by attending the ceremony.

Exercise 4

Answer the following questions.

1. What is implied by the threat of many white prizewinners to renounce their prizes if Simelane were to attend the award ceremony?
2. What can be inferred from Simelane's statement that in Orlando he can never drink his brandy slowly? (lines 29–32)
3. What can we infer about South African society from Simelane's reaction to being called "mate"? (lines 48–49)
4. What is implied by van Rensburg's reaction to hearing that Simelane has a degree?
5. What is implied by Simelane's comment that "We didn't exactly walk abreast, but he didn't exactly walk in front of me"? (lines 77–78)
6. Why does Simelane find it hard to be angry with van Rensburg for offering him a drink in the passage? (lines 129–130)
7. In what language does Simelane talk to the woman (lines 142–146)? How does he address her? Why does he choose this form of address?
8. What can we infer about Orlando from van Rensburg's decision not to drive Simelane home?

C Judging for Yourself

Express yourself as personally as you like in your answers to the following questions.

1. Did you find it surprising that van Rensburg offered Simelane a drink but wouldn't invite him inside? Explain your answer.
2. In your opinion, should Simelane have defied his family's advice and accepted his prize in person?
3. Is it likely that Simelane's life will change drastically after winning the prize? Justify your answer.
4. Did you find any reason for optimism about the future in the story?

D Making Connections

Answer the following questions in a small group.

1. Does your country have a history of protest against injustice? What have some of these protests been about? Which groups have taken part?
2. Has a work of art such as a book, painting, sculpture, photograph, or opera elicited controversy in your country? Give details.
3. How do people show hospitality toward guests in your culture?
4. Is there a diversity of races in your country? If so, how do people view interracial friendships or marriages?
5. Do you have laws that restrict the sale or consumption of alcohol in your country? If so, do you agree with these restrictions? If not, say whether you'd like to see such laws.

E Debate

Decide whether you are for or against the following statement. Be prepared to argue your case in a class debate.

The pen is mightier than the sword.

CONDITIONALS

A conditional sentence consists of a dependent clause, usually starting with *if*, and an independent (main) clause. The dependent clause contains a condition that may or may not be fulfilled, and the independent clause expresses the result of fulfilling the condition. Conditionals are divided into real and unreal situations.

1. A **real conditional** contains a situation that occurs regularly or is reasonably likely to happen. When the verb in the conditional clause is in the present tense, the verb in the main clause can also be in the present, or it can consist of a present modal (*will, shall, may, can*) plus the base form of the verb.

   *If Simelane **feels** inspired, he **works** late into the night.*

   The sentence expresses a generalization about an action that occurs regularly.

   *If Simelane **feels** inspired by a new idea today, he **will/may work** late into the night.*

   The sentence expresses a particular action that is likely to happen.

2. An **unreal conditional** contains a situation that is impossible or unlikely to happen, or that is contrary to what actually is happening or has happened.

   - To express an unreal situation in the present or future, the verb in the conditional clause is in the past tense, while the verb in the main clause is formed by using a past modal (*would/could/should/might*) plus the base form of the verb.

   *If van Rensburg **lived/were living** abroad, he **might/would see** blacks and whites living together peacefully.*

   This is an unreal conditional because van Rensburg does not actually live abroad.

   *If I **were** Simelane, I **would accept** the prize in person.*

This is an unreal conditional because I can never be Simelane.

If you use the simple past of the verb *to be* in an unreal conditional, use *were* for all persons. Do not use *was*.

- To express an unreal situation in the past, the verb in the conditional clause is in the past perfect tense, while the verb in the main clause is formed by using the perfect modal *would have/could have/should have/might have* plus the past participle.

"If I **had had** a bookshop, I **would have given** that boy a window too." (lines 109–110)

This is an unreal conditional because van Rensburg never owned a bookshop.

Exercise 1

Look at the following conditional sentences. Underline the conditional clause and say whether the conditional is real or unreal.

1. The committee of the sculpture section . . . was told by a very high personage . . . that if Simelane's work "was indisputably the best," it should receive the award. (lines 10–14)

   _____

2. We got out and walked along one of those polished concrete passageways, I suppose you could call it a stoep if it weren't so high up, let's call it a passage. (lines 111–113)

   _____

3. Even if I could have been, I might have found it hard to be angry with this particular man. (lines 129–130)

   _____

4. "If I were the artist, I would be so proud of myself," said van Rensburg.

   _____

5. If the committee had awarded the prize to a white sculptor, it would have been very unfair.

   _____

6. If there is another opportunity, van Rensburg will invite Simelane to have a drink with him again.

   _____

7. And I thought it was a pity, for if men never touch each other, they'll hurt each other one day. (lines 216–217)

   _____

Exercise 2

Complete the following dialogue with the correct form of each verb in parentheses. There may be more than one possible answer. If the condition used is real, write R above your answer. If the condition is unreal, write U.

VAN RENSBURG: If you _____ over tonight,
I _____ you my best cognac.
(come, offer)

SIMELANE: Why do you want to invite me home?
Everybody knows that it would be a violation
of the apartheid laws. If one of your neighbors
_____ me, the police
_____ me for drinking alcohol
and being in a white area. (notice, arrest)

VAN RENSBURG: No, you won't have a problem tonight,
although last Saturday was certainly different. If
you _____ me then,
you _____ into trouble because of
the protest near my flat. (visit, get)

SIMELANE: In my opinion, you're too optimistic. If you
_____ so desperate to talk to me, I
_____ your invitation at all. (not be,
not consider)

VAN RENSBURG: Perhaps if you _____ more
Afrikaners in your life, you _____
we aren't all prejudiced. (know, see)

SIMELANE: I have never believed in stereotyping anybody.
If I _____ you, I
_____ your words more carefully.
(be, choose)

VAN RENSBURG: If only I _____ that artist Simelane,
I _____ to him heart to heart about
his beautiful sculpture. (meet, talk) But that's an
impossible dream.

SIMELANE: Not necessarily. I hear he walks by the bookstore
every evening. If you _____ there
after dinner, you _____ him.
(go, meet)

Exercise 3

With a partner, write a few more sentences to finish the dialogue in Exercise 2. Use the conditional in some of your sentences. Read your dialogue to another pair of students in your class.

VOCABULARY BUILDING

PREPOSITIONS

A **preposition** is a connecting word that shows the relationship of a noun or pronoun to another part of the sentence. Prepositions most frequently show place, time, and manner, but they can also illustrate agent (*by*) and purpose (*for*). Some prepositions consist of two or three words, including *because of, instead of, in front of,* and *with regard to*. Although these **complex prepositions** consist of more than one word, they still function as a single part of speech.

Prepositions can be quite complicated to master because you can use different prepositions to express the same meaning. For example: *He was in the house when the bell rang* or *He was at the house when the bell rang*. And you can use the same preposition to express different meanings. For example: *He spoke to me for an hour* and *He is smart for his age*.

Exercise 1

Complete the sentences with the correct prepositions. All the expressions appear in the story. Try to do the exercise without looking back at the story.

1. The prize was given at a public ceremony that brought the celebrations _____ a close.

2. Simelane didn't feel _____ ease when in the company of white strangers.

3. Simelane waited _____ one of the neighbors' doors to open.

4. There wasn't a soul _____ sight in van Rensburg's building.

5. Anger could have saved Simelane _____ the embarrassment of being served in the passage.

6. Van Rensburg confided that he was frightened of Orlando _____ night.

7. Simelane decided that he could not act like an inferior black man _____ all the money in the world.

8. Simelane was afraid that _____ any moment someone in the building would see him drinking a brandy.

9. Van Rensburg spoke to Simelane _____ a strained voice.

10. It is tragic that black men only touch white men _____ accident in South Africa.

Exercise 2

Look at the list of complex prepositions below. Then complete the sentences that follow with the correct complex preposition. The first two prepositions appear in the story.

along with (line 15)	on behalf of
in front of (line 78)	prior to
in spite of	such as
instead of	up against

1. Simelane felt he was _____ laws of apartheid and was therefore afraid to drink the brandy in the passage.

2. Van Rensburg had often looked at the sculpture _____ his meeting with Simelane.

3. Simelane's wife _____ his mother recognized the tragic consequences of apartheid.

4. The chairman spoke _____ the committee when he said they had decided to recommend first prize to Simelane.

5. Simelane was used to swallowing his brandy _____ sipping it.

6. Simelane felt embarrassed to admit _____ Van Rensburg that he had a university degree.

7. A sculpture _____ *Mother and Child* makes a universal statement and moves people of all colors.

8. _____ the controversy over the prize winner, the majority of the public felt that it was right that Simelane still receive the award.

1. In an essay of one to two pages, discuss a controversial measure that has recently been proposed in your city or country. Outline the measure, place it in a historical and/or social context, explain why it is controversial, and offer some suggestions as to how to get it accepted or rejected. Such an issue might be legalizing gay marriage, strengthening or weakening state censorship, or abolishing the death penalty. In your conclusion, say where you stand on the issue and explain why.

2. Write a one-page description of a person you have met unexpectedly at some point in your life who is very different from you. Explain how you met, what makes you different, and whether you feel enriched or not by this encounter.

3. The arts have frequently been a potent source for highlighting injustice and effecting change. For example, the novel *Uncle Tom's Cabin* by Harriet Beecher Stowe is credited with influencing the antislavery movement in the United States in the nineteenth century, and Picasso's iconic antiwar painting *Guernica* helped arouse the conscience of the world regarding the massacre of Basques during the Spanish Civil War. Write a one-page essay on a work of art in your country, such as a novel, play, painting, or photograph, which has contributed to raising consciousness about an important issue.

16 ∽ The Catbird Seat

James Thurber
(1894–1961)

Born in Columbus, Ohio, James Thurber used his hometown as the setting for many of his comic writings. His mild-tempered father and domineering mother served as the prototypes for his frequent explorations of the war between the sexes. Thurber's career took off after he began working for the *New Yorker* in 1927, and he became widely known for his humorous essays, stories, cartoons, and illustrations.

Today Thurber is considered by many to be one of the greatest American humorists since Mark Twain. Beneath the humor of his work lies a concern with the consequences of marital humiliations, the destructive effects of technology, and the dangers of fascism. His large body of work, for which he won numerous awards, includes *My Life and Hard Times* (1933), *The Middle-Aged Man on the Flying Trapeze* (1935), *Further Fables for Our Time* (1940), *The Thurber Carnival* (1945), and *Thurber's Dogs* (1955).

The Catbird Seat

A man whose job is threatened takes drastic and ingenious measures to protect himself.

Mr. Martin bought the pack of Camels on Monday night in the most crowded cigar store on Broadway. It was theatre time and seven or eight men were buying cigarettes. The clerk didn't even glance at Mr. Martin, who put the pack in his overcoat
5 pocket and went out. If any of the staff at F & S had seen him buy the cigarettes, they would have been astonished, for it was generally known that Mr. Martin did not smoke, and never had. No one saw him.

It was just a week to the day since Mr. Martin had decided to rub out[1] Mrs. Ulgine Barrows. The term "rub out" pleased him because it
10 suggested nothing more than the correction of an error—in this case an error of Mr. Fitweiler. Mr. Martin had spent each night of the past week working out his plan and examining it. As he walked home now he went over it again. For the hundredth time he resented the element of imprecision, the margin of guesswork[2] that entered into the business.
15 The project as he had worked it out was casual and bold, the risks were considerable. Something might go wrong anywhere along the line. And therein lay the cunning of his scheme. No one would ever see in it the cautious, painstaking hand of Erwin Martin, head of the filing department at F & S, of whom Mr. Fitweiler had once said, "Man is
20 fallible but Martin isn't."[3] No one would see his hand, that is, unless it were caught in the act.

Sitting in his apartment, drinking a glass of milk, Mr. Martin reviewed his case against Mrs. Ulgine Barrows, as he had every night for seven nights. He began at the beginning. Her quacking voice and
25 braying laugh had first profaned[4] the halls of F & S on March 7, 1941 (Mr. Martin had a head for dates). Old Roberts, the personnel chief, had introduced her as the newly appointed special adviser to the president of the firm, Mr. Fitweiler. The woman had appalled[5] Mr. Martin instantly, but he hadn't shown it. He had given her his dry
30 hand, a look of studious concentration, and a faint smile. "Well," she had said, looking at the papers on his desk, "are you lifting the oxcart out of the ditch?"[6] As Mr. Martin recalled that moment, over his milk, he squirmed[7]

---

1 **rub out** slang meaning to kill
2 **he resented the element of imprecision, the margin of guesswork** he did not like the fact that the tiniest detail could cause the plan to go wrong
3 **"Man is fallible, but Martin isn't"** a humorous reference to the notion that usually only God makes no mistakes

4 **profaned** treated something sacred with vulgarity
5 **appalled** horrified
6 **"are you lifting the oxcart out of the ditch?"** are you attempting the impossible?
7 **squirmed** moved uncomfortably

slightly. He must keep his mind on her crimes as a special adviser, not on her peccadillos[8] as a personality. This he found difficult to do, in spite
35 of entering an objection and sustaining it.[9] The faults of the woman as a woman kept chattering on in his mind like an unruly witness. She had, for almost two years now, baited[10] him. In the halls, in the elevator, even in his own office, into which she romped now and then like a circus horse, she was constantly shouting these silly questions at him. "Are you
40 lifting the oxcart out of the ditch? Are you tearing up the pea patch? Are you hollering[11] down the rain barrel? Are you scraping the bottom of the pickle barrel? Are you sitting in the catbird seat?"[12]
    It was Joey Hart, one of Mr. Martin's two assistants, who had explained what the gibberish[13] meant. "She must be a Dodger fan," he
45 had said. "Red Barber[14] announces the Dodger games over the radio and he uses those expressions—picked 'em up down South." Joey had gone on to explain one or two. "Tearing up the pea patch" meant going on a rampage;[15] "sitting in the catbird seat" meant sitting pretty,[16] like a batter with three balls and no strikes on him.[17] Mr. Martin dismissed all
50 this with an effort. It had been annoying, it had driven him near to distraction, but he was too solid a man to be moved to murder by anything so childish. It was fortunate, he reflected as he passed on to the important charges against Mrs. Barrows, that he had stood up under it so well.[18] He had maintained always an outward appearance of polite
55 tolerance. "Why, I even believe you like the woman," Miss Paird, his other assistant, had once said to him. He had simply smiled.
    A gavel[19] rapped in Mr. Martin's mind and the case proper was resumed. Mrs. Ulgine Barrows stood charged with willful,[20] blatant,[21] and persistent attempts to destroy the efficiency and system of F & S.
60 It was competent, material, and relevant to review her advent and rise to power. Mr. Martin had got the story from Miss Paird, who seemed always able to find things out. According to her, Mrs. Barrows had met Mr. Fitweiler at a party, where she had rescued him from the embraces of a powerfully built drunken man who had mistaken the president of
65 F & S for a famous retired Middle Western football coach. She had led

---

8 **peccadillos** slight offenses
9 **entering an objection and sustaining it** In a court of law, an attorney may object to a line of questioning by the opponent and the judge may sustain (agree with) the objection or overrule (disagree with) it.
10 **baited** provoked
11 **hollering** shouting
12 **sitting in the catbird seat** enjoying an advantageous position
13 **gibberish** meaningless language
14 **Red Barber** a sports broadcaster, born in Mississippi, who covered the Brooklyn Dodgers, a well-known baseball team

15 **going on a rampage** getting violently out of control
16 **sitting pretty** being in an advantageous position
17 **like a batter with three balls and no strikes on him** In baseball, a situation where the batter is likely to do well
18 **had stood up under it so well** had successfully endured it
19 **gavel** a small hammer that a judge uses in the courtroom
20 **willful** deliberate
21 **blatant** offensively noticeable

him to a sofa and somehow worked upon him a monstrous magic. The aging gentleman had jumped to the conclusion there and then that this was a woman of singular attainments,[22] equipped to bring out the best in him and in the firm. A week later he had introduced her into F & S as his special adviser. On that day confusion got its foot in the door. After Miss Tyson, Mr. Brundage, and Mr. Bartlett had been fired and Mr. Munson had taken his hat and stalked out,[23] mailing in his resignation later, old Roberts had been emboldened to speak to Mr. Fitweiler. He mentioned that Mr. Munson's department had been "a little disrupted" and hadn't they perhaps better resume the old system there? Mr. Fitweiler had said certainly not. He had the greatest faith in Mrs. Barrows' ideas. "They require a little seasoning, a little seasoning, is all," he had added. Mr. Roberts had given it up. Mr. Martin reviewed in detail all the changes wrought by Mrs. Barrows. She had begun chipping at the cornices of the firm's edifice and now she was swinging at the foundation stones with a pickaxe.[24]

Mr. Martin came now, in his summing up, to the afternoon of Monday, November 2, 1942—just one week ago. On that day, at 3 P.M., Mrs. Barrows had bounced into his office. "Boo!" she had yelled. "Are you scraping around the bottom of the pickle barrel?" Mr. Martin had looked at her from under his green eyeshade, saying nothing. She had begun to wander about the office, taking it in[25] with her great popping eyes.[26] "Do you really need *all* these filing cabinets?" she had demanded suddenly. Mr. Martin's heart had jumped. "Each of these files," he had said, keeping his voice even, "plays an indispensable part in the system of F & S." She had brayed[27] at him, "Well, don't tear up the pea patch!" and gone to the door. From there she had bawled, "But you sure have got a lot of fine scrap[28] in here!" Mr. Martin could no longer doubt that the finger was on his beloved department. Her pickaxe was on the upswing, poised for the first blow. It had not come yet; he had received no blue memo from the enchanted Mr. Fitweiler bearing nonsensical instructions deriving from the obscene[29] woman. But there was no doubt in Mr. Martin's mind that one would be forthcoming. He must act quickly. Already a precious week had gone by. Mr. Martin stood up in his living room, still holding his milk glass. "Gentlemen of the jury," he said to himself, "I demand the death penalty for this horrible person."

---

22 **singular attainments** unusual achievements
23 **stalked out** walked out proudly
24 **She had begun chipping at the cornices of the firm's edifice and now she was swinging at the foundation stones with a pickaxe.** She had started by slowly changing some aspects of the business and was now revolutionizing everything.

25 **taking it in** looking carefully at everything
26 **popping eyes** wide eyes that stick out
27 **brayed** made a noise like a donkey
28 **scrap** useless material
29 **obscene** vulgar, indecent

The next day Mr. Martin followed his routine, as usual. He polished his glasses more often and once sharpened an already sharp pencil, but not even Miss Paird noticed. Only once did he catch sight of his victim; she swept past him in the hall with a patronizing "Hi!" At five-thirty he walked home, as usual, and had a glass of milk, as usual. He had never drunk anything stronger in his life—unless you could count ginger ale. The late Sam Schlosser,[30] the S of F & S, had praised Mr. Martin at a staff meeting several years before for his temperate[31] habits. "Our most efficient worker neither drinks nor smokes," he had said. "The results speak for themselves." Mr. Fitweiler had sat by, nodding approval.

Mr. Martin was still thinking about that red-letter day[32] as he walked over to Schrafft's on Fifth Avenue near Forty-sixth Street. He got there, as he always did, at eight o'clock. He finished his dinner and the financial page of the *Sun* at a quarter to nine, as he always did. It was his custom after dinner to take a walk. This time he walked down Fifth Avenue at a casual pace. His gloved hands felt moist and warm, his forehead cold. He transferred the Camels from his overcoat to a jacket pocket. He wondered, as he did so, if they did not represent an unnecessary note of strain. Mrs. Barrows smoked only Luckies. It was his idea to puff a few puffs on a Camel (after the rubbing-out), stub it out in the ashtray holding her lipstick-stained Luckies, and thus drag a small red herring across the trail.[33] Perhaps it was not a good idea. It would take time. He might even choke, too loudly.

Mr. Martin had never seen the house on West Twelfth Street where Mrs. Barrows lived, but he had a clear enough picture of it. Fortunately, she had bragged to everybody about her ducky[34] first-floor apartment in the perfectly darling three-story red-brick. There would be no doorman or other attendants; just the tenants of the second and third floors. As he walked along, Mr. Martin realized that he would get there before nine-thirty. He had considered walking north on Fifth Avenue from Schrafft's to a point from which it would take him until ten o'clock to reach the house. At that hour people were less likely to be coming in or going out. But the procedure would have made an awkward loop in the straight thread of his casualness,[35] and he had abandoned it. It was impossible to figure when people would be entering or leaving the house, anyway. There was a great risk at any hour. If he ran into anybody, he would simply have to place the rubbing-out of Ulgine Barrows in the inactive file forever. The same thing would hold true if there were someone in her apartment. In that

---

30 **the late Sam Schlosser** the dead Sam Schlosser
31 **temperate** moderate
32 **red-letter day** excitingly memorable day
33 **drag a small red herring across the trail** plant a deliberately false clue in order to mislead

34 **ducky** delightful, cute (old-fashioned slang)
35 **But the procedure would have made an awkward loop in the straight thread of his casualness** But waiting until 10 P.M. would have overcomplicated his plan

case he would just say that he had been passing by, recognized her charming house, and thought to drop in.[36]

It was eighteen minutes after nine when Mr. Martin turned into Twelfth Street. A man passed him, and a man and a woman, talking. There was no one within fifty paces when he came to the house, half-way down the block. He was up the steps and in the small vestibule[37] in no time, pressing the bell under the card that said "Mrs. Ulgine Barrows." When the clicking in the lock started, he jumped forward against the door. He got inside fast, closing the door behind him. A bulb in a lantern hung from the hall ceiling on a chain seemed to give a monstrously bright light. There was nobody on the stair, which went up ahead of him along the left wall. A door opened down the hall in the wall on the right. He went toward it swiftly, on tiptoe.

"Well, for God's sake, look who's here!" bawled Mrs. Barrows, and her braying laugh rang out like the report of a shotgun. He rushed past her like a football tackle, bumping her. "Hey, quit shoving!" she said, closing the door behind them. They were in her living room, which seemed to Mr. Martin to be lighted by a hundred lamps. "What's after you?" she said. "You're as jumpy[38] as a goat." He found he was unable to speak. His heart was wheezing in his throat. "I—yes," he finally brought out. She was jabbering and laughing as she started to help him off with his coat. "No, no," he said. "I'll put it here." He took it off and put it on a chair near the door. "Your hat and gloves, too," she said. "You're in a lady's house." He put his hat on top of the coat. Mrs. Barrows seemed larger than he had thought. He kept his gloves on. "I was passing by," he said. "I recognized—is there anyone here?" She laughed louder than ever. "No," she said, "we're all alone. You're as white as a sheet, you funny man. Whatever *has* come over you? I'll mix you a toddy."[39] She started toward a door across the room. "Scotch-and-soda be all right? But say, you don't drink, do you?" She turned and gave him her amused look. Mr. Martin pulled himself together.[40] "Scotch-and-soda will be all right," he heard himself say. He could hear her laughing in the kitchen.

Mr. Martin looked quickly around the living room for the weapon. He had counted on finding one there. There were andirons and a poker[41] and something in a corner that looked like an Indian club. None of them would do.[42] It couldn't be that way. He began to pace around. He came to a desk. On it lay a metal paper knife with an ornate handle. Would it be sharp enough? He reached for it and knocked over a small brass jar. Stamps spilled out of it and it fell to the floor with a clatter.

---

36 **drop in** visit unexpectedly
37 **vestibule** the entrance hall of a building
38 **jumpy** nervous
39 **toddy** an alcoholic drink
40 **pulled himself together** got control of himself
41 **andirons and a poker** metal tools used in a fireplace
42 **would do** were acceptable

"Hey," Mrs. Barrows yelled from the kitchen, "are you tearing up the pea patch?" Mr. Martin gave a strange laugh. Picking up the knife, he tried its point against his left wrist. It was blunt.[43] It wouldn't do.

185   When Mrs. Barrows reappeared, carrying two highballs, Mr. Martin, standing there with his gloves on, became acutely conscious of the fantasy he had wrought. Cigarettes in his pocket, a drink prepared for him—it was all too grossly improbable. It was more than that; it was impossible. Somewhere in the back of his mind a vague idea stirred,
190 sprouted.[44] "For heaven's sake, take off those gloves," said Mrs. Barrows. "I always wear them in the house," said Mr. Martin. The idea began to bloom, strange and wonderful. She put the glasses on a coffee table in front of a sofa and sat on the sofa. "Come over here, you odd little man," she said. Mr. Martin went over and sat beside her. It
195 was difficult getting a cigarette out of the pack of Camels, but he managed it. She held a match for him, laughing. "Well," she said, handing him his drink, "this is perfectly marvellous. You with a drink and a cigarette."

    Mr. Martin puffed, not too awkwardly, and took a gulp of the
200 highball. "I drink and smoke all the time," he said. He clinked his glass against hers. "Here's nuts to that old windbag, Fitweiler,"[45] he said, and gulped again. The stuff tasted awful, but he made no grimace.[46] "Really, Mr. Martin," she said, her voice and posture changing, "you are insulting our employer." Mrs. Barrows was now all special adviser
205 to the president. "I am preparing a bomb," said Mr. Martin, "which will blow the old goat higher than hell." He had only had a little of the drink, which was not strong. It couldn't be that. "Do you take dope or something?" Mrs. Barrows asked coldly. "Heroin," said Mr. Martin. "I'll be coked to the gills[47] when I bump that old buzzard off."[48]
210 "Mr. Martin!" she shouted, getting to her feet. "That will be all of that. You must go at once." Mr. Martin took another swallow of his drink. He tapped his cigarette out in the ashtray and put the pack of Camels on the coffee table. Then he got up. She stood glaring at him. He walked over and put on his hat and coat. "Not a word about this," he said, and
215 laid an index finger against his lips. All Mrs. Barrows could bring out was "Really!" Mr. Martin put his hand on the doorknob. "I'm sitting in the catbird seat," he said. He stuck his tongue out at her and left. Nobody saw him go.

    Mr. Martin got to his apartment, walking, well before eleven. No
220 one saw him go in. He had two glasses of milk after brushing his teeth, and he felt elated. It wasn't tipsiness,[49] because he hadn't been tipsy.

---

43 **blunt** dull-edged
44 **sprouted** began to grow
45 **"Here's nuts to that old windbag, Fitweiler"** a disrespectful expression suggesting that his boss talks too much

46 **grimace** expression of disgust
47 **coked to the gills** filled with drugs (slang)
48 **bump that old buzzard off** kill that horrible old man (slang)
49 **tipsiness** slight drunkenness

Anyway, the walk had worn off all effects of the whiskey. He got in bed and read a magazine for a while. He was asleep before midnight.

225 Mr. Martin got to the office at eight-thirty the next morning, as usual. At a quarter to nine, Ulgine Barrows, who had never before arrived at work before ten, swept into his office. "I'm reporting to Mr. Fitweiler now!" she shouted. "If he turns you over to the police, it's no more than you deserve!" Mr. Martin gave her a look of shocked surprise. "I beg your pardon?" he said. Mrs. Barrows snorted and

230 bounced out of the room, leaving Miss Paird and Joey Hart staring after her. "What's the matter with that old devil now?" asked Miss Paird. "I have no idea," said Mr. Martin, resuming his work. The other two looked at him and then at each other. Miss Paird got up and went out. She walked slowly past the closed door of Mr. Fitweiler's office.

235 Mrs. Barrows was yelling inside, but she was not braying. Miss Paird could not hear what the woman was saying. She went back to her desk.

Forty-five minutes later, Mrs. Barrows left the president's office and went into her own, shutting the door. It wasn't until half an hour later that Mr. Fitweiler sent for Mr. Martin. The head of the filing department,

240 neat, quiet, attentive, stood in front of the old man's desk. Mr. Fitweiler was pale and nervous. He took his glasses off and twiddled[50] them. He made a small, bruffing sound in his throat. "Martin," he said, "you have been with us more than twenty years." "Twenty-two, sir," said Mr. Martin. "In that time," pursued the president, "your work and

245 your—uh—manner have been exemplary." "I trust so, sir," said Mr. Martin. "I have understood, Martin," said Mr. Fitweiler, "that you have never taken a drink or smoked." "That is correct, sir," said Mr. Martin. "Ah, yes." Mr. Fitweiler polished his glasses. "You may describe what you did after leaving the office yesterday, Martin," he said.

250 Mr. Martin allowed less than a second for his bewildered pause. "Certainly, sir," he said, "I walked home. Then I went to Schrafft's for dinner. Afterward I walked home again. I went to bed early, sir, and read a magazine for a while. I was asleep before eleven." "Ah, yes," said Mr. Fitweiler again. He was silent for a moment, searching for the proper

255 words to say to the head of the filing department. "Mrs. Barrows," he said finally, "Mrs. Barrows has worked hard, Martin, very hard. It grieves me to report that she has suffered a severe breakdown. It has taken the form of a persecution complex accompanied by distressing hallucinations."[51] "I am very sorry, sir," said Mr. Martin. "Mrs. Barrows is under the

260 delusion,"[52] continued Mr. Fitweiler, "that you visited her last evening and behaved yourself in an—uh—unseemly[53] manner." He raised his

---

50 **twiddled** turned them over in his hands nervously
51 **hallucinations** imaginary visions
52 **is under the delusion** falsely believes
53 **unseemly** improper

hand to silence Mr. Martin's little pained outcry. "It is the nature of these psychological diseases," Mr. Fitweiler said, "to fix upon the least likely and most innocent party as the—uh—source of persecution.
These matters are not for the lay[54] mind to grasp, Martin. I've just had my psychiatrist, Dr. Fitch, on the phone. He would not, of course, commit himself, but he made enough generalizations to substantiate my suspicions. I suggested to Mrs. Barrows, when she had completed her—uh—story to me this morning, that she visit Dr. Fitch, for I suspected a condition at once. She flew, I regret to say, into a rage, and demanded—uh—requested that I call you on the carpet.[55] You may not know, Martin, but Mrs. Barrows had planned a reorganization of your department—subject to my approval, of course, subject to my approval. This brought you, rather than anyone else, to her mind—but again that is a phenomenon for Dr. Fitch and not for us. So, Martin, I am afraid Mrs. Barrows' usefulness here is at an end." "I am dreadfully sorry, sir," said Mr. Martin.

It was at this point that the door to the office blew open with the suddenness of a gas-main explosion and Mrs. Barrows catapulted through it. "Is the little rat denying it?" she screamed. "He can't get away with that!" Mr. Martin got up and moved discreetly to a point beside Mr. Fitweiler's chair. "You drank and smoked at my apartment," she bawled[56] at Mr. Martin, "and you know it! You called Mr. Fitweiler an old windbag and said you were going to blow him up when you got coked to the gills on your heroin!" She stopped yelling to catch her breath and a new glint came into her popping eyes. "If you weren't such a drab, ordinary little man," she said, "I'd think you'd planned it all. Sticking your tongue out, saying you were sitting in the catbird seat, because you thought no one would believe me when I told it! My God, it's really too perfect!" She brayed loudly and hysterically, and the fury was on her again. She glared at Mr. Fitweiler. "Can't you see how he has tricked us, you old fool? Can't you see his little game?" But Mr. Fitweiler had been surreptitiously[57] pressing all the buttons under the top of his desk and employees of F & S began pouring into the room. "Stockton," said Mr. Fitweiler, "you and Fishbein will take Mrs. Barrows to her home. Mrs. Powell, you will go with them." Stockton, who had played a little football in high school, blocked Mrs. Barrows as she made for[58] Mr. Martin. It took him and Fishbein together to force her out of the door into the hall, crowded with stenographers and office boys. She was still screaming imprecations[59] at Mr. Martin, tangled and contradictory imprecations. The hubbub[60] finally died out down the corridor.

---

54 **lay** amateur, not professional
55 **call you on the carpet** criticize you severely
56 **bawled** shouted very loudly
57 **surreptitiously** secretly
58 **made for** attempted to attack
59 **imprecations** curses
60 **hubbub** noisy, confused scene

"I regret that this has happened," said Mr. Fitweiler. "I shall ask you to dismiss it from your mind, Martin." "Yes, sir," said Mr. Martin, anticipating his chief's "That will be all" by moving to the door. "I
305 will dismiss it." He went out and shut the door, and his step was light and quick in the hall. When he entered his department he had slowed down to his customary gait, and he walked quietly across the room to the W20 file, wearing a look of studious concentration.

A Thinking About the Story

Discuss the following questions with a partner.

> Did you sympathize with Mr. Martin's antagonism toward Mrs. Barrows? Do you think Mrs. Barrows did anything wrong? Explain your answers.

B Understanding the Plot

Be prepared to answer the following questions with a partner or the whole class.

1. Why does Mr. Martin, a nonsmoker, buy a pack of cigarettes?
2. What does Mr. Fitweiler's reference to Mr. Martin—"Man is fallible but Martin isn't"—tell us about Mr. Martin's character (lines 19–20)?
3. Mr. Martin compares Mrs. Barrows to a duck, a donkey, and a horse. Why does he choose these particular animals?
4. What does "sitting in the catbird seat" mean? How does the reference to "a batter with three balls and no strikes on him" (lines 48–49) relate to your answer?
5. Why is it important to the success of Mr. Martin's plan that he has "maintained always an outward appearance of polite tolerance" toward Mrs. Barrows (lines 54–55)?
6. What exactly does Mr. Martin accuse Mrs. Barrows of doing?
7. How did Mrs. Barrows initially come to the attention of Mr. Fitweiler?
8. What specific event led Mr. Martin to take action against Mrs. Barrows?
9. Why is it important for Mr. Martin to follow his routine on the day he plans to "rub out" Mrs. Barrows?
10. What is the "red herring" Mr. Martin includes in his plan (line 124)? What is the purpose of this red herring?

11. Why do the lights in the hallway and in Mrs. Barrows's apartment make Mr. Martin uncomfortable?

12. Why does he keep his gloves on but take his hat and coat off?

13. What goes wrong with Mr. Martin's scheme?

14. What idea "sprouted" and then began "to bloom" in Mr. Martin's mind (lines 189–192)? How does he implement this idea?

15. What does Mr. Fitweiler decide to do about Mrs. Barrows? How does he come to that decision?

PART 2 CRITICAL THINKING

A Exploring Themes

Reread "The Catbird Seat." As you read, look at how Thurber draws Mr. Martin with minute descriptive details and sets him against Mrs. Barrows in a battle of the sexes.

1. When Mr. Martin reviews his case against Mrs. Barrows (lines 22–102), what role does he adopt for himself in his imagination? In what setting does he see himself playing this role? What particular words and expressions does he use to help him sustain this fantasy?

2. What kind of relationship between men and women is Thurber poking fun at in the story?

3. What makes this story funny? Give examples from the story, and explain the different elements Thurber uses to create the humor.

4. From reading "The Catbird Seat," what can you infer about Thurber's attitude toward modernization? Justify your answer.

5. What parallels does Thurber draw between the characters of Mr. Fitweiler and Mr. Martin?

B Analyzing Style

UNDERSTATEMENT

Understatement occurs when a writer or character uses language that is less strong or direct than the situation deserves. In general, the men in "The Catbird Seat" are given to understatement, a trait that unites them in comic brotherhood against the loud, exaggerated ranting of Mrs. Barrows. Much of the humor in the story arises from the contrast between what Mr. Martin says and what he actually thinks and feels.

When we first encounter Mr. Martin, he is thinking about his decision to *rub out* Mrs. Barrows (line 9). This is an example of his use of understatement. In gangster slang, *rub out* means to kill, but Mr. Martin enjoys thinking about the expression in terms of its literal meaning, which is to "erase a mistake" as a clerk might erase a wrong pencil mark.

Exercise

Answer the following questions.

1. In what way is "project" an understatement (line 15)? What word could be substituted?

2. Mr. Martin describes the immediate consequences of Mrs. Barrows's appointment as "confusion got its foot in the door" (line 70). How could he say this more directly?

3. Explain Mr. Roberts's understated comment to Mr. Fitweiler, and say what he really meant to convey (lines 73–74). What does Mr. Fitweiler reply? Rephrase his answer, using more forceful language.

4. In a deliberate and humorous reversal, Mr. Martin unexpectedly stops using his naturally understated speech and talks in the exaggerated style of Mrs. Barrows when he says:

   • "Here's nuts to that old windbag, Fitweiler." (line 201)
   • "I'll be coked to the gills when I bump that old buzzard off." (line 209)
   • "I'm sitting in the catbird seat." (lines 216–217)

   How might he have phrased these three sentences in his naturally understated manner?

5. When Mr. Fitweiler tells Mr. Martin that Mrs. Barrows has accused him of behaving in an "unseemly manner" (lines 259–261) and has demanded that he be "call[ed] on the carpet" (line 271), what do you think she really said?

C Judging for Yourself

Express yourself as personally as you like in your answers to the following questions.

1. Do you think that Thurber was fair to Mrs. Barrows in the way he portrayed her? Justify your answer.

2. In your view, did F & S appear to need some restructuring? How would you characterize the business?

3. Were you confident that Mr. Martin would triumph over Mrs. Barrows? Explain your answer.

4. Do you feel that Mr. Martin acts ethically toward Mrs. Barrows at the end?

5. What do you think life at F & S will be like in the future?

D Making Connections

Answer the following questions with a classmate or in a small group.

1. How is progress viewed in your culture? Do people think that modernization is always desirable?

2. If a woman has a domineering personality, how is she viewed in your country? Are the same standards applied to an aggressive man?

3. What are the main reasons workers are fired in your country?

4. In Thurber's time, baseball was the most popular American sport, and it features in "The Catbird Seat." What team sports do people passionately follow in your country?

E Debate

Decide whether you are for or against the following statement. Be prepared to argue your case in a class debate.

The end justifies the means.

PART 3 GRAMMAR IN CONTEXT

NOUN CLAUSES

A **noun clause** is a dependent clause that functions as a noun. It can act as either the subject of a clause or the object of a transitive verb or a preposition. Since it is a dependent clause, it cannot stand alone in a sentence but must be attached to an independent (main) clause. Like all clauses, it has its own subject and verb.

1. The noun clause can be the subject of a verb.

   That Mr. Munson's department had been "a little disrupted" came as no surprise to the staff at F & S.

2. The noun clause can be the object of a transitive verb.

   He mentioned *that Mr. Munson's department had been "a little disrupted"* . . . (lines 74–75)

3. A noun clause may come after a clause beginning with *it*.

   . . . *it was generally known* **that Mr. Martin did not smoke** . . . (lines 6–7)

   This sentence could also be written in the following way:

   That Mr. Martin did not smoke was generally known.

4. Noun clauses are commonly used in reported speech and are introduced by the word *that*, which may sometimes be omitted.

> *"You called Mr. Fitweiler an old windbag and said **you were going to blow him up** . . . !"* (lines 283–284)

5. Noun clauses may also be introduced by the following words: *whether, if, where, when, why, how, who, whom, whose, what,* and *which.*

> *"Can't you see **how he has tricked us,** you old fool?"* (lines 291–292)

The noun clause is the object of the verb *see.*

6. If one noun clause is linked to another clause by a coordinating conjunction (*for, and, nor, but, or, yet,* or *so*), the second clause is also a noun clause.

> *Mrs. Barrows said **that Mr. Martin had visited her last evening** and **had behaved himself in an unseemly manner.***

The two noun clauses are the object of the verb *said.* Since the subject of both clauses is *Mr. Martin,* it is omitted the second time.

Exercise 1

Follow the instructions concerning the following sentences from the story.

1. It was fortunate, he reflected as he passed on to the important charges against Mrs. Barrows, that he had stood up under it so well. (lines 52–54)

   a. Underline the noun clause.

   b. What is the main clause in the sentence?

   c. Rewrite the sentence, placing the noun clause at the beginning.

2. "Why, I even believe you like the woman," Miss Paird, his other assistant, had once said to him. (lines 55–56)

   a. Underline the noun clause.

   b. What word is missing from the noun clause but is implied?

   c. Which clause is the noun clause dependent on?

   d. Is the noun clause the subject or the object of the verb in that clause?

3. It was at this point that the door to the office blew open with the suddenness of a gas-main explosion and Mrs. Barrows catapulted through it. (lines 278–280)

   a. How many noun clauses are in this sentence? Underline them.

   b. What word is omitted, but understood? Where would you place it?

   c. Which clause do the noun clauses relate to?

4. "You may describe what you did after leaving the office yesterday, Martin," he said. (lines 248–249)

   a. Underline the noun clause.

   b. Which clause does it relate to?

   c. Is it the subject or the object of the clause?

5. It was his idea to puff a few puffs on a Camel (after the rubbing-out), stub it out in the ashtray holding her lipstick-stained Luckies, and thus drag a small red herring across the trail. (lines 121–124)

   a. Are there any noun clauses in this sentence?

   b. If your answer is yes, underline them/it. If your answer is no, explain the grammar of the sentence.

Exercise 2

Complete the following sentences with a noun clause. Start each clause with the word in parentheses.

1. I don't know anyone _____ (who)

2. _____ is difficult to predict. (how)

3. The building _____ caught fire last week. (where)

4. It is taken for granted _____. (that)

5. She wondered _____ or _____. (whether)

6. Do you understand _____? (why)

PART 4 **VOCABULARY BUILDING**

IDIOMS CONTAINING COLORS

An **idiom** is an expression with a meaning that is different from the sum of its parts. English has many idioms that contain colors. For example, Thurber makes use of two idioms in "The Catbird Seat" that contain the color red. Mr. Martin fondly remembers a special occasion as a *red-letter day* (line 113), and he thinks it would be a good idea to drag a *red herring* along the trail to divert the police's suspicions (line 124). In both cases, the meaning of the expression cannot be deduced from its individual parts.

Use your dictionary to find out the meaning of the following expressions. Then complete the following sentences with the appropriate idiom. You may need to change the verb tense.

see red	a green thumb
white lie	get the green light
white-collar	in the black
out of the blue	black market
have the blues	get a pink slip

1. During wartime, people often buy scarce goods on the
   _____.

2. The animal rights activist _____
   whenever anyone is cruel to a pet.

3. In a recession, many people _____.

4. _____ my husband asked for a
   divorce. I didn't expect it.

5. Although people in _____ jobs don't
   do physical labor, sitting at a computer all day can be dangerous too.

6. It is common for new mothers
   to _____ right after the birth of their
   baby.

7. Our business has struggled for many years. Finally, we are
   _____.

8. I have always loved gardening. I must have been born with
   _____.

9. When my friend asked me how I liked her new haircut, I had to tell her
   a _____.

10. We finally _____ from our boss to go
    ahead with the new project.

Share with your class more idioms that you know containing colors. You may give examples from English or your native language.

LEGAL VOCABULARY

Frequently, specialized topics have their own vocabulary that you need to know in order to talk or write about them. "The Catbird Seat" contains many examples of legal vocabulary when Mr. Martin fantasizes about trying and sentencing Mrs. Barrows in a courtroom.

Exercise 3

The following words and phrases are from the story and are commonly used in a legal context. Work with a partner and complete the sentences using these words. Use each expression only once.

enter an objection (line 35)   gavel (line 57)

sustain the objection (line 35)   case (line 57)

witness (line 36)   jury (line 101)

charges (line 53)   death penalty (lines 101–102)

The judge formally read the _____. to the defendant. "These are serious crimes," he said solemnly. "You could even get the _____." At this, the courtroom erupted in noisy protest. "Order in the court," shouted the judge as he hammered on his table with his _____. The prosecuting attorney then began his examination of the first _____.

"Your Honor," interjected the defense counsel, "I wish to _____. The prosecutor is harassing this person and is trying to influence the _____ improperly."

"I will _____," said the judge. "Now let's get on with the _____. I want the closing arguments by the end of the week at the latest so that we can all get home in time for the holidays."

Exercise 4

Find a newspaper article that deals with crime. Pay attention to the expressions that relate to the law. Share two or three of these expressions with a group and explain their meaning in the context of the article.

1. Have you ever been the victim of a domineering personality? Perhaps it was at work, at school, or in the family. Write an essay of two pages outlining your relationship to the person, and say what he or she did to you. Describe how you felt and what measures you took to deal with the situation.

2. In an essay of two pages, pick an area of modernization that comes at a cost. For example, it could include computerizing businesses with a resulting loss of jobs or cheap energy that causes environmental destruction. Take a stand on whether you are for or against this modernization. In your first paragraph, describe the issue. In the body of your essay, explain your position. In your conclusion, say what you would do if you had the power to control this process. Try to include various types of noun clauses in your essay.

3. From William Shakespeare's play *The Taming of the Shrew* to the animated TV program *The Simpsons,* many books, movies, TV programs, and cartoons have dealt with the war between the sexes. Write an essay of two pages analyzing how men and women are presented in a work you have seen or read. Say whether you think a war of the sexes is the natural outcome of the society we live in.

4. A deception is at the heart of both "The Catbird Seat" and "EPICAC" (pages 198–204). Describe these deceptions. Then compare the deceivers and their victims. In each story, whom did you sympathize with more— the deceiver or the deceived? Explain why you felt this way.

Text Credits

Chapter 1

Arturo Vivante. "Can-Can." First published in *The London Magazine* February/March 1972, Vol. 11, No. 6. Copyright © 1972 by Arturo Vivante. Reprinted by permission of *The London Magazine*.

Chapter 2

Peter Meinke. "The Cranes." Reprinted by permission of the Ann Rittenberg Literary Agency. Copyright © 1987 by Peter Meinke.

Chapter 3

Woody Allen. "The Kugelmass Episode" from *Side Effects* by Woody Allen. Copyright © 1977 by Woody Allen. Used by permission of Random House, Inc. Any third party use of this material, outside of this publication, is prohibited. Interested parties must apply directly to Random House, Inc. for permission.

Chapter 4

Nadine Gordimer. "An Intruder" from *Livingstone's Companions* by Nadine Gordimer. Copyright © 1965, 1966, 1967, 1968, 1969, 1971 by Nadine Gordimer. Reprinted by permission of Viking Penguin, a division of Penguin Group (USA) Inc. and Random Century Group, London, and Russell and Volkening as agents for the author.

Chapter 5

Tobias Wolff. "Powder" from *The Night in Question* by Tobias Wolff. Copyright © 1996 by Tobias Wolff. Used by permission of Alfred A. Knopf, a division of Random House, Inc. and International Creative Management, Inc.

Chapter 6

Grace Paley. "Mother" from *Later That Same Day* by Grace Paley. Copyright © 1985 by Grace Paley. Reprinted by permission of Farrar, Straus and Giroux, Inc. and Elaine Markson Literary Agency, Inc.

Chapter 7

James Joyce. "Eveline" from *Dubliners* by James Joyce. Copyright © 1916 by B. W. Heubsch. Definitive text Copyright © 1967 by the Estate of James Joyce. Used by permission of Viking Penguin, a division of Penguin Group (USA) Inc.

Chapter 8

Frank O'Connor. "My Oedipus Complex" from *The Collected Stories of Frank O'Connor* by Frank O'Connor. Copyright © 1981 by Harriet O'Donovan Sheehy, Executrix of the Estate of Frank O'Connor. Used by permission of Alfred A. Knopf, a division of Random House, Inc., and Writer's House, LLC on behalf of the proprietors.

Chapter 9

Monica Wood. "Disappearing." First published in *Fiction Network*. Copyright © 1988 by Monica Wood. Reprinted by permission of the author.

Chapter 10

Kate Chopin. "A Pair of Silk Stockings" from *Bayou Folk*. Published by Houghton Mifflin & Co, Boston and New York, 1894.

Chapter 11

Alice Walker. "Everyday Use" from *In Love and Trouble* by Alice Walker. Reprinted by permission of David Higham Associates. First published by Harcourt Brace Jovanovich, Inc. Copyright © 1973 by Alice Walker.

Chapter 12

Lousie Erdrich. "The Red Convertible" from *The Red Convertible: Selected and New Short Stories*, 1978–2008 by Louise Erdrich. Copyright © 2009 by Louise Erdrich. Reprinted by permission of HarperCollins Publishers.

Chapter 13

Kurt Vonnegut. "EPICAC" from *Welcome to the Monkey House* by Kurt Vonnegut, Jr. Copyright © 1950. Used by permission of Dell Publishing, a division of Random House, Inc. and Donald C. Farber, attorney for Kurt Vonnegut.

Chapter 14

Ann Petry. "Like a Winding Sheet." Reprinted by permission of Russell & Volkening as agents for the author. Copyright © 1971 by Ann Petry, renewed 1999 by Elizabeth Petry.

Chapter 15

Alan Paton. "A Drink in the Passage." Reprinted with the permission of Scribner Publishing Group from *Tales from a Troubled Land* by Alan Paton. Copyright © 1961 by Alan Paton. Copyright renewed © 1989 by Anne Paton. All rights reserved. Copyright © Alan Paton Will Trust.

Chapter 16

James Thurber. "The Catbird Seat" from *The Thurber Carnival* by James Thurber, published by HarperCollins. Copyright © 1945 by James Thurber, and renewed by 1973 by Helen Thurber and Rosemary A. Thurber. Reprinted by arrangement with Rosemary A. Thurber and the Barbara Hogenson Agency.